MEDAL MONDAY
Special Presale Edition

Running Servant
My Quest to Run 50 Marathons in 50 States in
50 Weeks 5 Years After Being Shot 5 times

Aaron Burros
Loren Murfield

A Special Note of Thanks

In my quest to go where God has led, he has sent
angels.
Thank you for being one who uplifted, encouraged,
and supported me when I needed it the most.
You have blessed me so I can do God's work,
blessing others, encouraging them to do what they
never imagined.
Thank you.

Table of Contents

I'm Called to Help

"Go get the tool and put in work!", one criminal said to another. At that very moment, I knew what wasn't apparent to others, we were about to get ambushed, and our very lives were at stake. I noticed the two guys outside the store and instantly knew they were trouble. Unfortunately, my coworkers didn't recognize what the two were intending an armed robbery. My coworkers meant well, but they were no match. If I didn't intervene, they would die.

I'm a born-again believer in Jesus Christ and know that my eternal fate is secure. I'm a religious man and know that my eternal fate is secure. However, my coworkers are not, and that concerns me, especially in this situation. Someone must interrupt their actions, or they would spend the rest of their lives in torment.

That someone was me.

Why?

Because I'm the #RunningServant.

"Get inside" I shouted as I grabbed the first guy from behind, wrestling with him, dragging him down and holding him from behind. He was desperately trying to reach for a weapon in his pocket, so I frantically grabbed his hand in order to prevent him from retrieving it. Seeing a gun in his pocket, I frantically grabbed his hands, preventing him from removing it.

He reeked of the Newport cigarettes

Sensing he was outmatched, the thug showed his nature, "Go get the tool and put in work Get the tool and put in the work" he shouted to his accomplice who was standing by near the car.

I looked up to see the second thug approaching quickly with a gun. With urgency, I freed the last coworker from the grip of the head thug as I placed him in a choke hold to shield myself from the shooter. I look up to see the second thug with a gun aimed directly at my heart. Instinctively I roll to the left.

Bang.

In a split second, I felt the hot metal grace my left torso.

Falling backwards, I dragged the head thug back with me to keep a shield.

Let my nigga go, he demanded. I did.

I laid on the pavement, the rain gently falling on my face. I couldn't tell whether or not I was crying.

Bang. Bang. Bang. Bang. Bang.

The hot lead pierced my body four more times as I rolled to protect my heart from receiving the kill shot.

I knew I was bleeding, sensing where the bullets came and went or whey they stopped.

I feared I was dying.

Family members point out bullet holes in my work clothing.

Help!

"Get the tool. Kill him."

In many ways I shouldn't be alive. But I was destined to live. You see, if I hadn't started running, I would've died on that rainy evening in Houston.

It all started when I was huffing and puffing struggling to make it up the church stairs. "What's the matter with you Aaron. You are too young to struggle with a few stairs." Larry Edwards was 20 years older and had biked the MS150, 150 mile ride in Texas from Houston to Austin. He was fit and trim and I'm 39 years old and praying that the scale won't touch 400 pounds. I knew diabetes ran in my family, but I was most concerned with the strain on my heart. I took out my phone and called my doctor.

"You have to lose 40 pounds, or it will lose you." He made it clear that if I didn't get busy and lose some weight, my life would end too soon.

I guess that would make anyone sit up and take notice. It would also make anyone drop to their knees and beg, "God, please help me. I don't want to die."

As much as I wanted to, I struggled. You see, no matter what I did, I wasn't motivated. I just sat around knowing I needed to do something. I knew what needed to be done but did not have the drive to get going. I tried to start exercising on my own, but I just couldn't make myself do it. I tried walking and jogging but couldn't get going or keep going. I knew what I needed to do but couldn't.

3

Debra, my niece, and I weigh in at a staggering 380 pounds.

It wasn't that I didn't know what to do. I was a great good quarterback and an even better power forward in basketball during high school. I would have had a scholarship had it not been for my coach, but I'll get to that later.

So, there I was, sitting at home, discouraged because it was too much work to move. I was so heavy that I couldn't lift myself much less any weights. All I could do was pray, "Help me!"

God answered my prayer, but in a strange way. He does that a lot, as you will see in this book.

I drove drive a Ford Explorer, known by my mechanic as a "Ford Exploder." One day it just stopped. No matter what I did, it wouldn't run. My mechanic said, "You need a new engine."

"Hallelujah! That was the answer to my prayers."

I realize that sounds like a strange response, but I knew it was the answer I needed to get my motivation.

"I'm not getting that fixed," I told myself. "I'm just going to move closer to work, that way I can walk to and from work. That's my motivation to start moving."

It worked. I walked to and from work, logging four miles each day.

A few months later, a friend, Alonzo Bickerstaff, gave me a ride home from church. While I loved walking, I did appreciate a ride since church was about 10 miles away. A funny thing happened on the way home. It was raining and for some reason, that light rain triggered a desire inside.

"I haven't run in the rain since high school football. I think I'll run after I get home."

That day I ran 3.5 miles. I had been walking for 2 months so I had the stamina. But where did the motivation come from?

There was something relaxing in that rain. I found it easier to breathe so I took my time and enjoyed myself. A mile from my house, I stopped at Starbucks, rang my shirt out, got my coffee, and found a seat outside. That was also relaxing.

Like Forrest Gump, I just started running and kept going.

It wasn't long before my shirts started to hang on me. No longer tight, I knew it was working. That was my measure since I didn't bother to weigh myself. I would know I reached my goal when I liked what I saw in the mirror.

I like learning so I made a call. There was a young man named Justin, who I called "Just Ice," that ran cross country at Kempner High school in Sugar Land, TX. I knew him from church and shared with him about my new venture into running.

"I'm so proud of you," he was beaming with encouragement.

"Thank you."

"Let's make you a plan to keep you running. Do you think you can run 3.5 miles a day?"

"Not if it isn't raining." That rain really made a difference for me.

"What about 2 miles?"

"Yeah, I can do 2 miles." That was the distance to and from work so I reassured him, "Yeah I can do 2 miles."

"Do 2 miles a day, Monday through Saturday. Then rest on Sunday and we will talk at church."

I ran two miles each day starting on Monday, and continuing on Tuesday, Wednesday, Thursday, Friday and then on Saturday. Sunday, I rested and looked forward to providing a successful report, although it seemed a little strange since I was his spiritual mentor.

"How do you feel?" he asked.

"I feel great. I averaged about 10.5 minutes per mile." I thought that was pretty good for a guy my size.

"Do you think you can do 3 miles?"

"No, let's stick with 2 until I get comfortable."

5

Understanding my reservations after only one week of running, he quickly agreed but offered a few conditions. "Do it again this week. If you get tired, do a mile in the morning and mile at night. It's ok to split it up."

"Cool!" I liked the idea that I had choices but also knew I was content pushing myself. On Monday I ran two miles." I ran a mile down my street and then a mile back. "No need to split it up," I thought.

The following Sunday we met again.

"How did you do? How are you feeling?"

"My time dropped to 9.75 minutes per mile."

Without hesitating, he asked, "Do you think you can do 3 miles this week?"

"Yes," I answered without thinking, "I can do 3."

"Remember you can split it into two or three times," he reminded me. "You can even break it up and run a mile at a time or you can do a mile and a half at a time or even two miles in the morning and one at night. You have several options."

I went to work that afternoon, plotting my path, and running every day around my neighborhood.

The following Sunday, as had become our routine, he posed the same questions.

"How did you do? How did it feel?"

"I feel great. I also dropped my time from 9.75 minutes per mile to 9.5.

"Great. Let's repeat that for the coming week. Let's do 2 weeks on 3 miles. But this time, on Saturday, try to run 5 miles instead of 3."

I liked the challenge, so I quickly agreed. "Alright."

But this week would be different. A passion was beginning to stir within me. I ran three miles every day except, on Saturday, as instructed, I didn't just run five miles. I ran seven. I couldn't wait to tell him.

"How did you do?" he asked.

"I did what you asked but on Saturday I ran seven miles."

"Great job. How long did it take you?

"Just a little over an hour, actually one hour and one minute."

"That's under 9 minutes a mile. You are not only running father, but you are also running faster. This week, do you think you can run four miles each day?"

6

I knew I could because I walked that far to and from work each day. I didn't even consider splitting it up as he had suggested earlier. But again, this week, that passion intensified. I ran four miles on Monday but on Tuesday, I ran five. Then I ran another five on Wednesday before running seven on Thursday and Friday. Having already surpassed my daily mileage, I welcomed my Saturday "raise your limits" day when I ran just short of nine miles. Instead of running 25 miles for the week, I had run 37 miles. "Pretty good for only my fourth week of running."

My new mentor raised the stakes the next week, asking me to run five miles each day and then kick it up to nine on Saturday. Remember, I'm also walking four miles a day to and from work. That is twenty miles a week in addition to the 35-38 miles running per week

I increased my miles each weekend and, before long, was running 10-13 miles each Saturday. That means I was running a half marathon on most Saturdays.

Terry Hershey Park in Houston quickly became my favorite place to run. With almost 500 acres that stretches twelve miles, it has great running, hiking, and biking trails. I found the trails and nature very relaxing.

Being gregarious, I greeted other runners, but they were hesitant and even rather reluctant to engage. Friends told me to just mind my own business and run. But that's not who I am. I love engaging others and even challenging them. After all, as I like to say, "It costs nothing to be neighborly and nice. I'm not going to let their silence dictate my behavior."

It wasn't long and my friendliness was reciprocated and invited me to run with their groups. "That's cool" I thought, "That gives me even more options."

On days where I worked, I biked the seven miles to the park and then ran a 5k. On my days off, usually Tuesday or Thursday, I ran to the park and then ran with the club members, and then ran back home.

To make it more interesting, I nicknamed people based on running style or characteristics. It is all in a good spirit. There is one guy I call Tiptoes. He runs half marathons in the park by starting at the gazebo and running to the Beltway 8 entrance and then back on his toes. The first time I witnessed his running style, I hollered, "Hello Tip Toes." He wondered who I was talking to. Once he realized I was referring to him, he smiled, and now he greets me. I don't know his real name, nor does he know mine, but we have a good laugh.

I progressed to where I ran 17 to 24 miles regularly. If not working, I'd do 30 miles, 15 out and 15 back on the trails. That's not easy but I love the trails. They bring me so much peace, in part, because I grew up enjoying the trails in Akron, Ohio. But it's more than nostalgia. Running trails is much more peaceful, relaxing, and interesting than pounding the pavement through urban or suburban streets. Without worrying about cars, I commune with God and nature. It is beautiful.

But don't get lost. The first time I got lost running was at Terry Hershey Park after sunset. Without streetlights, when it gets dark, you cannot see a thing, much less find your way out of the park's bike trails. I was turned around, so I didn't know which way was north, south, east, or west. Fortunately, I ran across a couple that pointed me in the right direction. I was so turned around that I was headed west when I needed to go east. In a park that covers nearly 500 acres, I would have been walking a long time in the wrong direction without their help. By the time I talked to them, I was already five miles from where I needed to be. To help from getting lost again, I now call that part of the park, "Punch Bowl" since it has a crater that fills with water.

By this time, summer had turned into fall and the wet rains of winter were approaching. I wasn't too worried about it, but a friend thought I needed more than just my shoes for transportation. You see, I was enjoying running so much that I had not bothered to fix my Ford Explorer. Wherever I went, I ran. I had clothes stashed at my mom's and other homes, so I changed when I arrived, and then changed back into my clothes to run home. I had it all figured out. But with winter coming, I appreciated my friend's generosity and foresight.

You would have thought I was a kid with a new toy. I cycled everywhere. But this was no leisurely ride. I pedaled as hard as I could to work, mom's house, and even to church. Remember I used to catch a ride. I didn't need that anymore because I had wheels again. Every Sunday and then again on Wednesday, I cycled the 10 miles each way. Enjoying my newfound freedom, I also taught a bible study at a Minuti Coffee shop in Sugar Land Texas during the week which, if I left from work, was only 8 miles.

In the meantime, I was still running the same number of miles. I cycled 18 miles on Tuesday, normally worked Wednesday night, if not cycled to church and again on Sunday. Then started cycling 65 miles at a time, just going wherever. Sometimes I got a flat, often many miles from home, I had no choice but to pick up the bike and carry it. Anyone who has tried to push a bike on a flat knows how irritating it is to be hit by the pedals. It wasn't uncommon that the flats occurred five, eight, or ten miles from home. Despite that, I loved biking. I also loved how the pounds fell off.

The Biggest Loser

I love challenges. That fall *The Biggest Loser* was a new show that was captivating the country. As with many companies, my job joined the craze and had a health challenge. Wanting to join the fun, I made an offer I couldn't refuse.

The challenge was to who could lose the most pounds in twelve weeks. Given all the exercise I was doing each week, I had a head start. But the challenge forced me to start doing something I hadn't done before – weigh myself weekly. I preferred just to measure my progress by how well my clothes fit but that doesn't work for a weight loss competition. So I quickly adapted the practice.

By the end of eight I had already lost 40 pounds. Looking at myself in the mirror, I liked what I saw. It was confirmed by looking at the scale, which by now was closer to the 300-pound mark than the dreaded 400-pound mark.

By 2011, I marked my first anniversary of running. Looking at the scale, it read 297. I had lost 100 pounds. Running and cycling made a big difference, but I also changed my diet.

My New Diet

My previous life revolved around eating fast and processed food. I frequented the usual places, and it added up. I was particularly fond of drinking Mountain Dew and Mountain Dew Code Red. But my absolute favorite comfort food was a king-sized bag of Peanut M & M with a pint of the best ice cream on the planet, Blue Bell Vanilla Bean. Mix them together and then wash it down with a Mt. Dew. Mmmm. That was delicious but a potential killer. If I continued to eat like that, as Dr. Bond said about my excess weight, "If you don't lose it, it will lose you."

That bad habit had to go when I started biking and running. By the time I entered the challenge, I was studying the government website to learn what foods I should be eating and how to put them together to make a great meal. It has all worked well but every once in a while, those Peanut M&Ms call my name. I'll nibble a little but can't fall back into that habit. I just say, "No thanks, I need to eat healthy." Besides, now when I eat that, I don't sleep very well. That makes it easy to say, "No thanks."

Today my drink of choice is a Starbucks blonde roast with 4 raw sugars and a steamed breve. The caffeine helps prevent and alleviate migraines, so it is not only enjoyable but also therapeutic. I gave up soda entirely.

"Get the tool. Kill him."

Losing 180 pounds saved my life. Had I not lost that weight, I couldn't have moved quickly enough to avoid the kill shot.

Before we go any farther, you need to know the background story. I was saved even before he pulled the trigger the first time.

Photo: I was accompanied by plenty of Los Angeles Hotwheels players at the 2015 Barker Ripley's Houston Turkey Trot.

Salvation

"Run. Get in the building?"
I intervened not just to stop a robbery/homicide, but to save my coworkers
from the fires of hell

Why would I do that? How did I come to a point where that was even an option? Maybe it starts with another question asked of me several years before. I was sitting alone with a loaded weapon.

"What about your eternal life?"

I grew up the farthest one could get from the church, yet I encountered God several times. You might even say I've been saved several times, even though I didn't grow up in the church. Yet that question wasn't even in my vocabulary. Why was it so important on that rainy night in Houston?

Great Potential

I grew up in Akron, Ohio, the son of a man who had everything a woman desired. He was tall, dark, and handsome and every woman's dream. He was a disc jockey in a club and availed himself for several of those women's dreams. Maybe that is why he has seventeen children.

I only remembered going to church one time and dad scolded me for going to sleep in the front pew. You see, by that time, Dad had "gotten saved" after years of prayers by his parents. In the meantime, he was a rolling stone, very sinful, living life to what he thought was the fullest by enjoying the sins of the flesh.

11

My mom and dad never married. She did get married later to a man that was a pimp and a player, surrounded by a family known for their criminal connections. Without any spiritual foundation, I sat alone, depressed, with my index finger on a hair trigger.

But I wasn't satisfied with ending my own pitiful life. I was planning to take a half dozen others to hell with me.

That is, until God intervened.

The short story is that I had reached the end of my emotional resources. Everyone had let me down. Too many had promised and not delivered. Despite great potential, they dismissed me. By the time I held that decisive weapon in my hand, I had given up on a world that cheated me over and over and over.

It started with my school counselors who placed me in remedial classes even though I could excel at a much higher level. I had to fight to be placed in regular classes and eventually earned my way into honors classes. I thought counselors were supposed to be there to help students

In high school, even though I was more talented as a quarterback and got better results, the coach played the white boy. This was 1980s Texas and our coach proudly proclaimed, "I ain't going to help an nigger get anything." I could have easily been offered scholarships at division one colleges, but he wouldn't do his part. Time and time again, the head coaches kept me and other blacks on the bench until his white boy with the stereotypical All-American look messed up. Then we trotted in and got our nationally ranked teams back in the game. Instead of being rewarded, he benched us again so the white boy could get the glory. That coach cost me a college scholarship and possibly an NBA or NFL career. That wasn't right. Someone had to pay.

Not to be outdone, during my senior year, my high school basketball coach lied and cost me a college scholarship. He also embodied the 1980s Texas hatred and prejudice. Although I was a very talented high school quarterback, my best sport was basketball. As a power forward, I was unstoppable. I dribbled around and dunked over guys four to six inches taller. I also had the grades, having proven myself beyond remedial education to work my way into honors courses. I should have been promoted for a college basketball scholarship. But instead, the coach wouldn't even let me dress and play when scouts came to town. The one time I did, I showed up his star player. You guessed it, a white boy that coach wanted to be his first player to go straight to the pros. He was good, but I showed them I was better. Forgive me for believing in myself. To make matters worse, when I was offered a basketball scholarship at New Mexico, he claimed teachers had given me grades that I didn't deserve. The school pulled the scholarship. In all candor, I believe I could have played in the NBA. That's not arrogance. That's how much talent and drive I had. When someone denies that potential, someone needs to pay.

Without an opportunity to play college sports, my options were limited, so I joined the army. Then, when my older brother was diagnosed with a terminal disease, I was given a discharge to take care of him. After he passed, I was 21. Still passionate about playing sports, I pursed and secured a basketball scholarship at Knoxville college. Unfortunately, the school lied to me, others, and the government. A third of the way through the semester they presented me with a large bill for tuition, fees, and housing. When I told them I had a scholarship, they simply claimed, "That was a mistake." I dropped out but they still forged my name on a student loan. Despite proving the forgery and the Department of Education removing the school's accreditation, they still garnished my wages. I had to pay for a loan I never asked for. Someone needs to pay. I'm tired of being denied.

Saddled with debt after being denied tremendous opportunities, I did the only thing I knew to make a living. I started dealing drugs. I didn't care about crossing a legal line. I took what life owed me.

But it came with a cost.

I made a pact with the devil.

I'm not exaggerating. I literally had a conversation with the devil where I made a deal to get what I wanted. He promised that if I worked for him, I would never want for money. I would have cars, cash, and clout. All I had to do was play my part. That sounded like a great deal to me. After all the lies and betrayals from those who were supposed to have my best interest in mind, how could I say no?

A Voice

"I don't want you doing that anymore."

I literally heard God's voice. It was 1994, sometime between the birth of my two sons, when I heard an audible voice say, "I don't want you doing that anymore." There was no question, he was referring to my dealing drugs. I knew it was God because the voice was much different from the devil, who I had also heard. The voice came from every angle imagined and literally consumed me. It wasn't a James Earl Jones' booming voice, nor was it a still, small voice. It was one of command but one of a father expressing desire for his child. I remember it clearly because I remember exactly where I was, diving on a regular drug run between Lexington and Florence, Kentucky.

Then, just one week later, on the same road and about the same place, I heard God's voice again. Only this time, it wasn't as patient. It was more of a stern, impatient, and intolerant warning.

"I told you and expect you to do it."

I sensed that if I didn't stop dealing drugs, I was going to die. Shaken, I continued down the highway to do my drug deal, but everything I saw reminded me of death. I saw roadkill and quickly genuflected, even though I wasn't catholic. I saw a sign for Exxon, took the exit, crossed the highway, and looked through the entire store frantically looking for anything religious. I was hoping for prayer beads or anything to tie me to God. I was frantic. I had an overwhelming fear that I was about to die, and I was going to do whatever I could to prevent that.

I was scared straight.

I would eventually quit dealing drugs and accepted a low paying job remembering the warning. At that point, I just wanted to live my life and take care of my family. I forgot my pain and focused on preventing the ultimate pain of dying.

It was years before God spoke to me the third time.

Meanwhile, I was living with the woman who I made into an idol. I was 26, had two beautiful boys and knew the missing piece was the commitment of marriage. But that wasn't to be.

Her mom didn't like me, in part because my skin was too dark. This was a different version of hatred and prejudice. This was black-on-black prejudice based on shade of black. Despite my love, affection, and efforts to convince my girlfriend, her mother sealed our destiny. I had proposed and my girlfriend had accepted. We were planning the ceremony when her mom intervened again. That was enough for her daughter, the love of my life, to pack up the boys and her belongings and leave.

I wasn't just angry. I felt the ultimate betrayal. Once again someone had inferred and ruined my life. This was the final straw. I was distraught and defeated.

Once again, I turned to an old voice. No, it wasn't God but his archenemy. I entered into negotiations with the devil. Sealing our deal, the prince of darkness provided the instructions for a murder-suicide. With the assurances that my boys would be in heaven and all the adults would go to hell and wait on him, I set my mind on the plan.

First, I was to tie up the mother of my beautiful boys. Then I would kill our sons in front of her. I wanted her to suffer. I also wanted my boys to enjoy eternity in heaven.

Next, I was to go to the home of my godson and kill him. This was punishment for his mother who had interfered with my relationships. She too would suffer.

Third, I was to travel to another woman's home that used to be a friend. Once again, she had interfered with my relationships and must pay the price. She would suffer the same fate of watching her son die and living with the pain.

I wanted to make others experience the pain they had caused me.

Far from done, the next would be the most satisfying. I was to kill my fiancé's mother and then go to the high school where I would kill my high school coach who had cost me a college scholarship. Then, I was going to go back to my fiancé's place, kill her.

With vengeance complete, the plan called for calling a friend that worked for Channel 2 (NBC) news in Houston. I was to send him a message to share on the air. The message – don't play with people's lives. In exchange for his airing the message, I would tell him everything I had just done. I intended to send him everything I had done.

That only left one step left in the plan.

I sat there with a loaded 9mm Glock, as I would when I came to the last step in the plan.

"What about your eternal life?"

Then God spoke to me for the third time.

"What about your eternal life?"

Life was a blur. I had no concept of time up to that point, just the sting of emotional pain and the brutal stab in the back of betrayal. The words of my coach rang in my ears, "I won't help a nigger get anything in life."

I also remember my hateful words to him, "If I ever kill anyone in life, I will come back to kill you."

15

The tipping point was my fiancé's betrayal. I don't want anyone making decisions for me. If you are lying on your word, you don't have anything. For her to do it twice, that was too much

"But what about your eternal life?"

Up to that point, I considered myself to be a good person. By the time I made a pact with the devil for the murder-suicide, I knew I was a sinner but never knew that I needed salvation.

Yet I pushed back, complaining to God about everyone who had betrayed me. God countered in a conversation with shades of Job's ancient argument. God replied, telling me about sending his son who died and was resurrected and sits at God's right hand.

"If I can forgive after those who I've created have betrayed me, can't you forgive?

Time stopped.

I had no words to counter that.

Mankind killed his son when he generously came to save us.

They killed him. We killed him. I killed him.

Yet God is willing to forgive me.

I laid down my weapon and my hate. God removed the demons from me, shattered the pact with the Devil, and gave me the Holy Spirit. I was saved.

Go and Preach

I went to bed and slept peacefully.

The next morning, God woke me with a compelling message.

"Get up and go preach at the Stop and Go." Like Moses complaining of his stutter, and Abraham offering a sacrifice, God told me not to worry about what to say, he would provide it. I obeyed. I arose and went to that same location, preaching every Friday and Saturday night for the next five or six years. I didn't prepare a message. God supplied it. Although it was an act of obedience, and making the difference in the lives of others, it was my private time with God.

There was so much I needed to learn. He told me to get a Bible and start studying it. Then he instructed me to listen to 105.7 FM, KHCB. I had been listening to 97.9 the box, a favorite in Houston before switching over. Oddly enough, KHCB was broadcast in Spanish, and I did speak Spanish. Yet I understood everything. How can that be? It was not of my own doing. To this day, I have never turned off that radio or changed it to a different station.

From there I became a regular listener to Chuck Swindoll at 8:00 and Tony Evans at 8:30. Tony came back on at 9:00 pm. and I stayed tuned. I quickly ordered and completed Tony's studies. For those first 5 years, I had many, many questions so I went home and studied. Eventually I entered the College of Biblical Studies – Houston for formal study. By then I had learned so much on my own that some thought I already had a doctorate. I was ordained in 2009.

Am I Crazy?

Many doubt my story. They think I'm fabricating a fanciful lie. They doubt it can be real. After all, who actually hears God's voice? Who talks to the devil? Who would plan a murder-suicide like that?

Some even question my sanity and behavior. Even more disappointing, some question my character, choosing to believe that potential murderer is still a threat to them.

I grieve for them because they refuse to believe what I know is the truth. Yes, this is an unreal story. Yes, it might be hard to believe. But not if you have experienced both God's intervention and the radical transformation I have. As the author of Amazing Grace penned, "I once was lost, but now I am found." This wasn't just being lost in the darkness of Terry Hershey Park. I was so lost in life that I was believing the prince of darkness.

It doesn't matter what others say. They can doubt I heard the voice of God. They can argue the theology of whether God speaks in an audible voice or not. They can doubt the athletic talent I once had and doubt the radical change I've made. But that doesn't change my faith. I've experienced too much to live an ordinary life within the parameters of their measly vision. I know the extent to which God has pulled me from hell and for what purpose.

"Get the tool and put in work."
Those words still ring in my mind.
Why was I here? What was I wrestling with this thug who was telling his accomplice to kill me? Why didn't I avoid the situation?

Running Servant

Hearing the words get the tool and put in work, I recognized the situation developing. Unfortunately, my coworkers were oblivious. They didn't grasp the gravity of what was unfolding. If I didn't intervene, there would be casualties. To make matters worse, my coworkers didn't know the LORD Jesus; I knew I was going to heaven, but, if they were murdered, they were not. That meant I needed to intervene and quickly.

What would Jesus do in a situation like this? Would he stand idly by and wait for someone else to save the day. Of course not. He would intervene. Jesus Christ came to give his life as a ransom. for our eternal souls. As a follower of his, my duty is to follow his example and obey. My role is to serve others. That means, to be committed to him gives me no option. I must obey.

Make no mistake, I love serving and helping others. That's why I was mentoring that young man in youth ministry. Serving is what I was doing by preaching outside the Stop and Go. God told me to go preach, and I did out of obedience to him. In the process, I enjoyed helping others find peace with God and the peace of God. To me, that is a win-win-win. God wins. Others win. I win. You can't beat that with a broom stick if it hung outside on a clothesline.

I'm an outgoing guy who loves to bring a smile and a helping hand to those that need it. To know and understand Aaron Burros is to appreciate how service to others makes the world better. You might not have understood that when I sat at my dining room table, filled with hate from betrayal, ready to write the horrendous last page of my life story.

No, service to God wasn't a part of that story. It was a service to the devil. Maybe that is why my salvation story, my critical life pivot, was so dramatic and why I am now totally committed to God.

I've seen the hurt and evil in life.

I've been betrayed over and over and then over again.

I've witnessed broken wedding vows by a mate.

I've experienced family turning their back on me in my hour of need.

I've personally suffered from school counselors holding me back from my ultimate potential.

Then there was the coach who cost me a scholarship and the college who forged my signature. Remember the government demanded I pay back a loan I never asked for or received. To make matters worse, I've been on the receiving end of the white cop's callousness, being harassed for no reason other than their prejudice, pride, and inconvenience.

But God changed that story.

I know what I would have done in those situations apart from God saving grace. It wouldn't have been pleasant. However, God has given me a different perspective and a renewed heart. By saving me, he changed my attitude, behavior, and trajectory.

Instead of hating, I forgive.

Instead of serving the devil, I obey God's commands.

Instead of focusing on my needs, I serve others.

I purposely reached out to each of those individuals mentioned and offered my forgiveness. It wasn't just words. I purposely released them from the anger, bitterness, and hatred.

Instead of taking, I give.

Instead of waiting to receive, I initiated kindness.

Instead of waiting for someone to serve me, I take the initiative and serve others.

I was not a troubled child, actually just the opposite. Although my father was a man about town and my stepfather was a hustler and a pimp, I followed the rules. Focusing on my education, I tried to live my life the best I could. That is why I was honorably discharged from the Army to come home and care for my dying, older brother. I carried and cleaned him. I waited on him, tending to his every need even though growing up was a battle every day with him. He was several years older and made my life miserable. Even before I became a Christian, I realized that I needed to forgive him. One day, I paused and took time for that powerful conversation with him. I said the words, "I forgive you" and I meant them. I am eternally happy I did that before he died. Imagine how damaging it would have been to carry that bitterness and anger with me for the rest of my life.

With service as a big part of my life in my B.C. (Before Christ) days, you can imagine how it has been multiplied since my conversion. With God, it is a part of my identity, the essence of who I am.

Nicknames

As I began running in the parks, especially Terry Hershey Park in Houston, I automatically began reaching out to others. Remember, I greeted other runners even when they wouldn't return the pleasantries. That was my way of connecting but also serving. As we cracked that icy unfamiliarity between strangers, an apathetic distance melted into a smile. One after another, strangers became acquaintances and then friends. In the process, I gave others, and they returned the favor of assigning nicknames. That's what friends do. I didn't know their real names for months and that didn't matter.

Of course, as you can already see, I am not shy. I arrive with a burst of energy and never let up. In the middle of that energy, I am open and honest about my faith, quickly and freely talking about serving God. That led to my nickname "Paz" (short for Pastor) from the Houston running community. Other nicknames popped up like "Happy Feet" and "Run Doctor", but they didn't stick.

One of my favorite nicknames came from a fun experience with The Terry Hershey Kisses, one of the Black Girl Run Houston running groups. As they watched me losing weight, one lady said, "You're getting sexy."

I responded, "I'm getting big" because I was gaining some weight back. Eventually the two were combined where they called me "Big Sexy."

"When are you getting sexy again?" she continued.

"Big sexy is getting slim" I countered.

One day I was getting hot and said I needed to take my shirt off. Others overheard the recurring banter joined in, "Don't hurt 'em." We all laughed knowing that they might faint and hurt themselves at the very sight of this Big Sexy body. Like I said, it is all in good fun.

The nickname of "Big Sexy" was more than just a little fun. The banter was a stress release for the hell I was going through. The shooting had not only left a bullet in my right glute but also a fragment in my left buttock tissue. The pain was an irritating companion that won't leave. No matter what I did, sit, stand, or walk, the pain was there. Sometimes a discomforting throb and at other times a needle stabbing. Equally, if not even more painful, PTSD left me isolated, agitated, and then debilitated. Running became a service to myself that would bring one of the best therapies for my pain.

But let's not jump ahead.

My favorite park was easily Terry Hershey Park. I loved the trails and scenery. It is so peaceful. I loved it so much that even when I ran other parks in Houston, I kept talking about Terry Hershey Park. "You all should check it out." My exuberance knew no bounds and I quickly earned the nickname, "Park Ranger."

My circle of friends was growing as fast as I was losing weight. Many of those new friends were very active in the running community. For example, one individual started Run Houston, another the Bayou City Half series, and yet another the Houston Running Company. They needed help and I gladly volunteered. People started to notice and said, "You are always running and serving." From there, the nickname "The Running Servant" stuck.

As with any good story, that was only the beginning. I would have never guessed that this Streetwise Pharmaceutical Sales Entrepreneur, drug dealer, would become a passionate street preacher for the gospel of Jesus Christ and the glory of God. Neither would I have ever predicted that this nearly 400-pound wheezing man would accept the urge to run the six world major marathons. Who does that? Why do they do that? How did that story unfold?

World Majors

I grabbed the intruder and held his arms so he couldn't reach in his pocket to get his weapon. That's when he hollered to his buddy, "Go Get the tool and put in work…." I turned around to see him aiming directly at my heart, and fire.

As I began this new relationship with God, I got to know him through daily prayer, meditation, and bible study. Through it all I learned to listen to him. Remember, he spoke to me twice on that Kentucky road just weeks apart. Both times the message was clear, "I don't want you doing that anymore." (Selling drugs.) Directly after my conversion in November 1996, he told me to preach at the Stop-n-Go I responded immediately. But then, in August of 2018, God said something that I had no idea what he meant.

"Run the World Majors."

"Say what?"

He didn't need to repeat himself, even though I had no idea what he meant. I would obey whatever he said. Unlike the previous messages, this one wasn't an audible voice. I knew it was from God.

Let me explain.

Every morning I start my day with meditation and prayer. I quiet myself, read scripture, and focus on God's character. That morning, a thought came to my mind that made absolutely no sense. It was not something I had thought about. It wasn't a childhood dream or a recollection of a conversation with another runner. No, it was something so unfamiliar that I had to google what it meant.

"Run the World Majors."

It wasn't in my heart, mind, or world. I know some of you might suspect I overheard a conversation while running. After all, I was now part of a running community. But that wasn't the case. When it came to the World Majors, I was completely in the dark. That's why I knew this message must be from God. How else could I explain it?

Part of my faithful obedience to God following my dramatic "Damascus Road" experience took me to the College of Biblical Studies - Houston where I received a bachelor's degree in Bible and Transformational Leadership. Later I was ordained through the Friendship Community Bible Church, Sugar Land. Add that to my daily bible study and you begin to see that I honed my listening to God. The only way I could explain this message to run the world majors is to see it as an unction of the Holy Spirit.

If it would've been up to me, I would've run trail runs. I love trail runs and only do road runs to serve others by pacing and encouraging. So, if he would have told me to run trails, I could see how some would say, "That's just what you wanted to hear." But road runs? Naw, that isn't Aaron Burros. I tell anyone who will listen, "Put me on a trail and point me in the right direction." I don't need a message from God to run trails because that is heaven to me.

But running road races? And running the six major world road races? That's not something I'd dream up.

But if that's what God said, I'm in. Just like preaching at the Stop and Go. He said it and I did it. I imagine many would be like Jonah and say, "God, I don't think I heard you right" and go the other way. So, I didn't have a problem accepting the challenge to run the World Majors (whatever they were) because I would gladly do that to serve God.

This unction was incredibly strong. It wasn't just a fleeting thought or a cool idea. It was so strong that I felt I needed to do it. Without waiting, I picked up my phone and googled it. I discovered "The Abbott World Marathon Majors is a series consisting of six of the largest and most renowned marathons in the world: Tokyo Marathon, Boston Marathon, TCS London Marathon, BMW Berlin Marathon, Bank of America Chicago Marathon, and TCS New York City Marathon." (https://www.marathontours.com/abbott-world-marathon-majors)

"Ok" I thought, "that's big." Then I read further. When linked together, that is a challenge that less than 8,000 people have completed.

What made me think I could do it?

I had taken quickly to running and found a hidden gift for running fast and far. I had been a member of the running community for several years, and more importantly, had run not only marathons but ultramarathons. For those wondering, an ultra is technically anything longer than a traditional marathon, which is 26.2 miles. The ultras I ran were 50 miles to 100-miles. There was no question in my mind that I could run the six world majors in one year.

Searching further on my phone I began to plan. Knowing it was the fall of 2018, I looked at the 2019 schedule.

Tokyo: First weekend in March

Boston Mid-April Armed Forces Day

London: Last weekend April

Berlin: Last weekend in September

Chicago: Third weekend in October

New York: First weekend in November.

Then I researched each for the application process. Unfortunately, the Tokyo Marathon was already closed for registrations. On to the next one on the list, Boston. It too was closed. That led to London. I connected with a charity in London and secured a spot. I was excited to start the world majors in April of 2019.

Now on to the Berlin Marathon. I learned that the Teen for Kids charity had openings. Not being shy, I quickly dialed and chatted with a very nice lady at the charity. To my surprise, she asked if I wanted to run all of the world majors for them. That sounded great, except for the commitments I had already made. She understood but welcomed me to the ones I could run.

In my excitement, I posted on social media that I had gotten into all the world majors. Naively, I didn't realize the impact of what I had done, or should I say, what God had done. I had no clue how difficult it is to get into all six in one year. Later I learned that some runners apply several years in a row and still don't get accepted. I had done this in a matter of a few weeks.

As you might imagine, that brought out jealous and angry people. Some posted, claiming I was lying. "That's too hard to do." To me, it showed how much God was working. Evidently it was impossible, or at least very unlikely, that any human could do it.

One particular individual targeted me as his enemy. He was relentless and ruthless with his slander. It got so bad that I had to confront this news reporter that attacked me online. Unfortunately for me, he was very influential with the Abbott World Majors. He claimed I was lying and stealing money under the disguise of a charity runner . His influence came in part because he hadn't run all six and didn't have his 6 stars (the medal earned by running all six.) Many considered him an authority on the topic, so if he said I was lying and cheating, they believed it.

I hadn't lied and I hadn't stolen anything. I had no other choice but to send him a cease-and-desist notice. Eventually he took down all his negative posts, But the damage had been done. Today, as I run and raise funds for charities, his attacks still create a problem. They still doubt me. I challenge people to contact the charities themselves and ask them if I am indeed running on behalf of the charity. The money goes directly to them when paying online, which I prefer. The problem comes in that a majority of African Americans don't want their information online, so they send the donation via CashApp to me. I'm transparent with every donation but the suspicion persists. His lies are based on his unwillingness to believe how God opened the doors has made my fundraising efforts difficult. The silver lining is that it affirms why I know God called me to this. If it was easy, I wouldn't need God. If it were easy, I wouldn't be slandered.

You can imagine how excited I was, looking forward to becoming a 6 Star Finisher by the summer of 2020. By the time I left for London, I had all the races set except Tokyo

London Marathon.

I was excited to run London. Being such a world class city hosting one of the six world major marathons was an honor and an opportunity.

I set my pace based on my previous results but being conservative based on the shooting. I expected to run it in 4 hours and thirty minutes. To understand my mindset, a time of 4.30 was slower than I would pace. I paced groups ranging from sub 2:50 to 3:55 and occasionally to 4:10. (Races have pacers who mark the time for runners.) But I wasn't pacing this race, so I was free to set my own strategy. My plan was to run the first half slow and then pick up the pace in the second half.

Unfortunately, it didn't take long for my expectations to be shattered. Not long into the race, I had leg issues and my right leg began buckling. Then my glutes shut down. It was as if someone flipped the switch, shutting off the power to the major muscles in that leg.

Somewhere around mile 13 or14, I stopped at the medical tent.

"What do you need?" the doctor quickly asked.

"My glutes are not working."

"Do you need to stretch out?

"No, they aren't working. I was in a workplace shooting and still carry a bullet in the right glute."

She listened as she sat me on a small chair stretcher and examined me.

"You are right. Your glutes aren't even firing." Considering what most would do, she asked the usual question, "Are you calling it?" Most would've quit but I immediately responded.

"No."

"What do you want me to do?"

"Help me with my lower back and hamstrings. That will allow me to walk the rest of the race.

I figured it would take only another 3 hours, but that was optimistic. It was hard walking but then, with only 10 minutes left, I still had a half mile to go. I knew I had to pick up the pace. Although I couldn't run, I began to trot.

Running the first of the six world major marathons was absolutely iconic. Who wouldn't be impressed running by Buckingham Palace, Parliament Square and London Bridge?

But then the most iconic thing happened, the Queen came out. 2019 was the only time she had ever done that. A runner friend, Brunson Elliot, is a good friend of hers. He was going to be over there before the marathon and was scheduled to see the queen. I told him, "Tell the queen I'm coming for the marathon, and I want to see her." To my surprise, the Queen of Great Britain came out to see us run. I attributed it to Brunson. He lives in Atlanta now and serves as an adult pastor for Martin Luther King's church, Ebenezer Baptist. He has also worked for Sheila Jackson Lee.

Photo: This photo is included in honor of the now late Queen Elizabeth II who is a sister in Jesus Christ by like faith in the person and works of Jesus.

But there were some parts that weren't so iconic. While I had run plenty of races before, I wasn't prepared for a unique London Marathon tradition. It seems that the female spectators take great pleasure in smacking the bottoms of male runners. The first whack I received surprised me. With each subsequent one, I became more and more irritated. I couldn't believe they did it and they couldn't believe I didn't like it. Then when we ran by the bars, the pedestrians hurled abusive comments, especially toward those of us in the back of the pack. To me, that gave London and the London Marathon an ugly eye.

Think about it. Women smacking male runners on the butt during the race. Who does that? What would happen if it were men slapping women runners on the butt? I can tell you that wouldn't and didn't end well for one guy. He was a runner that decided to smack a female news reporter's bottom during the race. Showing a double standard, he was banned from two races.

I was expecting that the Abbot World Majors would be run with the highest standards. I couldn't have been more disappointed. Because of the bullet lodged in my right glute, I wasn't able to match my pre-shooting pace and that left me toward the back of the pack. To my surprise and disappointment, while many of us were still on the course, workers began tearing down the racecourse. That's where the verbal abuse happened. Near Buckingham Palace, the person who was supposed to be directing us disappeared. With the gates broken down, we had to ask pedestrians which way to go. In the process, the brave souls on their comfortable perches hurled alcohol inspired insults toward us running the race.

Tearing down the course at that point makes no sense. The race was still officially open, the "sag wagon" was still behind us. In most races, a car or bus marks the end of the race. Those that cannot meet the time are asked to exit the course and board the bus. But we were still ahead of the sag wagon. That meant the race was still open. In the ultimate insult, contractors were spraying chemicals on runners. This was far from the experience I expected.

Struggle

Alone on the course, my past success haunted me. I expected to easily run a 4:30 marathon and now I'm fighting to finish. I was surprised by my body shutting down. Normally, whenever I asked my body for a surge of energy, it responded. But no matter how much I pushed down on my mental accelerator, there was no gas going to the engine. I had no power and that demoralized me. Although I didn't realize it at the time, that was the beginning of my deterioration.

Something inside of me died at that moment. Maybe it was a bit of my identity, being a big, strong man who had lost a lot of weight and loved running all over Houston. Maybe it was the realization that I couldn't just hit the course and ignore the invading bullets. Just as if that thug's bullet hit the bullseye he had on my chest, the depression struck and debilitated me. Suddenly, like a fatal shot to the heart, all my mental, physical, and emotional energy drained from my spirit.

Then the Running Servant came to my rescue.

That is the strangest feeling. Here I am spent, but then I see another in pain, and suddenly, I'm recharged. The opportunity to others saves me when I need it most.

I met a lady in the second half of the marathon who was running to honor her father who had passed away recently. Her commitment was admirable, but her pain was intense. Yet, like me, she wouldn't stop.

Having lost track of her on the course, I was alone in my pain and depression when suddenly, as happens in races, we look up and there they were. I could see she was grimacing and working to fight through brutal pain. It hurts to watch her. One thing about Big Sexy is that I can't stand to see others in pain.

My mind pivoted instantly, and the Running Servant reappeared, encouraging her through those last few miles.

I wouldn't know the entire story until a few years later. She contacted me and thanked me for sticking with her and helping her. She discovered after finishing that she had fractured her foot, not during, but before the marathon. She was doing well until mile 20, but as the muscles fatigued, the stress of the race took its toll. Imagine running a marathon on a broken foot. I have to admire someone like that.

Finish line

As I crossed the finish line, I gladly accepted my medal and then they handed me my shirt. A quick glance revealed it was an XS, not the XXL I paid for.

"What do you want me to do with this?" I questioned the volunteer. "What do you want me to do with this, wrap it around my thigh?" I stood 6 feet two inches and weighed over 200 pounds and they gave me an XS shirt.

They looked back, stunned I didn't just take it. I continued, "What did you do with my shirt?" You see, to get an XXL, I had to pay extra. So why didn't they have my shirt that I paid for.

Obviously, they gave my shirt to someone that wanted a bigger one but didn't pay for it. Even my bib said the XXL for the size, but they tried to explain, "That's all we have left." Come on people. Why didn't you give people the size of shirts printed on their bib? I traveled thousands of miles and had to leave without a shirt. That was ridiculous.

Maybe it was one indignity too many after them breaking down the course early, booty smacking women, and audience insults. But I wasn't alone. Runners took to social media, posting on various sites, including What's App, Facebook, Instagram, and others. The posts quickly went viral to the point that traditional news outlets picked up the story. The outrage was so quick, in part, because 75% of runners in the London Marathon are running for a charity. They aren't the elite runners but rather running to raise funds for worthwhile causes. Imagine how many friends and family were outraged by the mistreatment of their favorite runners. When the organizers received the angry calls and saw the negative publicity on the news that evening, they quickly investigated and changed their policies. Almost 800 runners were offered a complimentary entry into the next year's marathon. I was one of those and anticipated returning in 2020 to run it again.

At this point, demoralized from my weak performance, poorly run race, and the booty smacking, the Running Servant went into hiding.

Looking Back

Frustrated but yet pleased I finished the London Marathon, the first of the six World Majors, I set my sights on Berlin in September. I was hoping to have the summer to recover and train. That would help me recover, turn the corner, and return to my previous running success.

Berlin

The summer of 2019 flew by and soon I was walking out of the Berlin airport in September. Unfortunately, I ran right into a wall of cigarette smoke. I couldn't believe it. I hadn't seen this many people smoking cigarettes in public since the 1980s in the U.S. I came to understand it was more like the 1960s when they still advertised cigarettes on TV.

Everyone was smoking. When I say everyone, I mean it seemed like everyone was lighting, inhaling, and blowing out a cloud of smoke.

Catching my bus to the old airport where I was to pick up my race packet, was even worse than exciting the airport, as we were packed in

31

the bus like sardines. The smell of the smoke permeated everyone's clothes.

Photo: Trying hard not to breathe so much.

Why is that so annoying? Cigarette smoke is the worst trigger of my PTSD, and it brought back horrible memories. The guy I wrestled on that fateful evening in Houston reeked of Newport cigarettes. That specific smell of cigarette smoke triggers my PTSD very quickly.

After changing buses at the central station, I caught a train to the packet pickup at the old airport. Unfortunately, this was the same song, second verse.

I found my check-in and provided the required passport. They put my wristband on me with the instructions to not cut it off, lose it, or let it fall off. "You will not be allowed to run the race if you do not have the wristband on."

The next step was to get my racing bib. Given that 44,000 runners were here for the same purpose, I took my place in line. To my surprise, they were printing the bibs from a regular office printer. Unlike every other race I had run, the bib was nothing but an 8.5x11 sheet copy paper. Normally they are a special type of paper with fibers making it sturdy and waterproof. The bib usually has the timing chip on the back, but Berlin opted to have the timer attach to your shoestring. Maybe that is why they choose the cheaper option for the bib. The bib served only to identify us in the photos.

I decided prior to leaving Houston that I only wanted one souvenir, a running jacket that said Berlin Marathon. I found the merchandise area and found the biggest size they had, an XXL. That's when I fully realized where I was and that European sizes are cut much smaller. I guess it complimented my XS London shirt well. "Oh well."

I found my hotel, went out for a quick meal, and then returned expecting a restful evening. That wasn't to be.

Hours before, unbeknownst to me, the cigarette smoke had triggered the PTSD process and I was headed for a depressive episode. Unable to prevent the attack, I knew the only option was to get through it. I laid down and slept. I slept so long that when I woke up, I realized I had slept for eighteen hours. I had woken up a time or two, but it was as if I had no power. The batteries were dead. My motor unplugged. I tried but literally could not get out of bed. I prayed, asking God to prevent soiling myself. I tried again later with no success.

I was looking forward to running the 5k family and friend run that morning. Like Tokyo, anyone can run it and it is a great opportunity to meet elite runners, the superstars of the sport. Naturally, that is a great opportunity to get photos that you will fondly remember for years.

Unfortunately, I missed all that. It wasn't until that evening that my body allowed me to get out of bed. In a daze, I made it to the lobby before collapsing on the couch like a vegetable. Gathering my bearings. I slowly made my way to a pub, simply to force myself to move. I knew I needed to eat and squeezed my way through the crowd to find a place at the bar. The Reuben Sandwich tasted phenomenal. Knowing I needed to prepare for the race in the morning, I returned to the room and went back to sleep. I just hoped I had the energy to get out of bed in time for the race.

My alarm sounded and I opened my eyes. As if in slow motion, I tested my body to see if it would react. Yes, it responded. As I sat up, I realized I was refreshed and ready to run. Since I purposely chose a hotel close to the start, I just had to walk half a mile to the running area and then another 1.5 miles to the start. That was better than another smokey bus ride.

The Race

The Berlin Marathon offered a beautiful start. The heart pounding music was complimented with an enthusiastic emcee standing on a platform in the middle of the runners stretching. We all enjoyed the high energy.

That September day was preceded by two days of rain with no sight of relief. You would have thought the organizers would have forecast the problems. Copy paper running bibs quickly lose a battle with rain. Organizers should have known the rain would win that battle easily.

Photo: Representing Houston and Rocket Sports

Throughout the race, I smelled smoke. I tried focusing on the beautiful scenery, route, and people, but the smoke was always there.

Many runners let their bibs fall, even before the start line. The diligent few ran with it in their hand and held it up for photos. Meanwhile, the ground was littered with soaked and deteriorating bibs.

I felt defeated during the run. Sitting in the back of my mind was the lingering disappointment from London five months before. My running bottomed out in London. Expecting to run 4.30, I ran 6.30. I didn't quite match that in Berlin. I was extremely disappointed. I expected to at least better my time, not get worse. To my dismay, even though I was training, getting massage therapy, and stretching, my leg was getting weaker. Mentally I was asking myself, "What's going on with me?"

Fortunately, the chip timers were waterproof and securely attached to our laces. The only problem is that they expected you to return them at the finish unless you wanted to pay for it and keep it as a keepsake. As I finished, the lady offered help to untie my shoe, but I knew that wasn't going to happen. Fortunately, I had already decided to keep the timing chip. "You can charge my account because I can't bend over." I had my souvenir.

Looking Back

Despite the smoke, Berlin was iconic. It is hard to beat Germany during Octoberfest, even for a guy who doesn't drink. Now it was on to Chicago in October.

Chicago

"I'm just going to go out and enjoy it." Having been disappointed for my first two world majors, I lowered my expectations for the windy city marathon. Even though my time didn't change much, the Chicago Marathon stole my heart. — I'll share why later

London is more iconic, but Chicago quickly became my favorite marathon, a ranking that hasn't changed since. It is truly an American marathon because they do everything well beginning with the packet pickup to the finish. Along the way, there are so many people who cheer you on. That includes the police who banter and talk crazy to you. It's all good and left me feeling great.

The Race

The start and finish lines are located in Grant Park. Blocked off and filled with festivities, the whole area is one big party. As a runner, if you are staying in one of the big hotels nearby, all you have to do is wake up, walk out the hotel, and walk to the starting line. I stayed next to Expo, so I caught an uber to the start line. Still, it was easy. I was going to walk the 1.5 miles but caught uber to save stress on my right glute. I did, however, enjoy the walk back to my room following the post-race celebration.

The start is epic as you run through the city, along the lake, through downtown, ethnic neighborhoods, and back to the park. The skyline is great, inspiring runners to run the last 6 miles like Rocky running the steps in Philadelphia.

As I said, Chicago does it right. For example, athletes with disabilities start before the elites. I asked and they allowed me to start with the disability athletes without a big argument. They assigned me a volunteer who checked on me and helped navigate the start. They gave us clear instructions to stay to our right to let faster runners pass. I would come to understand they do what the New York Marathon does in respecting all runners the same, regardless of time.

Photo: Representing Atlanta based run "The RACE" for the Chicago 55K.

There was one mistake. For the 5k the day before, they gave runners beanies along with the medals. That wasn't the problem. Someone didn't stay there and hand them out, ensuring all runners got one. Instead, they just set them on the table and let runners, families, and spectators help themselves. Learning of the problem, they quickly sent an email apologizing. But then they stood tall and reordered beanie hats and sent one to each runner. That is doing it right. Meanwhile, I'm still waiting for my XXL shirt from London.

The Chicago Marathon is a runner's paradise. Let me finish telling you why it stole my heart. I had the privilege to pace the 2017 Chicago Marathon. I experienced the best and worst of the windy city's

weather, from ice cold rain prior to the start and beautiful clear blue skies with temperatures in the mid 40 at the start. After crossing the start line and being warned to run on the red carpet while crossing the bridge, I knew I was having a pacer's proud moment. Then it happened, total glute failure and muscle meltdown.

After utilizing the port-port-a-port-port-a-can, I found myself playing catch-up to my group for a mile or so before slamming face down onto the floor on the concrete jungle. My total understanding gave way and caused my body to begin spas; so much so, I had to be carried off the course. What a sight it must have been. But for the next few years, I never forgot the beautiful sight of running back into downtown. To me, the 2019 Chicago was a continuation of the 2017 course, a course which was more challenging because of my condition yet more rewarding because of my Six Star mission.

New York City

The New York City Marathon is also known as a phenomenal experience, but for another reason. Not only is it held in the Big Apple, but it is also known for attracting the most runners and largest crowds. Coming from Texas, and being called Big Sexy, you know that I love big things. Little did I know that the 2019 running would attract a field with 54,205 runners starting the race, and a Guinness Book of World Record 53,627 finishing it, surpassing the previous record of 52,813. That's an amazing 98.9 percent completion rate with only 578 dropping out. This is why I affectionately call it the people's marathon amongst other reasons.

But the race isn't the only thing big in New York City. So are the prices. I stayed at the Doubletree but quickly looked at other options for my next run (I knew I would run this one again.)

But let's not focus on the negative. This marathon is known for its big crowd participation and the big bridges. After all, this is New York. As Frank Sinatra sang, "If I can make it here, I can make it anywhere." The very thought of running the New York Marathon is taking my place on the big stage and finishing. Just arriving here was a phenomenal experience.

One part of running the marathon that surprised me was the reactions I received by raising funds and running for the Teams for Kids charity. First of all, I was surprised by how many runners were on their team. We filled an entire ferry taking us to Staten Island to begin the race. Then I was impressed with how many people in the stands saw the Teams for Kids singlet I was wearing and thanked me for my help. You see, without the funds we had all raised, their child wouldn't be able to receive coaching in important skills. Some learned to run, others to speak in public, and still others learned important life skills. They were grateful for their child's opportunity and my help in making that happen. I was struck by the countless strangers who said, "Thank you" for my involvement with Teams for Kids.

Teams for Kids provided a luncheon for their kids and their families. Runners were also included and enjoyed several speakers addressing the needed life skills. I particularly enjoyed meeting Meb. His full name is Meb Keflezighi, but serious runners know him by his first name. His story is quite impressive as his parents gathered their ten children and left the east Africa country of Eritrea as refuges. Making their way to San Diego, Meb started running at age 12 and quickly made his mark by winning races and setting records. He ran a 5:10 mile while in high school and won 4 NCAA championships in college. Turning pro he went on to win both the NYC and Boston Marathons. He also won a silver medal in the 2009 Olympics.

Photo: Meb and I gave a video shout out to my run coach Jetola Blair at the 2019 Team For Kids luncheon marathon weekend.

One of the highlights of the weekend was meeting Meb and recording a video with him to our mutual friend, Getola Blair. She was amazing as she ran 7 minutes and walked 2 minutes while running a sub four-hour marathon. Meeting Meb is just one of the things that make running the NYC Marathon and other world majors so fascinating. It attracts the best.

As you can imagine, moving 53,000+ runners is quite a logistic challenge. As assigned, I arose early on race day, left my hotel to make my way to the Team for Kids Ferry, filled with our runners. Landing at Staten Island, we boarded buses taking us to our staging area.

Following my disappointment in London and Berlin, I lowered my expectations in Chicago. I was realizing I wasn't the runner I once was and needed to accept that. But that doesn't mean I wasn't frustrated. I still wanted to do more. I still wanted to return to that pre-shooting form. So, I swallowed hard and accepted my condition and set my expectations accordingly. Beginning the race, I was content to do what I could do. For me, maybe for the first time running a race, time didn't matter. What did matter was enjoying the race and finishing.

The Race

The enjoyment started immediately because the start of the New York Marathon is off the charts. With the massive group of runners and staged near Broadway, you know this is going to be a great show. Helicopters hovered along all sides of the bridge, both the lower and upper decks, the music energized the audience and then, just after the national anthem concluded, two fighter jets flew over and a cannon blast to begin the race and each Corral thereafter. Those flyovers and Canon fires helped every runner feel like they were an elite runner at the front of the race. It felt like we were filming a Hollywood box Blockbuster. By the way, Team for Kids filled our own corral. That's impressive.

The New York City Marathon is known for their bridges connecting the five boroughs. Our first challenge was Verrazano-Narrows Bridge into Brooklyn. It has two decks and is usually reserved for vehicle traffic, but not today. The top deck was filled with the elite runners while us charity runners filled the lower deck. You can imagine the sight of that many runners starting a race. No wonder that is the iconic image used in the news media and marketing.

Photo: Start Lines for New York City Marathon, Lower Level

Running shoulder to shoulder, we ran up Fourth Avenue, then close to the Brooklyn waterfront. But this is no ordinary race because of this section. Brooklyn is the highlight of the entire race. The road is blocked off from curb to curb until the elite pass. Then, as if on cue, people push beyond the police tape and barricades to leave only a narrow path. Cheering wildly, they create a frantic chaos of excitement for miles. Imagine running through that hysteria. You want to run faster and faster. But with that many runners going through that narrow pathway, you would think there would be a bottleneck. But there wasn't. The energy of the crowd kept everyone running and running faster. The only challenge is to keep track of your running companion because it is easy to get separated.

Brooklyn is such a phenomenal experience I almost wished I could loop back and run through it again before continuing. Everywhere else, the whole street was open, but not Brooklyn. The fans are incredible. Make no mistake, there is nothing like Brooklyn in any other marathon throughout the world.

One of my favorite parts of the race is the DJ booth in the Brooklyn Safe Bank cheer group. In 2019 it was a male and 2021 a female. Gender doesn't matter, whenever I get there, I get jiggy with it. I stop for maybe five minutes and dance. The spectators and the runners always love it. You would think that a runner wouldn't want to stop and lose five minutes but for me, it is worth every second.

Photo: Running through the crowds in Brooklyn

Back on the course, at about the halfway mark, we crossed the Pulaski Bridge into Long Island City. We only ran a short distance through Queens, when we were back on another bridge, this one the Queensboro Bridge into Manhattan.

That was one of the most difficult parts of the race because of the deafening silence. Without the crowds cheering us on, our world went silent. All you hear is feet striking the bridge. It is eerie.

Other than a camera man taking race photos on the bridge, we were sequestered for these 2 miles. That might not seem long, but realize I was running about a 15-minute per mile pace. That meant for 30 minutes, all I encountered was deafening silence and the sound that reminded me of goosestepping Nazis in the Holocaust. There were no cars and no spectators. Just feet rhythmically pounding the pavement. Runners call that section the wall of silence. Before I stepped off the bridge, I vowed I would never run that bridge again in silence. It is mentally defeating.

That silence is suddenly shattered coming off the bridge and entering Manhattan. The world explodes as if we were shot out of a canon. That huge cheering crowd lit our short fuse. Wow, it was invigorating and the second-best moment of the race, surpassed only by Brooklyn.

After half, somewhere around mile 15, 16, or 17 we faced the last incline before turning into the park. I thought that the hill was never going to end and halfway up I had to break my pace and walk. My right glute just isn't as strong carrying that bullet. Finally reaching the top, it opened to a view of Central Park that was so beautiful that I just had to say, "Thank You" to my maker. I had not only finally made it to the top of the incline but gave thanks for the glorious view.

By that point, all that was left was running the last three miles through Central Park.

I crossed the finish line in approximately seven hours. Recognize the importance of that comment. First of all, I finished the New York City Marathon. Then realize it took longer than Chicago, Berlin, or London. For one of the first times since returning to running after the shooting, I was grateful to God for answering my prayers. The long incline tapped by glutes, but I had the strength to keep going. I finished. For a long-distance runner, that is ultimately what is important.

Running marathons lives up to the metaphor. It's not a quick or easy sprint. You need to prepare for the long haul, getting up in the dark, get to the starting line, begin, set your pace, resist temptations to run faster, persist and not quit, power through the challenges, finish, and head home in the dark.

Running the New York Marathon reminded me of a few lines in Frank Sinatra's famous song.

These vagabond shoes
They are longing to stray
Right through the very heart of it
New York, New York

One thing that I most appreciate about running the New York City Marathon is that, unlike Boston and other races, they keep the finish line open until the last runner is finished, no matter how long it takes them to cross the epic Central Park finish line. One woman finished in 8 hours because she started and finished the race on crutches. Why? She refused to quit, she tackled the challenge and finished. For a race to keep the finish line open for her meant a lot to me. So, I stayed and cheered her on as she crossed that finish line. What she did was incredible. So was what the New York City Marathon did.

Tokyo and Boston

Having completed London, Berlin, Chicago, and New York, I had two remaining to complete my six-star medal for the Abbot World Marathons.

Remember, I'm running these marathons through charities. I ran London with Team Scope. While going through their list of charities online, I was looking for a connection to those that were fighting for people with disabilities or fighting for our children. I specifically wanted to do something to support those helping with PTSD. I reached out to Crime Stoppers; however, their response was delayed. By then I was in contact with Team Scope. Then, for Berlin, I connected with Teams for Kids and that changed everything. They wanted me to run every one of the six world majors to support them. That was even better than I imagined. However, the lady didn't know if offered the Tokyo Marathon. It turns out they did not.

To my dismay, I found that Tokyo had already closed their fundraising for 22019. I also learned that unlike other world majors, submitting to run for a charity in Tokyo is based on competitive fundraising. My acceptance depended on how much I was willing to raise. In other words, it is a bidding war where they only take the top segment, and you don't know how much others are bidding. But that is only half of it. You must guarantee your donation by attaching your bank account. If your bid is accepted, they take the money from your account. If you don't have it, the bank pays it and you must pay it back. This is serious business.

That creates a challenge in any negotiation where you must know your limits. Most bid high, determined to gain entry and earn their star. But I know my limits and options. I know there are tours that offer entry as part of their travel packages. I started calling around and found that some tours are restricted for citizens of that country. That isn't the case for the United States tours but they had a waiting list. Continuing my research, I found a tour out of Jerusalem that had openings. The cost was $3000. That wouldn't have been enough in a charity bid so it was a good deal, especially considering it included a hotel, located near the start line and transportation from the finish line back to the hotel. I secured my spot and looked forward to running in the spring of 2020.

Boston and Tokyo both cancel 2020 with Boston not only going virtual for the first time but being canceled for the first time after being held annually for 123 consecutive years.

Unfortunately, the world pandemic shut everything down before I could board the plane. They refunded my money, and I signed up for 2021, the year Tokyo hosted the Summer Olympics, only to have the entire general population field canceled with only the elite field competing for Olympic Gold. The Tokyo Marathon put out a notice for 2022 that they were suspending charity runners until all those former fundraisers have run and would only allow Tokyo citizens and residents to participate, leaving me waiting until at least 2023. Currently, I have my tour package info and am waiting to purchase after the Tokyo Giveaway of 100 free entries.

Boston also canceled the race for 2020 and then postponed 2021 to the fall. I'll save that story for later but give you a teaser. Boston made London look good. I've never been so disappointed.

Having done all, I could with the world majors by the end of 2020, I needed another challenge.

My Audacious Challenge

Seeing the shooter aiming at my chest, I turned quickly, and the bullet missed its mark, I began to run, and he continued to shoot. The kill shot missed but the next four didn't.

"Are you crazy?"

"No."

"Who runs 50 marathons in 50 states in 50 weeks?"

"I do. It isn't crazy. I'm on a mission."

Following the shooting, I met weekly with a psychologist and, in a separate appointment once a month, a psychiatrist. The PTSD was not only debilitating but threatening to shut down my life and close me off to the world. The psychologist and the psychiatrist both urged me to begin putting my life back together.

But there was another problem. In my efforts to prevent my coworkers' deaths, I interrupted the killers' illegal and selfish goals. To say they didn't appreciate it was an understatement. Filled with anger and retaliation, they made additional threats on my life. They came back to the place of my employment and asked about me. They were definitely not concerned about my health. Another time they left evidence from another one of their criminalized crimes on my stoop and hanging from the fence just outside my front door. Yet another time, they stalked me, with the intention of killing me. This is partly why I spend my days at a Starbucks frequented by Houston police officers and Constables. Never feeling safe, like you're going to be murdered at any moment by people you can't identify but know is out to silence you, is a torturous living hell — I knew I had to do something to escape it.

By January of 2020, my doctors wanted me to come up with something that would give me a reason to live, to get up in the morning, and rebuild my hope in humanity. Realizing I was turning 50, I wanted to be grateful to God for being alive. I didn't know what I wanted to do, but knew I had to do something every day of each and every week.

Covid hit in March, limiting where I could go and what I could do. Not only had every gym shut down frustrating the rats, but even the parks were off limits for the ranger. The only thing I could do was go to Starbucks and sit outside. If I didn't do something, I could expect nothing more than what I had experienced the last 5 years. I needed to get out of that hell.

The only thing that motivated me was to get back into my fitness and wellbeing. I remembered the exhilaration of losing approximately 180 pounds and discovering the joy of running. I remembered how alive I felt meeting the running community and enjoying the trails of Terry Hershey Park. For me, running is a release, a freedom that celebrates my strength, talent, and spirit. To return to that became my priority.

That's when the 50-50-50 challenge entered my mind. I challenged myself to run 50 marathons in 50 states in 50 weeks to celebrate my 50th birthday. I also set a goal of finishing each marathon in 5 hours and 5 minutes.

Why run marathons? Why not run half marathons? Why run every week? Why did I need to make it that audacious of a challenge?

Why?

There existed four compelling reasons to tackle this audacious goal.

1. As I mentioned, I was running to get back to what I was prior to being shot. I was on the verge of turning professional in trail running, before the shooting squelched that opportunity. Any competitive athlete who has suffered an injury or an illness wants to return to the previous level if possible. That is my quest.

2. I also run to counter PTSD, build my mental health, and restore my health. I have found running to be the best medical, mental, and emotional treatment. Runners know running a marathon is a

mental game and I am determined to win this battle — I suffered an extreme case of runner's depression in addition to PTSD. That is my task.

3. I am the running servant. This isn't for ego but to live out my heavenly mission. As a man of faith, I believe I am running to help others as God directs. My goal is to help others make the changes they want and need to make. I serve my LORD Jesus, the Suffering Servant, by helping others. Remember my nickname, and online brand RUNandSERVE, #RunningServant. That is my purpose.

4. That led me to take the attention off of myself and onto others. I chose St. Jude's Hospital and, in particular, one little boy as the recipient of my fundraising. Aiden is a little boy afflicted with several childhood diseases. I first heard of his story while running the Chicago marathon as part of the Abbot Majors. Something about him touched my heart and I immediately prayed for him. God quickly spoke, telling me to help. To this day, that image of Aiden is imprinted on my mind and spirit. Very quickly I joined the movement, #IrunforAiden. That is my focus.

My Plan

My plan was to begin in my home state of Texas and complete my challenge like all the Super Bowl MVPs do, by going to Disney World. Only I would be running Disney's Dopey Challenge for their marathon weekend.

As I looked ahead, I realized a critical part of the challenge is navigating the logistics. Running 50 marathons in 50 states in 50 weeks will require considerable planning each week. My initial plan was to sublet my apartment to a cousin and hit the road for a year, traveling from race to race. Given many races would be along the east coast, I intended to visit family in South Carolina and Ohio. Even then, the schedule presented itself as a giant jigsaw puzzle, finding the right race at the right time. Then arranging the hotel, airfare, and ground transportation on a reasonable budget made it even more complicated.

My early schedule takes me through the southern states of South Carolina, Alabama, and Mississippi in consecutive weeks. Then I go west but stay in the warmer weather with Arizona and California, before returning closer to home in Arkansas and Louisiana. Then it's west again with Nevada and New Mexico after a side trip to Delaware. Each of those marathons require a flight, hotels, and a return flight.

That gives me a couple days at home before doing it all over again. Of course, there is also continual training and attending to personal issues.

That's not even considering the physical and emotional demands of running a marathon a week. Given that only one percent of the population ever run one marathon, I was attempting to run one a week for fifty consecutive weeks. That posed a significant physical challenge for my nutrition as well as my physical training and recovery.

That would be forbidding for most, but then I had to consider I wasn't in the physical and emotional condition that I was before the shooting. Remember, I ran all over Houston and its surrounding areas in those days. I never drove. When I wasn't running, I was riding my bike. But now I was in constant pain from the bullets invading my body. Interestingly enough, that wasn't my biggest concern.

I didn't consider how the Covid shutdowns would multiply the problems and complicate the process. Not only would I be faced with running a marathon each week in a different state, but I was also faced with the chaos of rescheduling races that were postponed or canceled. Add to that the rescheduling of air travel, hotels, and ground transportation. Oh yes, then all along the way, I was raising funds in honor of Aiden for St. Jude's Hospital.

Make no mistake, I am a dreamer, thinker, and planner, all necessary traits for those willing to do what others never consider possible. Even though I wasn't a Boy Scout, I knew I needed a backup plan. I researched and identified races as my plan B, C, or D. That proved immensely valuable in the chaos that unfolded.

Through it all, I had one condition. I refused to run a virtual marathon. Instead, I scheduled additional marathons that would ensure I exceeded 50 marathons. In some cases, I was scheduled to run multiple marathons in a week, even running them on successive days.

For example, on May 1, I scheduled the Pittsburgh Marathon before quickly hitting the road to run the Frederick Running Festival Half Marathon in Frederick, Maryland the very next day, May 2. Then, on May 3rd, I traveled to Washington, D.C. to compete in the Potomac River Run Marathon. Since one fell on Saturday and the others on Sunday, they count for different weeks. Never-the-less, that's demanding.

Plan B also included the New England Challenge in early May. Beginning on Monday, May 17, he scheduled the Pine Tree Challenge in Portland, Maine, and the next day the Granite State Marathon in nearby Nashua, New Hampshire. That's less than a two-hour drive but marathons in consecutive days are brutal. Like the commercials tell us, "But wait, there's more." I had a day off before another short drive to run the Old Colony Marathon in Westfield, Massachusetts on the 20th, the Old Nutmeg Marathon the 21st in Hartford, Connecticut, before finally finishing this brutal stretch with the Red Island Marathon in Warwick, Rhode Island on the 22nd. That's five marathons in six days, resulting in running 131 miles in six days.

Because that is all in one week, I will only count one of those runs toward the 50-50-50 challenge. Remember, that was my backup plan to ensure I reached my goal. I'm a man of my word and am unwilling to take shortcuts.

Then there was the unfinished business of running the last two of the Abbot Six Majors from 2020, the Tokyo and Boston Marathons. Both were scheduled to be run in October of 2021. Again, I wouldn't count them toward the 50 because they were part of my previous challenge to run the six world marathons.

Am I crazy?

No, I'm on a mission. I know I can do more than what most believe is possible when I've learned to think bigger, reach higher, and work to exceed expectations.

With my plan set, I went to work training during the remainder of 2020. After all, what else could we do during that shutdown year? Like everyone else, I was hopeful the pandemic would ease, and we could return to some semblance of order.

A Shaky Beginning

I gladly said goodbye to 2020 in anticipation of a phenomenal 2021. But I held my breath, knowing that many races were canceling or postponing or going virtual. I knew there was one thing I wouldn't do in this challenge and that was to run a virtual race. Part of my motivation was to get out of Houston to begin rebuilding my life. I realized very quickly how difficult that would be.

I wanted to start at home by running with the Houston Chevron Marathon for my birthday weekend. That would be a great way to celebrate my birthday and kick off my audacious quest. Unfortunately, like many races around the world, Chevron canceled in-person races, choosing to opt for the sweeping virtual trend due to the pandemic. I hadn't even gotten to my first race and was scrambling to reschedule. I scrambled to find another run but very few have escaped the fear and frustrations of the pandemic. I found one after another run but as time grew closer, one after another was canceled. Finally, I found the Daufuskie Island Marathon off the coast of Georgia, next to Hilton Head Island, South Carolina. As they say with business strategic plans, it needs to be a living and breathing document, therefore it must be flexible.

With the early revision, I was now starting in Georgia and ending with Houston's 50th Anniversary Chevron Marathon. That would be a fitting birthday present.

As you follow my challenge, notice how many expectations were not met. That is life in many ways. We expect one thing, and another happens. It wasn't because we didn't work hard enough or set our goals high enough. Our success or failure depends on how we pivot those expectations and make the most of the opportunities. While we cannot control many elements of our lives, we can control our attitude and make our own decisions.

Week 1: Daufuskie Island, South Carolina, January 16

It's my birthday!

What better place to spend it than on a warm, beautiful, almost magical island? Daufuskie Island was the perfect place to begin my quest as it is like stepping out of the present and traveling back in time to the old, low country of yesteryear. Sitting off Hilton Head Island, South Carolina, it is the southernmost point of the state's barrier islands. Savannah, Georgia sits to the south and is just a stone's throw away, if you have a strong arm.

Photo: Surprise, surprise, the volunteers sang happy birthday to me.

The island is only five miles long and 2.5 miles wide. What makes this island so unique is that it can only be reached by ferry. There are no bridges or tunnels to get to the island. The only way you can get there is by ferry. That means, there is no car traffic on the island. You can either rent a golf cart, bring your bicycle, or walk.

I learned that the name "Daufuskie" comes from the Muscogee language and means "sharp feather", for the island's distinctive shape. I figured with a name like that, the roads had to be nice and soft. I wouldn't be disappointed.

Stepping off the ferry at the southernmost tip, Haig Point, I quickly appreciated the architecture of this former plantation. I learned that there were once eleven plantations here.

My plan started out well, flying into Hilton Head and staying at a hotel just a short distance away so I could walk or take an Uber to the hotel. I had originally planned to walk the 2 miles to the ferry but called an Uber instead. That was valuable because parking at Haig Point is very limited.

Foreshadowing the New York Marathon, the only other race where I had to take a ferry to get to the start line, I made sure to be there early. That was critical because there were only three ferries that would get us to the island in time for the race. Fortunately, runners could start whenever they wanted, meaning they didn't have an official start for the half, full, or ultra-marathons. (In this race, the ultra is a marathon plus another half-marathon.) That also meant that the first two ferries carried runners pursuing various goals. The third ferry was reserved for spectators so if you missed the first two ferries, you had to wait for either the 4th or 5th.

Landing at Haig Point, a private club, I enjoyed the warm tent, catered breakfast, and great food afterward. The warm tent was nice but not necessary with a low of 63.

Knowing that I love running trails, you can imagine how excited I was to run through the ancient oaks never too far from the sandy beaches. What a special birthday present as God directed me to this throwback island. The course was flat and straight on mostly smooth, soft, dirt paths. Only miles one and five of the loop were paved. Normally running a trail requires close attention to detail lest you stumble over a root or a rock. Not here. I didn't even need trail running shoes. That dirt was so comfortable that many runners chose not to run on the pavement at all. Stepping off the side, they continued running on the dirt.

As a serious runner, I have my goals and know what times I need for each segment. This course was so beautiful and predictable that there was no guesswork. All I had to do was run, and I did.

Quickly hitting my stride, I was feeling great before I knew it, I finished the first loop. But suddenly, I was confused as to where I needed to turn around and start the second loop. I made one turn, ran through the start gate, and kept going. That was different but then almost every marathon sets the course up differently. All the sudden people started cheering like I had won the race in record time. That's when I knew I had taken a wrong turn. I smiled, laughed, and welcomed directions to the second loop.

Back on course, I joined up with the 11 minute per mile pacing group. We crossed a bridge, and it was as if my legs said, "find me." They gave out and I hit the ground. People stopped and offered help, but I told them to keep going. "This happens every once in a while. Sometimes my right leg goes numb. I just need to wait, and it will wake up."

Photo: The flat me.

I did and it did. Getting back on my feet, I changed my pace to include a run/walk sequence before shifting to a straight power walk. In the end, I finished, but did not meet my 5:05 goal. That didn't bother me because I purposely set aggressive goals to push myself. It's no challenge if you know you know you can do it. Progress comes when we push ourselves beyond what we have already done. I'm not going to settle. I've known since London that my body wasn't what it used to be so mentally, I work on my mental toughness. With a bullet still lodged in my right gluteus maximus muscle, I know the second half of every marathon, usually beginning around mile 15, will be challenging. In Starbucks terms, the bullet is lodged in the biggest of the three glute muscles, small, grande, and vente (small, medium, and large). That means the muscle I need the most to push uphill is the most damaged. Even on this flat course, at some point that muscle will give me problems. But that doesn't mean I wave the white flag and surrender to a limited result. No, I set an aggressive challenge to push me father.

Remember, that is why I began this quest. Little Aiden and my niece Gabby can't quit when fighting their medical problems. If they can't quit, neither can I. I am the Running Servant because I want to help others. Part of that service is helping people see beyond their pain. I want to be an example for them. So even if I don't meet my aggressive goals, I am doing far more than I would if I settled for what I know I could do.

As I was approaching the finish line, I came alongside a lady running the ultramarathon. She was 63 years old and ran 39 miles in the time it took me to run 26. What an incredible story. She didn't listen to those that said she was too old to run or that she should be taking it easy. I love people like that. Better yet, she remembered me a couple months later when we were both running the Skidaway Island Marathon. She was pacing the two hour half-marathon group and when she saw me, she shouted out, "Oh My God, it's the Running Servant." We smiled and hugged and got a group photo with those nearby.

Photo: Skidaway Island Marathon Pacers sponsored by Howe 2 Run, running store.

Unexpected Logistical Problems

I love people but sometimes they test me. After enjoying the breakfast and the facilities, I boarded the ferry sweaty and tired. I was ready for a shower, clean clothes, and a good nap. But that wasn't to happen.

"Why won't this work? I guess I'll have to go down to the front desk and see what's wrong." After catching another Uber back to the hotel, I was locked out of my room. That wasn't what I was looking forward to.

By this time, I was hurting, wobbling, and freezing in the colder than I like hotel air. I approached the front desk and asked for another key.

"We will need more money."

"What?" I admit that I wasn't at the top of my mental game after running 26.2 miles with a wounded booty, but she didn't make sense.

"You need to pay." She gave me a number but that didn't matter.

"I paid." I tried to argue but she wouldn't budge. You see, for a variety of reasons, I choose to pay for each night rather than trust them with a credit card. I have learned that hotel accounting systems are weird and, depending on who does night audit, deliver unpredictable results. But the hotel workers want you to take their word based on what their system says.

"I'm not going to lose my job for you. I got bills, rent, and . . ." She continued, complaining about hotel problems.

I tried to politely reason with her. "I need to get out of these wet clothes. Can you at least let me in the room so I can change?" But she wouldn't accommodate me in any way. "Can you at least have someone get my bag so I can change?" Still not receiving any cooperation, I did what anyone in my situation would, I demanded to talk with the manager. Of course, Murphy's law prevailed, and the manager wasn't on premises.

Not to be denied, I took a seat in the cold lobby to get off my feet and wait. Eventually the manager called in and quickly set things straight. "Give him a key. His room is paid for." It turns out the stubborn person at the front desk was new to her job. The previous night manager was on her second to the last day of her job, leaving due to a terminal illness. The new lady didn't know the system and she didn't want to lose her job. No wonder she wouldn't even allow me to get my luggage. She was playing this one strictly by the books, even though the books were wrong.

Finally, I got into my room and enjoyed a hot shower, change of clothes, and rest.

The next morning the manager sat down with me and explained the situation. She was very nice and explained that Covid has changed a lot within the hotel industry. I was surprised to learn that people were stealing televisions from rooms, so the hotels needed to charge hold fees for incidentals. That added a higher hold charge than I anticipated. That was one logistical challenge I hadn't forecast. The manager handled it extremely well, understood my perspective, and apologized. I thanked her and offered, "This is a good time to coach your team." She agreed.

Then there was another logistical change. With family a short way away, I extended my stay to connect with them. Unfortunately, that didn't happen, so I had an extra day on the island. In my usual fashion, I sought out the nearest Starbucks for my Blonde Roast. That is my drink of choice because I need the caffeine to offset my migraines. I had suffered from most of my adult life but grew worse and more frequently with running.

Remember the problems I had in Berlin with the cigarette smoke triggering PTSD? I take precautions wherever I go to sit away from others, often outside, and definitely away from smoking.

But some people don't care. In fact, some people just look to make trouble for others.

I purchased my coffee and went to the patio that wraps around the building. I purposely sat by the drive up in order to separate myself. Then a guy walks out the door, lights up a cigarette, and stands a very short distance from me.

Trying to be polite, I ask, "Can you please not smoke on the patio?"

"Who are you? Why do you think that you can tell me what to do? It is legal for me to smoke here." Continuing his inquisition without even breaking, "Where is it written that I cannot smoke on the patio? Where does it say that you can ask me not to smoke?"

"I'm sorry but I have gone through a very traumatic workplace experience and cigarette smoke triggers my PTSD. All I'm asking is that you not smoke on the patio. At least don't stand next to me and smoke. Show some common decency."

Ignoring my request, his buddy continued the rant. "What kind of right do you have to ask him not to smoke next to you in public? Why don't you sit there and mind your own business" He expected me to knuckle under to his emotional outburst. I tried to be nice, now it was time to up my game.

I stood up.

He wasn't expecting what he saw.

His facial expression changed as I rose and my full 6 foot 2, 240 plus-pound body eclipsed him. I thought that would change it, but he and his buddy who joined him were not relenting.

His buddy, equally as belligerent as displayed by putting his foot in his mouth so far, he was sucking on his big toe, didn't stop. He filled in when the other one stopped to breathe and smoke. He was so agitated he stuck his head in the door and yelled for a manager, expecting backup.

The manager came out along with a couple of other guys. This sent a message to the two guys that they were outnumbered. One of the guys that came out was a detective from Florida here on vacation. He had noticed them and commented later that he knew they were looking for trouble.

The manager firmly explained to the two guys that they don't allow smoking on the patio.

The first guy returned to his previous argument, "Where does it say that in the constitution? And why do we have to wear these stupid masks?"

I don't remember what else he said but his lips kept moving and noise was coming from his mouth.

As it unfolded, it became evident that these two had a history with the manager. In the end, the guy complied but only to the letter of the law. He moved off the patio but near me, standing on the driveway, claiming, "You can't kick me off because this isn't Starbucks' property." Then for good measure, he looked at me and added, "I'll bet you voted for Biden. All you want to do is take away my rights."

I surprised him with my response, "Actually I didn't vote for Biden. I voted for Trump, you chump."

They both looked at each other, "At least we can agree on something." And then walked away, got into their truck decorated with confederate flags and bumper stickers, and drove off.

In conversation with the manager and the other two guys, they confirmed what I thought. They targeted me because I was the only black guy and they assumed I was a liberal who voted for Biden. All I cared about was that they didn't smoke next to me. If they would've listened, I would have told them they need to add this to the constitution. "No smoking next to the Running Servant."

I wish I could say that I went back to relaxing after that. But remember, cigarette smoke triggers my PTSD. Later that night, the trigger fired. I struggled to sleep as the nightmares arose from the dark of night. Anxiety followed and depression soon after. Lastly, I became hypervigilant about people approaching me. My only choice was to stay secluded in my room until going home.

I started this quest to escape my previous hell. But that incident put me right back into it, just in a different state. That was frustrating. I run to focus on others and, in the process, hope God will help me deal with my own problems. Tony Evans said, "Give and it shall be given unto you. What is the 'it'? It is the thing you give. Whatever you need from God, and you believe in God for, on whatever level you can be an answer to someone else's prayer, God uses you for that. Then do it because God is not interested in blessing selfish people. I've learned that God gives common grace for law, but he's not interested in blessing selfish children who are spoiled and think that they are the only ones who have a need. He gives to the needy, not the greedy.

I run to help others and that allows me to escape that hell. Unfortunately, sometimes escaping that hell takes every ounce of my being, every bit of faith I can muster.

With the Daufuskie Island Marathon completed, I returned home to Houston to prepare for Oklahoma.

Week 2: Go Short, Go Long, Go Very Long, OK, Jan. 23

With my first marathon in the books, I looked forward to making the short trip to Tulsa for my next stop. However, what I thought would be an easy venture turned into a series of problems.

First of all, I chose to drive. It made sense because Oklahoma borders Texas, so Tulsa is only about an eight-hour drive from Houston. I figured by the time I went to the airport, waited to board, flew, landed, and got transportation to the hotel; I could almost be to Tulsa. Besides that, I could save money. If only it was that easy.

Remember, I have the bullet lodged in my right glute. That means, I'm sitting on it the entire eight-hour drive to Tulsa while using my right leg muscles in driving. I should have seen that problem coming. Note to self: Don't do that again. Man was I in pain, so much pain that I wanted to take my leg off and throw it out the window.

My plan was to get there, lay down, and get some rest. That didn't happen because of another problem. The hotel was overbooked. How does that happen during a pandemic when very few are traveling? To make it worse, the front desk clerk told me, "Had you walked in before the guy in front of you, you would've got the last bed."

I quickly tried other hotels, but they were all booked. I couldn't believe this and surely couldn't have anticipated it. But, with no other choice, I climbed back into my car which would now be my bed for the night. To make matters worse, the forecast low was 29-degrees.

Making the best of it, I reclined my seat and tried to get some sleep. After all, I was running 26.2 miles the next day and couldn't do that without sleep. But there was one big problem. That means that I would be sitting on the bullet laden glute all night. It wasn't long and that already complaining glute was screaming at me.. I knew that once I finally went to sleep, I might oversleep and miss the start, so I positioned myself in a way that others would wake me up as they drove into the park entrance. After all this, I definitely didn't want to sleep through the start.

Photo: Friends, bib, and medals for Tulsa.

I was able to doze off and slept pretty well considering the situation. Runners arrived and made enough noise that I woke up. My accommodations were not ideal but at least I didn't oversleep. I went back to my car, grabbed my running clothes, and figured I would change in the bathroom. But anyone who has run races knows, the lines to the bathrooms before a race are quite long. Fortunately these were not port-a-potties, but the bad news was that the line was ridiculously long. Not wanting to wait nor take too long once it was my turn, I changed what I could without being arrested for indecent exposure and finished when I finally made it inside.

I made my way to the start and warmed up as much as I could in this 32-degree weather (not quite as cold as promised.) is tough.

It was a relief to get to the start and begin the race.

Once on the course, the overcast sky made for a great place to run. I mean, it was a beautiful, flat race except for one hill. Now that was a real hill deal when you went up the bridge then back off onto the trail. It was a challenge. But on the back side, now that was beautiful.

It is funny what you notice when you are running. Given that I slept outside like a homeless man on a cold night without an underpass, I quickly noticed a place ahead with a gas public utility plant with huge burners. I was sorely tempted to linger a bit. "When I get there, I'm going to take a nap." As runners, we have some strange thoughts on the course. But I kept running.

Like Daufuskie, the marathon required running two loops on the course. As I calculated my time, I realized that all the other marathon runners would be done by the time I crossed. I made the 3-hour cutoff to continue but by then, my glute was really screaming at me. I've learned that when my glute complains that loudly, the only way I can continue is to stop and rest. But since I was already the last runner and barely meeting the maximum time limit, I knew the best decision was to pull the plug on this race. I decided to not run the second loop, opting instead to settle for finishing a half marathon.

As much pain as I was suffering, I had to remember my mission as #RunningServant. I noticed a lady running with her friend. The lady was hurting really bad because of her right IT band. I helped her and encouraged her to go farther but she couldn't finish. Knowing the pain I encounter on a run; I do what I can to help others along the way. Sometimes it is a helping hand, other times, it is an encouraging word. I appreciate that others have their own story and purpose in challenging themselves to run farther and faster than they have before. I'm glad to help others in their quest. I just wished she could have finished.

The finish is always a great moment and often filled with incredible people. Tulsa wouldn't disappoint. Those people at the finish were simply phenomenal.

Looking back, week #2 on my quest was a prelude to the kiss of betrayal. Like Judas kissing Jesus, this race was a snapshot of what would follow.

It wouldn't be the last time I would be in this much pain.

It wouldn't be the last problem with a hotel.

It wouldn't be the last time I wouldn't be able to finish a marathon.

I did make a mental note that I would never drive to a race again unless I had at least an entire day to recover and a nice hotel bed.

With the race completed, I was anxious to get home. But this venture wasn't anywhere near done. I had to crawl back into my vehicle and drive those same 500 miles that had caused me so much pain. Only this time, I was driving it on very little sleep and having run 13.1 miles. I was tired, sore, and anxious to get home.

You might be thinking, "Get a hotel and a good night's sleep and head back tomorrow." Unfortunately, for whatever reason, there still were no hotel rooms available in Tulsa. The only thing I can think of was that with the cold weather, sometimes churches pay for rooms so the homeless have a warm place to stay in cold temperatures. I knew one thing. I wasn't about to sleep in my truck again in the cold.

As I approached Dallas, I considered stopping and getting a hotel room. But Dallas is only three and a half hours from my own bed at home. That seemed like a waste, so I pushed on. By the time I got home, parked, and got out, it was just in the nick of time. I could not have driven another mile.

With #2 checked off my list, I turned my attention to #3, the Big Beach Marathon in Alabama.

Week 3: Big Beach Marathon, Alabama, Jan. 30

One of the best parts of running is to see how each race is managed and the courses they lay out. Daufuskie offered a half, full, and ultra. Tulsa ran a 5k, 10k, 25k (15 mile), and 50k (31 mile). Daufuskie and Tulsa both ran a double loop course — the ultra at Daufuskie was three loops. Big Beach ran a 7K on Saturday and the marathon on Sunday. I ran the 7K, an absolutely stunning course, as a good warmup for the marathon.

Photo: Hanging with my friend.

Courses are often like a miniature golf course with some crazy obstacles. Big Beach implies a course along the beautiful Gulf of Mexico that is flat, sandy, and relaxing. It was beautiful but also had an incline to hell from mile 7 to 10. We started with a gradual incline into rolling hills to the lowest part of the park before inclining. At mile 7 we turn around and start going up for a steady, challenging climb. Just when I thought I was at the top, it levels off for a hot second, turns to the left, and then to the right, and then climbs even higher. That climb was torture.

Fortunately, there was an aid station at mile 10 that lifted my spirits. Remember, long inclines tax my glute muscles. Going down I use my quads and don't need the glutes so I'm fine. But this aid station offered far more than physical refreshment. Those exuberant volunteers boosted my spirits by cheering us on like it was the finish line and you ran the world's first sub-2-hour marathon. Made up of only a handful of people, they were one of the loudest aid stations I have ever encountered. I can't express how much I appreciated their encouragement. Without them, I'm not sure I would have made it up that incline.

From there we declined and ran on the boardwalk across the swamp. The scenery was beautiful, and the boardwalk was great because it wasn't slippery. Continuing on, we ran through a trailer camp where the wind picked up and we were forced to battle a headwind of 20 mph wind gusts. It was so strong that it stood me up and pushed me backward. I'm no small guy so you can see how strong those winds were. The 3 miles felt like a wind tunnel. Then I learned why. I had run up behind the man, the myth and the legend himself, Steve Boone, Texas' own. With one lap complete, all I had to do was run one more.

I was in pain from the incline to hell and battling the wind. My glutes were tight and were cramping in the back. I knew that to recover and continue, I needed 20-30 minutes of rest. But once again, I was in the back of the pack. In fact, I was so far back that the sweeper pacers passed me. The race director was at that point and told me, "You need to play catch up because we need to shut down the course. You can keep going but need to run on the sidewalk." It's nice that they allow you to keep going and would allow me to finish but they needed to keep to their time schedule too. I knew that with my glutes in this condition, I didn't have the strength to play catch up. So, for the second race in a row, I stopped at the half.

Photo: Mary Griffin standing between Texas Running Legends, the Boones, and founders of 50 States Marathon Club.

You might think I would be disappointed and even dejected. But I wasn't. It was actually very rewarding because this was one of the first runs where I ran 1.5 hours without walking or stopping. For my body with that injury, that is good. I was very happy with my progress and considered the race a success.

Challenge to a Quest

Mentally, by race #3, I was redefining success. Instead of seeing this challenge to run 50 marathons in 50 states in 50 weeks 5 years after being shot 5 times, I began to see it as a quest. It is not just finishing but how I am able to run, the progress I'm able to make, and the milestones I cross. I began to realize that I may not even finish. However, being able to run inclines, rolling hills, etc., if I make 15-17 miles, I'm happy. So, when I can complete 20 miles or run a 10k in 45 minutes, that is a success. I know that there is often a 6-hour completion time for a marathon. That means that if I make it to 20 miles, that is huge for me. That may not sound like a lot to others, like a friend who runs 135 miles, but it is for me.

I think about this friend, Marie Bartolecci. She is a friend on social media that is a triathlete who had a stroke and made it back. She wrote the book, *Perseverance: how a determined athlete tenaciously overcame a stroke* that was released in November of 2015. Her story is so impressive that she was featured on a Wheaties's box. Since then, she has completed 109 runs. I was surprised and pleased to learn she published the book the same month I was shot. There is a photo of her running at mile 35 and she looks fantastic.

Photo: With Marie Bartolecci.

Her drive comes from experiencing a runner's high during a race, her body responding well, and her sense of service. She markets her book to educate people about stroke prevention as well as raising funds for stroke society. She sent me a book and I gladly gave a donation. We are kindred spirits, because like the Running Servant, she loves to encourage others. Imagine how I felt when she told me, "I can't wait until you get back to running like you used to." I am also encouraged knowing that in her recovery, she had to redefine success and make new milestones. I had done that in this race, and I was pleased. It became clear to me that the process to recovery included the following six steps.

1. Survive
2. Thrive
3. Rebound
4. Overcome
5. Kick Butt
6. Encourage

At the beginning of all this, I felt like I was in the middle of a fierce emotional, spiritual, physical, and mental storm. But just three races into my quest, I am in a much better place where I am making progress.

With #3 checked off my list, I am continuing my Gulf Coast tour, this time visiting Mississippi.

Week 4: Mississippi River Run, Feb. 7

Had one thing been different, this tour of the Gulf Coast races would have been different. I wouldn't have returned to Houston. My original intent was to give up the lease on my apartment and travel from race to race. The rent and the extra flights would have easily paid for a few more hotels. But a cousin of mine who was going to sublet my apartment had a change of heart. Unfortunately, that didn't happen until just after I had renewed for another year. So instead of simply traveling to Mississippi from Alabama, I flew back to Houston, stayed the week, and flew to the next race.

This race is intriguing because runners can choose to either run the Arkansas or Mississippi half of the race. Choose which half marathon you want and run it. If you are on a quest to run all fifty states, you can run them both in one day. Or you can do as I was doing, running both halves for a full marathon.

I usually fly United because it is the most convenient. This time I took another flight that was cheaper. In the process, I had an opportunity I didn't expect.

Changing planes, I met Darrell Jones, president of Innocence Convicts. He was coming from Waco and also flying into Memphis. He would have been on an earlier flight but stopped to smoke and missed his plane. Darrell, as I learned on this fateful flight, was falsely accused, and wrongly imprisoned for 32 years. Railroaded by the Boston Police Department, he was finally acquitted in a 2017 retrial. At the time we met, he was looking forward to being featured in an upcoming HBO documentary. That's why he was in Waco, they were filming him while he bought a house for his sister.

It is definitely a small world because I have done business with his brother. Maybe that is why we hit it off, sparking a friendship that continues to this day. Telling him my story, he responded, "I'd like to run a marathon."

"I have a trainer in New York for you." I shared how I was raising funds for St. Jude's Hospital on my quest, and he quickly promised to donate $5,000 and put my story on his website. What a blessing. I love connecting with people who have the same sense of serving. (Note: I don't keep track of donations, so I never go back and check whether someone carries through or not. I believe that is between them and God. Personally, I give anonymously.)

The Race

The Mississippi River Run crosses two states and gives runners the opportunity to run both states or either Mississippi or Arkansas. The good part was that as I chose Mississippi, the only hill I had to climb was the two-mile bridge crossing the Mississippi River from where we started in Arkansas. The bridge is one mile up and one mile down. The halfway point in the marathon is just as you begin the steep incline of that bridge. The full Marathon starts in Arkansas, crosses the halfway point on the Mississippi River Bridge and finishes in Greenville, Mississippi.

Going up was tough but everything else was flat so I knew I would be fine. By the fourth race, I could feel that I was getting stronger.

There is always one person that stands out in every race as I look to serve. In this race, it was a lady I met at mile 17 who had prayed to the LORD Jesus to send her someone to help. Just then, I appeared seemingly out of nowhere. Not only was I in the back of the pack, but I was also the "Back of the Pack".

Cassandra Bennett was running her first marathon. I always enjoy meeting and helping those run their first long race. Everyone remembers running their first marathon, for both the joy and the pain. Unfortunately for this woman, had a cramp in her calf muscle. You don't have to be a marathoner to imagine how much that hurts. Runners especially feel the pain at mile 17 and know that you cannot run through a cramp. I approached her and offered encouragement and to massage her calf. Meanwhile, I've studied enough to know that cramps are caused by a lack of sodium, not just water. I massaged her calf but had to find something to replace the sodium. Not having sodium tables, I went in search of anything that would help. Picture this. A big black man with an even bigger afro running through an exclusive neighborhood asking, "Anyone got some pickles? I need the pickle juice." Fortunately, I found pickle juice and she gladly drank it. That did the trick. She finished her first marathon and was exhilarated.

By helping her, it took my mind off my own pain. That helped me do what I already knew, I was going to finish this race. Sure enough, I completed the marathon in the allowed time.

Photo: Cassandra Bennett proudly posing with her first marathon medal.

There were others that made that race memorable, especially the cop following the last runner who was jamming on Michael Jackson. I liked that.

The race was small with only a couple hundred runners total due to COVID-19 restrictions. Some did half for Arkansas and another group just running Mississippi. Some had two bibs, one for each state. I finished that run.

With #4 completed and having finished my second half marathon, I was encouraged, and I set my focus on the next race, Oak Island, North Carolina.

Week 5: Run Oak Island, North Carolina, Feb. 13

After returning from Mississippi, Texas, the entire state, including Houston where I reside, was hit with an arctic freeze. Not wanting to miss my flight, I drove to the airport, flew to Charlotte, then arrived in Willington, North Carolina. But with delays, I arrived very late, setting back my schedule. Since there were no hotels available on the island, I found a couch in the airport's comfortable lounge, and awoke early to catch an Uber to the race. Just like Tulsa, I laid down where I knew the activity would wake me up in time to make it to the race. It was just like I was sleeping at a friend's house because others were staying in the lounge as well.

Photo: Airport Lounge in Wilmington, North Carolina

I woke up and caught an Uber to Oak Island. Fortunately, even though the driver was at the end of his shift and anxious to get home on the other side of the mainland, he decided to take one last fare. He commented that he couldn't pass up the additional income. I appreciated his willingness as he was my last option to make it to the race on time. Here's a great piece of advice: never schedule an Uber or Lyft ahead of time; they don't come even though it says confirmed.

The foul weather, like a stalker, followed me, creating heavy rain, and flooding that slowed and snarled traffic. Meanwhile, time was ticking away, and I was cutting it close. I was still in my travel clothes and, knowing the window to start was closing quickly, I changed in the back seat of the Uber.

The rain was heavy and made driving difficult. Thanks to the attentiveness of the driver, I arrived but with only a couple minutes to spare. Dropping my bag at the gear check area, the lady cautioned me, "You only have 2 minutes to start."

The weather delayed several of us, but that wasn't the worst of it. The torrential rain flooded the original start line with 3 feet of water. Given this was a marathon, not a triathlon with a swimming segment, they relocated the start line, but it too was underwater, just not as deep. It "only" covered my foot. I started without the usual fanfare by sloshing through the water with a couple people behind me. Good thing it wasn't a "No Wake Zone." The water was so high that our only choice was to find the part of the road where the water only rose an inch onto our shoes. At least my whole foot wasn't getting wet there, as if it mattered by now.

It would have been bad enough to run in that much water, but the rain was relentless. To make matters worse, the temperature hovered near freezing. That meant that shortly into the race, I'm wet and cold. I came prepared with my gloves and gear, but it didn't matter. My North Face rain gear quickly lost the battle against the weather. My gloves were of little help as my fingers froze together. Looking at them in dismay, I thought, "I need better gloves."

The nasty weather, like the worst experiences in life, generates compassion. As you would expect, I met a number of diehard runners, plodding through the course. Most of those at the back of the pack people were running the half marathon while I was running the full.

I met one lady runner who owned an air BnB rental whose husband was running the full marathon. She was so nice that when she saw me coming back at mile 14, she asked, "Can I get you anything?"

"A banana and drink would be great." I took a moment to stop and shared what I was doing. I was pleased when they donated.

By the time I got to mile 15, I was spent physically and emotionally. "That's a wrap. I can't continue in this cold." I don't like to quit but this was cold beyond belief. It was supposed to be 45 degrees when we started but when that front came through, the temps dropped to just above freezing. I wasn't the only one as many others tapped out. Some people put plastic bags over their shoes and socks and over their bodies to stay warm.

The frustrating part was that my glute was doing well. Unlike the earlier races where my glute was my biggest challenge, this time it was the weather. Even though I had five miles left before the turnaround, I found a cut through and joined the runners headed for the finish. "This is ridiculous. I'm done. I can't continue in this weather." Even then, the street was flooded.

Having moved the start line due to flooding, I expected they would do the same with the finish. That didn't happen. I guess they figured you were wet by that time, so it didn't matter.

The strange thing is that I prefer to run with numb feet in trail running. So that wasn't the problem. It was my hands. I couldn't keep them warm. It was so bad that my fingers were becoming discolored. I was seriously concerned about losing a finger to frostbite. To make matters worse, the wind was blowing and creating a wind chill. It was bad enough running out and onto the island but turning around and running along the water was worse. Mercifully, I crossed the finish line.

Because Covid was still ravaging the country, masks were required once we left the course. I went to reach for it and didn't realize the mask was already in my hand. Fumbling with it, I asked a volunteer for help.

She said, "Put on your mask."

I had trouble responding and saying the words, "I need help with my mask." All I could do was point to my pocket. She insisted that if I didn't put my mask on, she'd have the police remove me from the grounds.

Sensing a problem, a lady behind her asked, "Do you need help?" She patted me down like a police officer, struggling to find the mask.

I could hardly talk. She helped me get my mask on and take off my gloves. My hands were like an ice tray. I wasn't surprised to see that I actually had ice between his fingers.

It took some time, but I finally thawed to where I could function. But remember, social distancing was still in place. So, I went to retrieve my bag, went to the race sponsored barbeque, and then under the tent. That felt better. Unfortunately, they wouldn't let you under the pavilion where I could've gotten out of the rain. That meant I had nowhere to go. I approached the guy running the barbeque who had a trailer. Unfortunately, by then he was done cooking and it wasn't giving off any heat. I half-jokingly asked, "Can I lay inside on the grill?" I was that cold and miserable.

I had to find somewhere to change. Without any other options, I went to the police station. Unfortunately, in this small town, no one was there. To make matters worse, there was no public bathroom. I searched and searched, walking a half mile in that cold rain before I finally found a Publix Grocery store. I quickly located the family bathroom. Peeling out of my saturated clothes, I stood in front of the air dryer and repeatedly hit the button until I got warm. You might say that I literally melted inside Publix.

As I stepped out of the bathroom in my dry clothes feeling somewhat human again, I looked back to see a puddle of water and mud. I couldn't leave it like that. To make matters worse, the lady janitor had just cleaned it and was finishing the other bathrooms. I set my clothes on the bench, got her mop from the unattended cart when she appeared. She was a woman in her 20s.

"What are you doing?"

"I have to clean up in there. I apologize."

She laughed. "No, that's ok. I'll take care of this."

"No mam. I was taught to clean up my own mess. You shouldn't have to do that."

She laughed and insisted, "No. This is my job. I'll take care of it.".

Finally regaining some feeling, I realized I was hungry and needed my recovery food. I asked a manager to help me and told him my story. He was impressed that I was running in this weather and asked for the items I needed.

"You just stay here. I'll get it for you."

My eyes must have lit up like a child on Christmas morning as he and another worker appeared with chocolate milk, power bars, and other items I cannot even remember. I was so grateful to them. They could have simply told me which aisle to go to, but instead, they told me to sit on that bench while they retrieved the items. I realized later they were a race sponsor in Atlanta, but they still went above and beyond in serving me. A lady rang up the items and bagged them before bringing them to me on the bench. I was warmer but still feeling only half thawed.

Ok, so now I'm dry, warmer, and have some food. All is good, right? Not quite. I am running on four hours of sleep, have just run about 20 miles, and need to get back to Texas as soon as possible.

With another storm approaching, I didn't want to get stranded away from home. If I'm going to get stuck anywhere, I want to be in Texas. That's not a selfish thing. It's because my mom isn't able to fully take care of herself.

I'll let you in on a secret. Texas isn't prepared for a big freeze, much less snow. That February storm of 2021 was historic in that the entire state was out of electricity and water for three days and parts of the state were out of power for a week. That's tough for everyone but especially the elderly who can't care for themselves, like my mom. Since I looked after her and the storm was coming, I knew I had to get back. There was no time for a much-needed nap.

I mentioned earlier that I caught an Uber from Wilmington to the race. Anyone would assume that I could just catch one and go back. The problem was that there were no Ubers or Lyft drivers on the island. That left me with the old-fashioned method of calling a cab. They charged a flat but expensive fee to the airport. I didn't mind because it was still far cheaper than renting a car. At that time, unless you had a reservation for at least 15 days, you were not getting a rental car. If you were one of the lucky ones, it would cost you at least $600-800 for a weekend. Taking the taxi, I arrived at the airport with only 45 minutes to board. I connected in Charlotte and felt good settling into my seat, knowing the next stop was home. But the drama of this trip wouldn't end until we had to make a significant detour, flying to the Oklahoma line to avoid the worst of the storm. That allowed us to approach Houston from the back side of the worst snow we had seen in 40 years. Finally landing, I walked to my truck and drove to check on mom.

Looking Back

Thinking back to this run is difficult, maybe in part because it was so cold. Survival was the order of the day. Of all the races I would run, this one was the worst for weather. The good news was that my glute didn't give me any trouble. But one important theme was emerging during this quest. For one reason or another, I was constantly reshuffling my schedule and working to overcome the logistical challenges. I was originally planning on staying a few days to see my aunt and cousin in the area before returning to Texas and then driving to my next race in Louisiana. But with the storm, I canceled those plans and caught an earlier flight. Realize too that the Louisiana marathon was originally supposed to be held on my birthday weekend in January, along with the Chevron. So, when Chevron canceled, I signed up for Louisiana. But then they postponed it so I found Daufuskie. Then when they rescheduled, I shifted my plans. It was like a crazy game of checkers with pieces disappearing and then appearing on a different part of the board.

Oak Island wasn't part of my original plan. Normally it is a very nice race, they call it BAM because they give Big A** Medals. If you run all the three island runs, you get a fourth. In the process, they raise funds to protect sea life, like turtles and sea fish. Unfortunately, because I cut my race short and didn't finish the entire race, I didn't get one of those big marathon medals. The race director was kind enough to drop me to a half marathon. But there was a hitch. They didn't have enough so they promised to ship it to me. I'm still waiting for the packet.

I was looking forward to sleeping a short but restful time in Houston. As usual, I got my massage, saw my doctors, and went to my trainer before leaving early for the Louisiana Marathon. I was starting to wonder, "What else can happen on this quest?"

What I didn't know is that the freeze left me home until March 5 when I drove to Louisiana.

Week 6: Louisiana Marathon, Mar. 7

Not wanting to reprise the Tulsa mistake, I left a day early to give my glute time to rest. That plan worked perfectly.

The Louisiana Marathon is a two-day event with the 5K, 10K, and quarter marathon (6.55 miles) on Saturday. The half and full marathon ran on Sunday. The shorter runs are a good warm up for the next day, but also a great way to meet a wide variety of runners, including elite runners relaxing before completing the next day. The shorter races also attract social, recreational, and spontaneous runners. The nature of the races is different. A marathon takes four to five months of serious training where the shorter races, especially the 5k, is more of a fun run. That's why it attracts those running their first race. I love the diversity and opportunity to meet many people, each with a great story.

I was running the quarter marathon. After postponing the race due to covid, the race required social distancing and masks, when not on the course.

Starting the race was like my body was still frozen from the week before. Then, as if it finally thawed, I found my stride and enjoyed the beautiful course. Crossing the finish provided a warm feeling that tomorrow would be a good run.

The Race

The full marathon course was even more impressive than the shorter ones. It wound us through the LSU campus and around a lake. The scenery reminds me of running trail runs and, of course, I love that.

By now you know that I am not a shy guy and that I love meeting people. On the course, you likely hear my burst of energy before you see me.

Photo: This is what John and Jerry say.

As you might imagine, running through a college campus like LSU is a tempting challenge for fraternity students at the end of a wild night of partying. Given they allowed late entries, this was the case. I can only imagine the alcohol induced conversation.

"Hey look, they are running a race."

"Let's do it."

"Ok. Where's my shoes."

"Wait a minute, how long is this race?"

"Who cares. It will be fun."

That last comment says it all. They were there to have fun. While some had bibs on for the half marathon, some brave souls had bibs for the full marathon. I didn't see them again. I'm sure they made stops at every place offering a shot of booze. I wonder how many of them finished. I wonder how many of them remember finishing.

I met one guy that I can't forget. Drew is an attorney who was once an avid runner. Did I mention he is 72 years old? After running many marathons over the course of his life, he took a different approach to running by the time I met him. He doesn't train for marathons. Read that sentence again. Yes, you read it right. He doesn't train for marathons; he simply signs up and runs them. While that

would be dangerous for the novice runner, he is in good enough shape to make it. He readily admits that the first 15K is good and then he struggles.

But along the way, he serves as an unofficial tour guide for the course, pointing out historic locations and regaling anyone who will listen about the events and characters. He shared fascinating tidbits about the campus, mansions, and churches, providing an experience unmatched in any other races.

Photo: Drew Louviere supporting my charity.

He heard me mention that I was fundraising for St. Jude's when we were running together. As we passed the first milestone, the 5K marker, he handed me a $20 bill for my fundraising efforts. Then at the 10K he handed me another $20 bill. He did this again at the 15K, half and then, at the finish, handed me yet another $20 bill. To mark the moment, we paused for a photo at every milestone. After the race, we talked in more detail when he promised to get some of his friends and mason friends to contribute. Then he offers another $20 and says, "Now I have to run and help you raise this $50,000."

"Thank you, sir," I shouted.

Just like that, I finished. Notice there was no drama from my glutes. My PTSD wasn't triggered. I met fascinating people and enjoyed the 26.2 miles. "Thank you, Jesus,"

With the race completed, I was ready for some great Cajun cuisine. There are people like me who catch the casino bus from Houston to Lake Charles, Louisiana just to eat at the buffet. That's how much some of us love Cajun food. So, when I signed up for the Louisiana Marathon to be run in Baton Rouge, my mouth was watering.

But it turned out to be a cruel joke. As you run this well planned, beautiful race, you will fall in love with the Cajun country capital. You will enjoy the running past grand old homes, including the old governor's mansion. It will capture your spirit as you run over a bridge, admire the churches, and enjoy the music of an outdoor worship service. But remember this one important thing. You won't find great Louisiana cuisine there. I had friends from Chicago who were licking their chops in anticipation, but it wasn't to be. My heart sank as I arrived at the food tent, There I saw what otherwise would have been a great spread to replenish hungry runners. But no Cajun cuisine. Was this a cruel joke? It was a shame that we were in the heart of Cajun country but had to drive to New Orleans to get our fix of the food we expected. It's like someone forgot to tell them they were in the Cajun food capital of the world.

We were so disappointed that we went to Chili's. We can do that anywhere. To show you how frustrated, dissatisfied, and disheartened I was, I told Mike who was running for a seat in the Louisiana congress that if his campaign is anything like the cooking at that restaurant, he is going to lose. Maybe it tasted so bad because I was expecting so much more. I couldn't believe it.

Heading back to Houston, I was looking forward to the next week when I flew to the gentle southern city of Savannah. I presume they will have great Southern cooking. They had better not disappoint.

Week 7: Skidaway Island Marathon, Georgia, Mar. 13

Here me when I say make Skidaway a getaway before you leave-a-way and wish on that day you had planned longer to stay.
— Aaron Burros, the Running Servant

I had never been to Savannah before and instantly enjoyed this historic and scenic southern Georgia city. I was ready for this experience. After checking into my hotel and enjoying a quiet evening, I was ready for another island run. To get there, I called a cab.

The cab driver, proud of his picturesque city, headed to Skidaway Island, lying a half hour south of downtown Savannah. Surrounded by the salt marshes, intercoastal, Skidaway River, and other barrier islands, this gem is filled with lush forests and several trails. I knew I was going to love running this race.

As we were approaching the island, he offered his version of the Chamber of Commerce greeting

"Welcome to the island where college students come to die and not graduate." Savannah is home to Savannah State University and SCAD, Savannah College of Art and Design, a prestigious and expensive college. Once I saw the island, I could understand why.

It's not huge as indicated by the fact that to run the entire island is only a 5k. That's only a touch over three miles. But make no mistake, this wasn't a state park open to all. Instead, it was exclusive, needing a pass to get on the island filled with fine homes, golf courses, and campgrounds.

81

As I exited the cab, there was a sound that lifted my spirits. It was a sound I rarely heard at races. Instead of the heart pounding, energetic rock music, the speakers were sharing Christian contemporary music. Don't get me wrong, I appreciate all kinds of music, and have heard it all as I have run. But to hear this was unique and refreshing. I'm a believer, so this music encouraged me to not only run the marathon, but to run the race of life.

That took the race to a new level, even though I hadn't crossed the start line. It was beautiful and became one of the most memorable runs in my life. The only one I could say rose above it was the Oklahoma City Memorial Marathon where they had a full worship service and prayer prior to running. At Skidaway, they held a two-minute bible study before the start where he read a bible verse and prayed for us.

Now in week six of my quest, world major runs, and previous runs I had pace, I recognized many friends and 50 State Miler group runners.

This was a smaller race and setting. New York City or even Baton Rouge seemed like it was on a different planet.

After a good start, I enjoyed running on these trails through this scenic island listening to Christian music. But it wasn't long before I struggled. Gone was the ease of the Louisiana Marathon. By the time I passed the half marathon split, I was alone, out of sight from the next slowest marathon runner. I struggled to swallow my pride and accept the limitations of my wounded body.

This marathon, like many, set a time limit of six hours. In my previous running career, that wouldn't have been a problem. After all, I used to run 8 miles in 45 minutes. But with a bullet lodged in my right glute, that became an issue. As I approached the mile 20 marker, I looked at my watch. I ran for 5 hours and 15 minutes. That left only 45 minutes left to run the remaining 10K, 6.2 miles. I knew I would never finish in time, so I stepped to the side and hailed the sag wagon.

It is nicknamed the "sag wagon" because asking them for help says you cannot complete the race in the time required. It also means you will receive an official "DNF" beside your name. You did not finish. For any runner, that hurts. We don't sign up, train, or start a race to accept defeat. While I appreciate the ride back to the finish when I'm spent, I'd rather be strong enough to finish the race in the time allowed. Even more, I wanted to average 5 hours and 5 minutes for each of the 50 marathons in 50 states in 50 weeks. Unfortunately, that wasn't to be.

Photo: The beautiful scenery of Skidaway Island, Georgia.

Despite my disappointment, I dearly loved running every minute of this race. The scenery and the music, along with the wonderful people made this thoroughly enjoyable. Well, maybe not completely enjoyable.

The sand mites were relentless. Despite a controlled burn and spraying to reduce the population, waiting for the race to begin was a battle that the sand mites won. Fortunately, once on the course, they weren't a problem.

"Next year." That's my motto for beautiful runs that I want to return and conquer. The setting filled with beauty and Christian music is worth a reprise. I wasn't that far off. I know I can do it.

As I headed back to Savannah, I realized how different the setting would be for the next chapter of my quest. It was like going from heaven to hell, from a spiritual retreat to sin city. Next up, Las Vegas.

Photo: Shirt I created to celebrate my birthday challenge.

Week 8: Labor of Love Marathon, Nevada Mar. 20

The canyon looked like heaven but was straight out of hell. Lovell Canyon sits on the back end of the beautiful Red Rock Canyon outside of Las Vegas. It is truly God's country, set in the arid desert with mountains and canyons filled with trees.

It's difficult to describe why I see this as God's country. In many ways it is dry, barren, and challenging. The weather was brisk, only 40 degrees and up to 48 mile an hour cross winds made it strong and cold. But I loved it.

Maybe it was because the first half was heavenly, running downhill. Serving as a vacation for my wounded right glute, my quads led the way, working fine. The hill descended into what anyone with bible training like me would imagine as entering the "depths of Sheol," a Biblical place for the dead. But running that one-thousand-foot decline between the 4.5- and 6-mile points, was pure bliss. The canyon dropped gently, before rising slightly, and then a deeper drop. The pattern continued, lulling me into a dream state where I imagined all marathons went downhill. I had no trouble completing the first half.

Along the way I met amazing people, runners, and volunteers. Colico Racing in Nevada has lovely folks. They got out early and set up the race. Unlike Louisiana, the cheering sections were limited to a few running groups and the aid station volunteers. I saw a rabbit but couldn't tell if it was Bugs Bunny or Roger. Then there was what I thought was a roadrunner teasing Wile E. Coyote. That might just have been a mirage.

We ran on a paved road that went without repair for many years. It might as well have been a trail, with cracks, dips, and holes. You had to be careful not to turn an ankle. Still, running down hill was a dream

Reaching the bottom, I awoke from my blissful dream to the hellish reality. In this race, what you ran down now requires that you run up. To finish the race, I had to run back up that 1000-foot incline. I instantly knew that would tax my glute beyond its ability. Having already run 20 miles, that peaceful dream was quickly turning into a nightmare, the yin (bad) replaced the yang (good), pain was about to shatter the peace.

As I turned around, I stopped. Looking ahead, I looked up and continued panning up until I saw the top of the canyon. "Lord, help me." I knew there was no other option. My mind pushed back, "You can't do this. You will shatter your glutes." I started when my destiny was determined. Even thinking of walking up wounded my spirit. I started but soon surrendered. I knew resting would not have made the difference. I knew my only option was to get a ride. Despite waiting 20 minutes, I gladly accepted the ride.

At the top, the driver offered to let me off so I could complete the run. Tapped out, physically and mentally, I replied, "Take me to the start/finish line." I can't lie and refuse to live a lie. I won't cut corners or shade the truth. Even though nobody would know or maybe even care, I can't claim I finished a marathon when I've had a ride up the worst part.

I asked and they gladly dropped me down to a half marathon finish, completing it in 3:40. That is the advantage of smaller runs. They are willing to make accommodations.

Despite the finish, I felt good about the run. I loved the challenge and the energy. I most appreciated how it gave me a realistic perspective of how far I have come in the healing process. I was learning that this quest wasn't just to see if I could complete 50 marathons in 50 weeks in 50 states. The quest was to return to my running form. The challenge was to get stronger and see if I could do what I once did. The quest was now becoming how much I could push my glutes. This race showed me I can already do more in week seven.

More than any other, I will always remember this Labor of Love Marathon for one important lesson. When it feels like Freddy Krueger is ripping my back apart and someone is twisting my hamstrings, that is when I need to stop. In this race, I stopped just short of that. Knowing when to stop is a critical lesson.

Another Hotel Problem

Having just encountered hell, I was looking for a heavenly time of relaxing. Little did I know that I was about to enter the second level of hell on this trip. In a Groundhog Day reprise of the Hilton Head hotel, the front desk refused to let me in my room. Once again, they claimed I hadn't paid in full. Only this time, they threatened me.

"If you don't have the money to pay for your room, I'll call the police."

"Go ahead and call the police," I countered, "that will be a great scene, because this is a civil matter."

Not to be outdone, she claimed, "You are making me feel uncomfortable."

Knowing that I am a big African American man and the stereotypes that go with that, I restricted my comments to non-threatening, discovery questions couched in a calming voice. "Mam, what am I doing that is making you feel uncomfortable?"

Without a better answer, she responded, "I feel threatened by you."

Gently probing further, "What am I doing that is making you feel threatened?"

"I have customers to attend to and so you need to move out of the way." She clearly didn't know what else to do but to get rid of me. Indeed, about ten customers had formed a line behind me, hoping to check out. But I wasn't going to let her out of dealing with me first.

Gently but firmly, I continued, "Am I not a customer? Do I not have a reservation? Have you not taken my money?"

In the end, I found out that their system showed there was a hold on my card but showed no dollar amount. The money had been paid out. What she was doing was charging the full amount of the whole stay, not just the one night, as has been agreed upon. I tried to tell her that, but she didn't want to listen.

Because I've had trouble previously, my practice is to pay for one night at a time. I use a bank card and transfer only enough money to pay for that particular night. Then each day I transfer what I need for the next night. In the process, I have recorded that the bill has been paid without letting them charge the entire stay up front.

So here I stood with a record of payment willing to show them what they needed to charge me. Still, she threatened to call the cops, said she felt uncomfortable, and threatened.

At that point, as with the Daufuskie Marathon hotel, I asked for a manager. Still belligerent, she told me to take a seat, or she would call the police and claim I was trespassing.

I know the law, so I wasn't afraid. I knew she wasn't a salaried manager so she can't ask me to leave. I also know I have a receipt showing I paid money and therefore am not trespassing. That means there is no criminal activity taking place so the police cannot ask me to leave.

Her belligerence pushed my buttons, but I continued in a civil but firm tone. "I have a receipt, which gives me the right to be here. As a matter of fact, why don't you call the police so the manager will have to come up here and we can get this squared away."

For some reason, that finally made sense to her. She called the manager who arrived and stated simply, "Give him the room."

I smiled, knowing that the manager had taken my money earlier that morning. The manager continued, "Charge him for the next two nights, not the entire stay."

Somehow, she still couldn't understand his directions. The manager, also growing frustrated, looked at me and said, "Look, this is what I'm going to do. I'm canceling his reservation. Put in another reservation for 2 nights at $99." She complied with his orders. More than that, every time I encountered her after that, she was cordial.

This was beyond frustrating. It was ridiculous because certain staff are not used to the hotel system. They only know one way to complete the transaction. They think that as a consumer, you are doing them a favor by spending your money with their company. They are not used to an informed consumer who knows their rights. In the end, I used to work retail, so I know the rules. I have taken the time to learn there are many different ways to complete a transaction.

Yet, something seems amiss. It's like the managers know but the employees don't have a clue. I've paid for my room, but they won't accept that. The managers are happy to let me pay for one night at a time, but the staff can't comprehend how to do that. Or maybe it is that they don't want to know. Maybe they just want to do their jobs the easiest way they can and are unwilling to accommodate anyone requiring a different way.

Having climbed out of that little piece of hell, I went to my room, cleaned up, and started preparing for the next week. I knew the next week was a challenge unlike any I had tackled so far on this quest. But with the unexpected turn of events, I had encountered so far, I was beginning to cringe at what next week would hold.

Week 9: Two Rivers Marathon Race Festival, Pennsylvania, Mar. 28

I already knew this was going to be a catch-up weekend where I ran two marathons in back-to-back days. The big freeze in Texas took out two weeks of running and I implemented my back up plan. But even my back-up plan required a back-up plan. That's the way the quest was unfolding.

My plan was to run the Two Rivers Marathon in Pennsylvania on Saturday, March 27 and then the New Jersey Ultra Festival on Sunday, March 28. In defining my 50 weeks, I decided that a week would run as most calendars, starting on Sunday, and ending on Saturday. Therefore, running a marathon on Saturday and another on Sunday, counted for two weeks.

Unfortunately, my memory and ego worked together to blind me from the toll the quest was taking on my body. I honestly thought I could do it.

The first challenge was logistical, finding an affordable place to stay. Lackawaxen, Pennsylvania. Given the obscure name, you can imagine it is located in the Pocono Mountains near what some call the "wild and scenic" Delaware River. Whenever someone uses "wild" to describe a place, you know it is remote and finding lodging will be difficult and expensive.

That held true. I did find a 3-bedroom lodge for $1, 000 a night but couldn't find anyone to share the costs. Again, what's Option B? The only relatively inexpensive place was a little inn in a small town approximately 30 minutes away. I took it knowing it is better than sleeping in the park by the start line.

Photo: Two Rivers Pocono Mountains Upper Delaware Scenic and Recreational River Zane Grey Museum

I felt good mentally approaching this race because I sensed I could knock this out after running that canyon outside of Las Vegas. Even though I hadn't run up that 1000-foot incline, I was beginning to believe I could. So, I was hyped for the Two Rivers Marathon.

Running during the covid pandemic has created several changes, the least of which is masks. I am appreciating how some races communicate the requirements, like a sign at 2 Rivers. "Masks are mandatory. Running shoes optional." Runners respected that, wearing their masks in the start and finish areas.

I started out strong and finished the first of the double loops. Usually this was a point-to-point race but that changed with covid. Along with that came running on an open road with cars and bikes. Unlike almost every other marathon in the 50-state challenge, they didn't close the road for runners. They did have township constable watching out for us and the repeat runners seemed to be fine with it. I appreciated how the people in the cars and on the bikes cheered as they passed us. But some runners were apprehensive and shouted for drivers to slow down. I felt pretty good when I saw the volunteers and staff riding bikes on the course. Overall, while it was a bit unnerving, it was great to see the entire community involved in the race.

The second loop was difficult. I knew pain was starting to take a toll. As with the previous races, the second half shows the stress on that glute. I slowed to the point that one of the 50 state walkers passed me. I knew that was a bad sign, so I picked up my pace. Catching back up, I tried to walk with him, but he was walking at a 10:30 pace. That was faster than I usually run. Trying my hardest, he quickly was a dot on the road ahead of me. That was demoralizing.

I ran 3.12 miles farther to the 10k turnaround mark. I stopped by the guardrail going over the bridge. I knew I was finished when I went to take off again but couldn't. It felt like my lower back and hamstrings tried to kiss each other but the glutes got in the way. My I.T. bands on both sides were tightened like piano strings. Then, as if other body parts became jealous, I developed hip pointers, feeling an evil torturer drilling a needle into my hip point. Every step became agony. I waved the imaginary white flag and surrendered to the course.

But if a tree falls in the forest and no one is present, does it make a sound? In the same way, if you are running in a marathon on remote mountain roads without cell phone reception, will anyone know you need help?

As I did in the Las Vegas canyon, I waited for someone to pick me up. It turned out to be a local constable, who was originally from

New York, but was now living in the township. I still laugh when I think of the first time I saw him. He was eating a bagel, no, not a donut, in Lackawaxen Park near a beautiful tribute to one of the hometown soldiers. While I laughed at our introduction, I greatly appreciated him rescuing me and taking me to the finish line.

The good news is that I believe I am getting stronger. How can I say that? Because I feel sore from my shoulders to my knees. Even my ribs were sore. That means I am engaging more muscles and being able to run more than I walk. That encourages me.

In what was becoming an unwelcome trend, I ran 16 miles and received credit for finishing the half marathon. But I had another marathon to run the next day. I began to doubt running the New Jersey marathon.

"Self, I think I should've done the New Jersey Marathon first."

New Jersey

I wanted to run the New Jersey Ultra Festival for two important reasons. First, the race was started by Princeton graduates to expose city youth to nature, tracking, and trails. As the #RunningServant, I love supporting people and organizations who selflessly make the world better. Second, I love running trails.

But when I arrived in New Jersey, intending to get the packet, and run a little bit, I was welcomed with rain littering the course with mud and debris. My already overtaxed glutes stopped me in my tracks and seemed to say, "Are you sure?" They didn't give me much of a chance to reply before continuing, "Not today buddy." I would need to reschedule.

I checked in and told them I couldn't run. As much as I didn't want it, I received another DNF.

I questioned my planning. Maybe I should have run New Jersey first, before the rain and on a rested body. I wondered if I could have run cyclical 5k bursts followed by rest and still finished in time. But when I did run two miles, my body convinced me to sit this one out.

Was this plan B, C, or D? I stopped counting. Even though I didn't finish the marathon in Pennsylvania, I was pleased with how well I did. However, each race seemed to be setting a new Personal Record (PR) for pain.

In the days that followed, I found the Bi-State Challenge (New Jersey and New York) and put it on my schedule for May.

"Just Run a Half"

By now, you might be asking a question that tests my patience. "Why are you wasting your money? Why don't you just sign up for a half if that's all you are going to do?" The answer is simple. Half marathons do not mentally challenge me. Yes, I could do a half and challenge myself to run it faster. Yes, I am confident I can do a half. But if you know you can do it, it isn't a challenge. It is only a challenge if you don't know you can do it.

Besides, I like being out on the course, meeting the runners, cheering them on. I am the #RunningServant and that means more when I'm out there longer. A 5k is great but I am only out there a short while. The  same goes for a half marathon. By signing up for and attempting to run a full marathon, I have more time to interact with runners. That is my calling as the #RunningServant. Just like I was called to preach on the streets of Houston, I'm now called to run marathons. Besides, once you cross the finish line for a marathon, it is different.

The critics don't understand why I run.

I used to hate running. But I developed a love for it after calling out to God for help. I was literally crying and going to the doctor. In the end, I learned to appreciate the physical and spiritual aspects of running. Of course, compared to now, running was easy. Now it is my way of handling stress because it is my time alone with God.

That took some trial and error. I tried listening to preachers and teachers. I used headphones but didn't like the way it sounded in his head.

Now I look for God to speak to my spirit. It is my meditation, bringing thoughts and words to mind in a spirit of prayer. I find my time alone on the course as an avenue for thanksgiving. It is also a time where God speaks to me and shows me lessons through all of nature, birds, hornets, animals, and even God's garbage men, the turkey buzzards. I am renewed with awe of his creation, admiring the squirrels protecting their den, reminding me of Rocky and Bullwinkle. I enjoy the presence of God when running and run more because I am communing with God.

Then there are the people. From my early days of running Terry Hershey Park, I have constantly watched people. The first thing I noticed back then was that most runners didn't look like me. A decade later, I see far more diversity. Something else changed. At first, I freely greeted others, but they failed to return the courtesy. I quickly learned I'm not responsible for their reaction. Besides, some people are tuned into their own private space. But now, I greet others with a word or simply give the runner's wave and we connect for a moment. I have found the runners to ultimately be a friendly and supportive group where I belong.

Of course, serving is critical for me. I love to help people, especially those who are new to running and those struggling. Everyone needs a helping hand from time to time. As I seek to minister, like-minded people reach out to connect. Already in my first two months of my quest, I'm building strong relationships with fascinating runners, race directors, and volunteers.

In the end, running has allowed me to become much more socially connected. As runners, we endure the pain, because pain is temporary. We enjoy so many life lessons that we have learned by running. Just when we think we can't learn any more, new lessons emerge.

For example, both of the race directors ran well-executed races. The Two Rivers and NJ Ultra-Trails reflected their integrity as well as their love of the sport and serving the community. They focus on every detail of the race. For example, they cared so much about every little detail of the race – before, during and after. And although the racecourse was changed due to covid-19, the cause did not get interrupted, or side stepped. There were no excuses given, only encouragement and expectations of what would come.

Week 10: Carmel Marathon Weekend, Indiana, Apr. 3

Covid forced many races to cancel or postpone to a later date. Even then, masks were required, rolling starts ensured social distancing. Many even changed their courses. The Carmel Marathon's previous course took runners through open fields for a very peaceful run. I think I would have liked that. But it was a bit too peaceful as some who complained it was boring. Personally, I enjoy the peace of nature more than the grind of the pavement through urban centers.

The new course wound through neighborhoods that allowed for more spectator participation. I appreciate that, as you know from my love of running through Brooklyn.

However, running through the park also brought a rather dangerous situation. We ran on a two-way paved road with four people abreast. That was tight but with only the middle line separating those us running from cyclists speeding by, that was too close for comfort. I'm a big guy but I don't expect to do well competing with a cyclist moving over 25 miles per hour. Race officials were not permitted to close down the park. That meant as runners paying to run a race accustomed to having room to run, we were suddenly competing for space with the general public. Between the cyclist and those enjoying games, relaxation, and picnics, this race was becoming a challenge.

But that wasn't all. In a one-mile stretch, elite, sub-3-hour marathoners were vying for the same space as back of the pack, slower runners. It was a recipe for disaster. I'm glad we made it but not sure how somebody didn't get hurt.

A New PR

The external threats, however, were nothing compared to my internal battle. The Carmel Marathon brought me a new PRP (personal record for pain). As I entered my third month of the quest, I was sore, but that was fine because I knew my body was getting stronger. However, the pain reached farther and concerned me. My whole body hurt, from my ears to my toes. My glutes were the culprit, shutting down, requiring my back muscles to twist and tighten my hamstring.

I wondered if this was from running almost 3 months of weekly runs.

What bothered me was that I know I'm getting stronger, but the pain is also getting stronger. Why? It seems as if my body is in the middle of a race to see whether the increasing strength or pain wins. I was wondering what the future held when a friend, a barista at my corporate office, who battled cancer told me, "At some point you are going to have to learn to "live with the pain, and not for it." I will never forget that. My pain isn't going away. I can work to minimize it but live through it.

Each time I lace up my shoes, I have to drag the pain with me. Instead of letting it drag me through life. I don't wake up and let the PTSD and pain dictate what I do with life. I learned that in fighting the cancer that caused me to almost make my leg dead weight, I had to push my right leg, drag it, and flip it in front of me. That's what I needed to do with my glute and life. I have to take the pain, trauma, PTSD and drag it with me, not letting it limit my life.

One of the ways I minimize it is working with my massage therapist. This is no relaxation massage with mood lighting and relaxing aromas. Instead, she hits those spots and makes me want to say "uncle." In my pain, I want to kick her in the face. ('Sorry if that sounds mean, but my body wants to fight back against the pain.) I let her work and afterwards I feel good. She is an angel but sometimes I see the smirk on her face, and I wonder if there isn't a little devil in her that gives her pleasure in causing me pain.

Pacing

I looked forward to this run for one specific reason. I was going to be running with a pacer, Marie Bartoletti (in photo). You see, I had paced many races, and at one point, was working to be the first person to pace a race in all 50 states. Then I was shot and that allowed others to beat me to it. So, for the first time, the pacer was going to have a pacer.

But this wasn't just any pacer. Marie had authored the 2019 book, *Perseverance: How a Determined Athlete Tenaciously*

Overcame a Stroke. Prior to her 2015 stroke, she had completed 315 marathons and 25 ultra-marathons. By 2016, she was back running marathons and by 2021, she had already run another 169 marathons. She was even featured on a Wheaties's box. I was delighted that she would be my pacer.

As Marie and I got to know each other in recent years, I realized this was no coincidence. We had too many connections. First of all, she had her stroke the same month I was shot. Then I realized she was pacing the exact time that I had originally set to run each of my marathons, 5:05. Lastly, she was a natural runner who had overcome a serious health threat. I needed her example. Indeed, meeting her was a divine introduction.

She paced a marathon like it was a stroll for her. Running with her allowed me to know how others felt when I was pacing them. I love pacing because I wanted to be the rabbit that made others run, drew them into the run, engaged them, not run away from them. Now, at the time when I struggled, denying my fading ability, not strong enough to finish, I needed her to help me through this obstacle.

Photo: Marie Bartoletti Six Star finish and Wheaties

Marie paced 5:05 and was on point. You may wonder how a guy who hasn't finished marathons could run at a 5:05 pace. You see, the pace wasn't too fast, it was just that my glutes will only last so long. They are getting stronger but it's like driving with a gallon of gas. You can drive hard and fast, but it will eventually run out. Time is my enemy and once started, it's like sand through an hourglass. Once the last grain has run through the hourglass, time is up. I'm finished.

Running with a pacer, being a pacer, was so beneficial. It kept me on an even keel, focusing on my form and feeling my glutes firing. I didn't have to pay attention to time but instead, trusted Marie for that. Going into Carmel, I set a goal to run 11.5 miles in 2 hours. In the first 10k, I had a good time and was on target. I was able to literally sense it, feel it, clock it, and run until the sand started to run out. I dropped a little behind but still kept my eyes on Marie and the group. Unfortunately, with the sand running thin, eventually I lost sight of them. It wasn't long and my glutes played out. I did well for the first hour but only made five miles the second hour. In the end, I was excited to turn in 11.5 in 2 hours. That would have been great instead of half in 2:50 or 3:00 like I had been doing. At that pace, I could have run a half marathon in 2:10. Although I was excited about those results, I knew I couldn't continue without hurting myself. It wasn't just that I couldn't run that far and that fast, if I pushed myself, I would injure myself to a point where I couldn't run for weeks. I didn't want that.

I tried to push through the pain but when walkers were passing me up, it was mental and emotional torture. I am used to running more miles than people drive.

That's when the internal argument starts. The same questions I've heard from others, come back to haunt me. "Are you sure about this audacious goal? Aren't you failing miserably? After all, you have only completed a couple races. Why not give up?" You might be surprised by how many well-meaning people ask those questions. Then you can also imagine how those questions visit me in my most difficult times, like Jesus in the wilderness or Scrooge in the middle of the night.

But like Jesus tempted by the devil to sacrifice his mission, I won't relent on mine. I firmly believe that if I aim for the moon, I may never leave earth's atmosphere, but I will at least reach the top of the trees. Then I will try again, shooting for the moon. I'm not going to give up. It is a goal. It's a passion. It's a commitment. I am not tempted to quit.

Understanding My Drive for More

Please understand this about me. I always push for more. When I was in school, I was pushed back when others denied me at Boone Elementary, Ollie Middle School, and Elsik High School. This is the high school that Beyonce and Lizzo, Rashad Lewis and Donovan Greer and Tobe Nwinwe and Mo Amer all attended. I was placed in remedial classes and told I was dumb, primarily because of my skin color. To say that upset me is an understatement. Actually, it lit a fire within me because I was making great grades.

By the time I was in junior high, a counselor asked, "Why not leave well enough alone." I answered, "Because I'm not learning anything. If I go in and leave without learning anything, even though I made an A, what does that prove?" By 8th grade and middle school, I was able to get out of some of those remedial classes.

But in Elsik High School, once again, they put me in remedial classes. I kept telling them, "I don't want or need these classes. I don't have a disability." By then I was making A's in all of my classes. Still, they wouldn't take my word for it but insisted I get letters of recommendations from my middle school. Then I had to secure letters from my current high school teachers. They all quickly wrote the letters because of my excellent grades. Still not satisfied, they required I submit all the letters to convince them to leave the remedial classes and join the regular classes. They still were not sure I could succeed. Had I been just another student willing to settle for the easy grades, I would have become a product of a questionable system. But I was relentless and eventually was allowed to take regular classes.

To their surprise, I still made A's. So, I pushed farther by asking to be admitted to honor classes, "I'm not learning anything." They still refused until eventually I ran into a Mr. Dallas, a professor at the University of Houston. He taught one class at Elsik each semester, a demanding science class. Everyone knew it was rigorous mainly because of his high standards. There I would join 100 other students in a college-like classroom.

Mr. Dallas made the high expectations clear on the first day. "Most of you don't even want to be here because you know who I am. If you don't want to be here, I suggest you get up, gather your things, and go to your counselor now." I was surprised to see about half the class leave only because of this guy's reputation. With the last of the students leaving, he turned to those of us remaining. "I'm guessing you all want to be here because I'm not the type of prof you would choose." He was wrong. I was staying there because I wanted to learn, and he was exactly the type of teacher I wanted.

It became apparent why many didn't want him. He set the standard high for students and expected them to work for the grade. On that very first day, he gave a quiz that was worth one third of our grade. We came to understand quickly that he only gave three quizzes during the semester. One on the first day, one at midterm, and one for the final. Each was worth a third. To complicate matters, he never returned the grade, so we never knew how well or poorly we were doing. For the semester exam, he entered the classroom with a box and sat it on the science table, containing a variety of science items. He proceeds to write a question on the board. At appointed times, he announces how much time we have left. We were free to use whatever we needed from the box to answer the questions. When finished, we placed our completed exam face down on the table and left. He gave no other instructions.

At the end of the semester, I learned that I had received a "B-"for the semester. Pleased, I was also curious when I ran into one of my classmates. He was a Chinese kid who was the smartest kid in the school. I assumed he received an "A" but was shocked when he told me he had failed the course.

"I'm smarter than the smartest kid in our school?" I wondered without speaking a word out loud. Then I couldn't resist, "How did you fail?"

He recounted what Mr. Dallas told him. "You received an 'A' on the initial quiz. You also received an 'A' on the midterm and the final."

"Ok, how do 3 A's turn into an F?" I'm sure he had asked Mr. Dallas asked the same question I had asked him. The kid shook his head and walked off.

Still curious, I went to talk to Mr. Dallas. In my mind, I'm thinking about my friend who failed when I received a B-. This whole process wasn't making sense.

Mr. Dallas welcomed me in and showed me my exams. The first one shocked me. The bold 'F" stood out. My eyes blurred as I tried to make out whether it was a 43% or 53%. Either way it stunk. It was clear that I didn't know anything about the science he was teaching. I flipped to the second quiz. This was better, with a score of D and a score in the 60s. Feeling a bit encouraged but still not confident, I flipped to the final where I scored a C+. I was still confused about how I earned a B- with those scores.

Mr. Dallas gladly explained. "You applied yourself. The progression of scores shows that you worked hard and learned during the semester."

"But what about my friend?"

"He didn't apply himself. He ended the semester not knowing any more than he did walking into the class."

I tell this story to illustrate an important aspect about me. Before the shooting, I was graced with "A" level talent for running. I was running and losing weight and got better naturally. I was like my classmate who didn't have to apply himself. He was not learning anything new. But since the shooting, I've had to work much harder to get lesser results. Even so, I've learned the difference between running with pain and running when you are tired or tired of running. I also learned that there is a totally different mindset among the elite runners than in the back of the packers. Beginning with the London Marathon, I began to appreciate people's stories, their amazing courage, and relentless tenacity. I learned the discipline of those who struggle to finish. I now realize and appreciate that if the elite runners had as much determination, passion, and joy as the back of the pack, the 2-hour marathon would've been broken by now. Back of the pack runners are on the course for far different reasons than the elite. Elites only run out of their ability. Yes, they get out of their comfort zones, but they are not running from purpose, passion, and pain as the back of the pack folks are. Some are just uncomfortable when they have given up. Instead, those that struggle like I do now, understand what it takes to improve beyond our wildest dreams. Elites expect success. Back of the pack runners overcome doubts every day to do what Elites don't even think about.

That reminds me of a classic movie, *Chariots of Fire*. The saga of the 1924 Olympics found Harold Abrahams frustrated when Eric Little beat him in a preliminary race. According to the movie, Abrahams sat dejected when his girlfriend approached him. Feeling sorry for himself, he proclaimed, "I will not run if I cannot win." His girlfriend wisely responded, "if you do not run, you cannot win." If I give up running because I cannot do what I once did, how will I know what I can possibly achieve now?

I met one lady who asked, "what happened to you?" She saw me early in the race but didn't recognize the person who couldn't finish. That disappointment is what I felt running London in 2019. I was so embarrassed that I hid in the bathroom. I ran the first half in 2:30, and at that pace, would have finished in 5 hours. But still, I couldn't finish in the next 4 hours by walking the rest. That made it real.

I was used to being an elite runner who regularly ran ultra-marathons, my favorite distance being 50 milers. Not being that elite runner is a very painful emotion to handle. But now as a back of the packer, I'm running with those that are doing what they never thought possible. Their goal isn't necessarily a time, but just finishing. So now, it's not the person who has the natural ability that impresses me. It isn't even the mid pack runner who confidently knows they will cross the finish line. No, the person that impresses me is the person who doesn't have the ability but still crosses the finish line, despite how they feel at that very moment. All they can think about is, "When is my next race?" They want to get back out there, despite what others would consider a pathetic time.

I've been on both sides of the spectrum and remember those that have inspired me. In one race, I was coming up on the finish line, approaching this steep hill, maybe a 30-degree incline, when my pacer for the 3-hour group approached the hill and told his group, "Everyone get in front of me now." To our amazement, the guy runs up the hill backward, keeping the pace, at the 3-hour marathon pace. Meanwhile, many others struggled with this pace, and he is running backward, up a steep hill while encouraging each person by name.

I miss being that type of pacer. I've been on that side, but it's only as good as the people I'm pacing. Running the Tampa Hot Chocolate race with my biographer, everyone was engaged. We sang boot camp songs and during our run/walk sequences I asked them to tell us their story. "What's your name and what's your claim to fame?" Everyone on the course wanted to be in my group. I miss the pacing that way.

I also remember having this approach to goals even when I worked in business. "If you can meet a goal, was it really a goal?" The company I used to work for gave managers operational bonuses. But they failed to make it a challenge. Instead of using bonuses to increase the sales, they used the operational budget to fund increases in salaries. They couldn't get the employees to engage so they lowered the bar. Instead of cutting the wages and potentially losing the employees, they lowered the standards and claimed the employee was meeting their bonus.

Isn't that stupid? Of course, it is easier, but the bonus doesn't serve its purpose. If you know you will meet your bonus without trying, why try or try harder? A bonus should be over and above what you usually have coming to you. A bonus is not your daily paycheck. "You are robbing yourself."

I saw this and, as you might have imagined by now, I spoke up, explaining how their process was flawed. My supervisor, doing what many in management do with someone who complains, put me in charge of bonuses. To their surprise, within six months, we went from the bottom store to the top store in the company in 18 months. My boss couldn't figure it out, so I explained it to him. "You must invest in the machine that is making the product. You are muzzling the ox who is treading the grain and then wondering why you are not getting as much grain. The ox is hungry. You gotta let the ox eat." The reason the company suffered at that store was because leadership didn't have confidence in their own authority. Therefore, they didn't challenge their employees and reward the eventual success.

Not finishing every race doesn't make me a failure. I'm on a quest, a journey of a servant whose purpose is to meet and encourage everyone. The running servant's purpose is to meet and encourage everyone. So finishing is desired but serving is critical.

I was encouraged, now understanding far more about running than I ever imagined. I was ready to take the next step. With that new attitude, it was time to Go to St. Louis.

Running with Pain

"We are now faced with the fact that tomorrow is today. We are confronted with the fierce urgency of now. In this unfolding conundrum of life and history, there "is" such a thing as being too late. This is no time for apathy or complacency. This is a time for vigorous and positive action."
Martin Luther King, Jr.

Martin Luther King, Jr.'s quote reminds me that character is not forged in times of complacency but rather from going through pain. That is where character is purged, formed, and forged.

To be a runner, you have to have to enjoy pain at some level. Yes, you are going to be sore because you are pushing your body to new heights. Muscles are going to develop, and you will appreciate that. But in the process, if there is no pain, there is no gain. Runners appreciate that process. Ultramarathoners face even more pain, pushing their bodies farther. They come to a point where you get so accustomed to pain that it is actually more painful to stop than it is to run. It is like you are Fred Flintstone trying to stop a big truck with your feet.

I always have pain when I'm running or sitting on my glutes too long. That's why I can't drive 4-5 hours to a race. It is too much sitting. People always ask, "Why don't you have surgery to remove the bullet?" The answer is simple, "because that would make the pain worse. The scar tissue from surgery, as the doctor explained, will cause more damage than leaving the bullet in. As part of the surgery, they would have to cut the muscle to get the bullet and that would cause even more pain."

111

Then there is the emotional pain from the self-proclaimed critics. They pretend to know best. As one runner heard, "What are you training for, a bad heart or bad knees." What those critics don't realize is that if you don't use it, you will lose it. Sitting on the couch will cost more problems because you are not conditioning those muscles and joints. I have heard that fish that get trapped in a cave go blind because they don't use their eyes. Even if you put them in a lighted environment, they fail to regain their eyesight. Some people want to keep you blinded, protecting you so you remain blind. Sitting on the couch protects you from initially experiencing pain but the long term is worse. Those people are purposely resisting or avoiding immediate pain but inviting long term pain.

Remember how I lost 178 pounds by running and biking. The immediate pain of exercise was far better than the lingering pain of almost weighing 400 pounds.

That required experiencing a different type of pain. When I learned that gluttony is a sin, my spiritual sensitivities were heightened. You might say it was a pain of embarrassment when I realized my eating habits were self-satisfaction. God wants you satisfied but not to the point where it is in excess. Instead, eating is designed as physical fuel for the body. It is NOT salve for our emotional wounds. Too often we eat to immediately satisfy our tongue and mouth, not nourish our bodies. It was painful for me to realize I was living with the wrong goals. I was living for pleasure, not for service.

That was a very important lesson. Be thankful for the food God provides and use it to live God's purpose.

Learning that lesson is painful for many, so painful that people never change and enjoy the benefits. I was glad that I was able to push through that pain. I'm thankful that I learned to live beyond pleasure to enjoy a life of service.

As I returned to Houston, I was experiencing a new pain. I wasn't sure about the day of the week or where I was. My schedule was so confused from scheduling, rescheduling, and then rescheduling again that I wasn't sure where I was or where I was going next.

Week 11: Go! St. Louis Marathon, Missouri, April 11

As was becoming the trend, I met a lot of great people in St. Louis. By this point in the quest, I was seeing many runners from other races. Each meeting was an opportunity for another conversation that would expand our relationship. I was also making new friends.

While waiting to board the buses for the race, people started telling interesting and funny stories. Of course, I couldn't stay silent. I told a woman from Houston, who lives in Victoria, "they call me nipples" in Trail Runners over Texas. Of course, that is quite the opening line that intrigues everyone.

"I learned the hard way that you don't run with cotton shirts on a long-distance run. Feeling the pain during one race, I stopped at an aid station, lifted up my shirt and said, 'I need help.' One of the lady volunteers grabbed the Vaseline, rubbed it on my nipples with an applicator, and that took care of me. While I greatly appreciated her help, it turns out her boyfriend was out there with her. He didn't appreciate it nearly as much. So, the next year when I saw her at another aid station, she advised me that I had to apply the Vaseline myself." Despite her boyfriend's concern, the others tagged me with the nickname, "nipples." I loved it because it was all in fun.

Everyone seemed to enjoy the stories and we made our way to the buses. It was a smaller race with approximately 240 marathoners and over 1000 others half marathoners. That didn't include the 5 & 10K day run the day before.

The First Domino

But there is something happening at that point that I need to back up and explain. The day started off on the wrong note. As with most races, we got up and arrived at the pickup point early, while it was still dark. We boarded the buses to the drop off point. That's when something strange happened. I had a notion to pray. I shrugged it off, not sure what it meant. But the notion persisted and got stronger. I knew this was something that couldn't be ignored, even though I didn't have a clue what this was about. I prayed while the bus was waiting at a stop light. I finished just before the light turned green. Before the driver could enter the intersection, two cars suddenly screamed through the intersection, illegally racing over 100 mph without headlights, narrowly missing the bus. The stunned driver cautiously looks both ways and hesitates, even though the green light remained. Without saying a word, everyone in the bus watched for additional cars. Hesitantly, the driver inches the bus forward. By now everyone in the bus is on edge. Suddenly a third car flew by, slowed to about 80, saw the bus was stopping, and then speeded up. Everyone let out a collective sigh of relief. All 3 cars were driving without lights on.

Striking up a stress relief conversation at the drop-off point, a woman said, "God has a plan." I had looked at my watch while we waited at the light and noticed it said 5:33 a.m. I wondered, "why am I doing this?"

Little did I know that was just the first domino to fall that day.

We collected ourselves and started the race. From the very beginning, the running was good. I love it when that happens because it is like my body is a finely tuned machine. Everything is working as it should.

I connected with Debbie who I learned is a schoolteacher. Unfortunately, her husband dropped her off at the half drop-off instead of the full. The Race Director came to her rescue and gave her and another lady a ride to the full drop-off point. It seems like everyone has a story at this race.

Running alongside each other, she commented, "My goal is 5 and a half hours."

"I'm hoping to finish in 6."

"We can finish together," she smiled.

"I'll try to keep up," I responded.

114

This race, like Mississippi, crosses two states, Illinois and Missouri. We were running together in Illinois, and it felt great. She shared that she knew she would be walking the big hills that came later in the race.

We learned from others on the course that due to covid, the course had been altered from the previous year. But that was a good thing. People liked how the new course was more scenic, peaceful, and easy to engage other runners. There was also less congestion on the course and less traffic stops, especially by the iconic Arch.

The Second Domino

The first domino had been a near miss. This once was a direct hit. To say the wind was disrespectful was being too kind. It was a mean-spirited monster of biblical proportions, hell bent on destroying anyone willing to challenge it. Far more than a stiff breeze or a gusty irritation, it was a murderous, relenting wind that nearly knocked me off my feet.

It was also very devious.

All was calm as we started in St. Louis, luring us into a false confidence as we crossed the bridge into Illinois. At mile four, we followed the tow path along the Mississippi River for two miles before turning around, retracing our steps. Here we met the monster, a fire breathing dragon with a fierce breath gusting up to forty miles an hour. The wind threatened to tip us over, just like the port-a-potty at mile five.

It was there that I noticed people running toward me, having completed the turnaround, but oddly running with the right arm stiff at their side. It was as if it was glued to their side and leg. Just then, a gust caught me mid stride and blew me a foot back and to the side, almost blowing me into the path of an oncoming runner. We both smiled and laughed in astonishment. "Watch out for the wind."

Coming back, I heard a guy say, "I really need to use the restroom." Unfortunately, the outhouse that was upright just a minute ago, now lay on its top with all the putrid contents leaking out.

"Use it if you want, but I wouldn't." I cautioned.

The Result

The double-barreled attack leveled its load. I looked at my watch as I spotted the aid station and restroom ahead. My watch read 8.25 miles. We had run across the bridge, which was a mile long before going up a slope and then back down. Combined with the difficulty pushing against the wind, a familiar monster appeared. The PTSD kicked in about the middle of the bridge making me nauseous and dizzy. It was as if someone stood behind me, grabbed my head on both sides, and squeezed it relentlessly. The vision in my right eye blurred and the tears flowed faster than the Mississippi river.

It's hard for some to understand, but the struggle against the wind along with how the inclines tax my glute serves as a signal to my body to relieve the anxiety and fear of losing my life. The trauma is trapped in the muscle memory of my body, forcing me to relive that rainy night in Houston five years previous.

Not only did I feel horrible, but others could see the meltdown and kindly asked, "Are you ok?"

I said, "No."

"Do you need help?"

"No" is all the words I could muster. I knew what I'm going through and that there was nothing else anyone could do for me at that moment. I just need to get through it. It's like Winston Churchill said, "If you are going through hell, keep going." There was nothing else anyone could do. But I appreciated the kindness of people pausing their run to help me.

There was one person whose help I did welcome. A medic rode by on a bike and stayed with me as I made my way back across the Mississippi River bridge. As we reached mile 11, back in St. Louis, we stopped at the aid station when the medic left me in the care of another kind lady. I recognized her from a video from the Black Girl run and Black Girls Bike.

She graciously offered to take me back to the start/finish line, but I refused.

"We can get you the medic and he will take you back." "

"No, I have to make it to 13.1."

"Why, you aren't going to finish the marathon."

"I just have to. I at least need to do a half."

I was in too much pain to not at least finish a half. That might sound crazy. After all, if I was in that much pain, wouldn't I want to quit? The answer is a definite, "NO!" Interestingly enough, the medic understood.

"You are invested now. I understand what you are saying," she explained.

I was thinking about my great niece Gabby who has cancer. She is just two years old and already had surgeries to remove cancer in her kidney and tumors under her skull. She doesn't have the luxury of just stopping when she is in pain. I kept her on my mind and knew I had to at least get to 13.1.

So, I continued. Defeat or quitting wasn't an option.

It was in that last stretch where another runner brought a smile to my face. At mile 12, he seemed to appear out of nowhere, shouting, "Hey nipples." It turns out he overheard my story at the start line. That brought a smile to my face and warmness to my heart.

I made it to 13.1 and finally calmed down. Being with a medic helped because he was asking the basic questions to bring me down off the anxiety the right way. The cycle is the same each time, Anxiety – Depression - Crying.

"I apologize" I said to the medic.

He had none of it. "You don't have to apologize to me."

But I was extremely appreciative. He broke the cycle by being there and reassuring me I wasn't crazy. He checked my blood pressure, eyes, and demeanor. He wisely asked to make sure I was cognizant of who I was, where I was, and what I was doing.

After the race I learned there were a lot of people who quit because they didn't want to battle the wind. Like I had done at Oak Island, they doubled back at a convenient point and enjoyed the wind at their back, almost flying to the finish, where it was much calmer.

Prior to the race, I really wanted to finish. I felt good through that first eight miles, but the last four and a half miles were difficult. It took that entire time for me to get off that extreme PTSD cycle where I felt like my life was being threatened. I felt that hypervigilance for the next two days, constantly looking around, not paranoid but gut feeling that my life was about to end. It was the same feeling I had during the shooting.

In retrospect, the PTSD might have been triggered by the bus incident. That bothered me because it seemed like the number of triggers was increasing.

Reflection

As I reflect back on this race, I'm so thankful for Karen, the volunteer medical aid that took me back to finish to get my packet. She could've quit there but insisted that she take me back to my hotel.

"I couldn't just leave you."

'Thank you so much."

Everyone was so hospitable it made me feel like I was on a trail run." Trail runners feel like family while runners in road races usually don't get that involved. Trail runs are usually much smaller, so it is easier to make the connection. For example, this race was small but many trail runs only have about 1000 runners compared to 15,000 for many road races.

Go! St. Louis did it right. The Aid stations and medics were first class. The police officer followed me the last half mile to see me finish and handed me off to the medic. I appreciated that assistance. I'm not sure how I would have done it without her.

Although I was disappointed that I couldn't finish the marathon, I was pleased with the results. It helped knowing that I wasn't the only one that struggled. Knowing others turned around to avoid the wind, affirmed my pain.

It is disappointing to learn that some runners take shortcuts and then claimed they finished the entire race. Some do it to get an added advantage to place in their age division. Still others do it simply to claim the medal and pride of finishing.

I wouldn't have done that. It is against my beliefs and character to do that. I need to be an honest runner for Aiden and Gabby. They cannot cheat or bypass the pain in their marathon battle fighting cancer. I wouldn't blame them if they could, but they can't. Meanwhile, I know the marathon I'm running will be over in about six hours. They don't know when their pain will subside. They don't know when their illness will be done. I just run until the time expires or my energy runs out. Then I stopped. Even though the pain was excruciating, and it was the worst PTSD in a long time, I'm glad I ran.

A God Thing

The next morning, I called for a Lyft driver to get me back to the airport for my return flight to Houston. Little did I know a "God Thing" was about to unfold.

My Lyft driver asked if a couple could share the ride with a couple that couldn't get a rental car. I said, "as long as you can fit us." As #RunningServant, I'm always happy to help. The driver, Michelle, was driving a van so we had room. I boarded the van and John, the husband of the couple needing a ride, said, "You ran the marathon yesterday."

I looked at him and said, "Yeah" I remember you" and then looked at his wife, and continued, "you too."

"Let us pay for half the ride" they offered generously.

"No, I'm good. But instead, you can donate on the website." I filled them in on the details of my fundraising for St. Jude's Hospital.

"Consider it done." I was pleased when John said he quickly agreed.

In the process of telling them about my mission, the Lyft driver Michelle, who is a nurse, shared about her 6-year-old granddaughter. Kyra has an incurable cancer but is in remission. Michelle quit her nursing job so she could help care for her family. Needing the flexibility in her schedule, she started driving for Lyft.

Meeting Michelle, John and his wife was definitely a God Thing. Everyone exchanged information and we arrived at the airport on time and were inspired. I was blown away.

But it didn't stop there.

God definitely has a plan and I need to simply keep doing what I can do. That is amazing and applies to everyone. That seemed to be the theme of the entire weekend.

The next morning, as is my habit, I went to my "office" at Starbucks. There I saw a guy wearing a Houston Chevron marathon shirt from the year before last. I wear mine all the time, so when I see him across the patio, he looks back at me, our eyes connect, and we both laugh. We are wearing the shirts from the same marathon. Unlike women who would be embarrassed, we connected. I learned he was Joel Davis who is on my Strava running app. I shared my story with him, learned that he too is a believer, and he asked to pray for me. I'm honored whenever someone offers to pray for me. His prayer said that God has something bigger and encouraged me to stay the course.

I felt blessed with that week's theme. Lately, I have been second guessing myself about the 50-50-50 quest. I wondered if I should have simply stayed in Houston and donated the money I would've spent traveling and running. Maybe that would have honored God more. But this clearly told me that I was on God's path and needed to continue.

That week I posted about the upcoming Akron marathon in an online running group forum, appealing for donations for Akron Children's hospital. A guy from Germany responds. It turns out he is from Akron, so I invited him to come home and run the race. Unfortunately, he couldn't make it, but he sent a link to a book he has written. It turns out he is Geoffrey Simpson who once set the 10K world record holder, running it in 26 minutes. I ordered a book and kept in touch. He messaged and thanked me then donated to charity. Once again, God is really networking and connecting me to people.

One thing that I failed to mention happened when I was in St. Louis. I met a guy at Starbucks, Justin, who owns Talasek Home Builder. He called to encourage me and see what else they could do to help me. It is refreshing when someone believes in you and your message so much that they make an open offer. "What do you need? Plane tickets? Hotels?" Knowing that October was becoming overloaded with races and expenses, I asked him to help with roundtrip flight and hotels for Boston. He quickly agreed. "If you need anything else, let me know. The business is going well, and I am willing to help." My heart overflows with his and others' generosity.

Meeting people like Justin put me on top of the world. Now it was time to literally run to the top of a mountain.

Week 12: Foot Levelers Blue Ridge Marathon, Virginia, Apr. 20

Roanoke, Virginia is beautiful with the trees, valleys, and streams providing a magnificent panorama from atop the mountain. Getting to that mountain top, however, is the challenge.

I maybe shouldn't have signed up for this race given how it would tax my glutes, but in the end, I was very glad I did.

Photo: Roanoke Mountain ascends approximately 780 feet in two miles with multiple switchbacks

Walking from the hotel to the start line in a cool 42-degree temps, people wondered how I could do it. While bundled up, cringing from the cold, they couldn't believe I stood dressed only in my t-shirt, shorts, Strava Pacer Shirt, and running gloves.

"I've learned never to make a temporary decision based on what you are going to wear running the marathon. Better to suffer for that hour than to suffer for hours." I like to wear pacer shirt when the race doesn't have a pacer. Yes, it was cold, and I suffered a bit, but was happy later when I didn't get overheated.

The Foot Levelers Blue Ridge Marathon is known as America's toughest road race. It deserves that moniker since runners scale three mountains totaling 7430 feet in elevation gain. The first is a gradual incline, the second a series of switchbacks up the tallest mountain, and the last, almost straight up. Running this marathon proves your mettle as a runner.

Those seeking to push themselves even harder ran it twice in one day. I met a Chinese guy who started at midnight and finished his first marathon, rested, and started his second marathon at 6:00 a.m. That meant from midnight to 10:30 a.m., he ran two marathons, each in a time of 4:19 while scaling a total of 14, 860 vertical feet. Meanwhile, the elite runners completed the marathon in a little over three hours.

While waiting to begin, I met two young guys in their 20s. One had trained, but the other one hadn't. I gave them some pointers but seriously wondered who would run this particular marathon without training. To my surprise, both ended up finishing.

I started with the regular marathon at 7:30 a.m. Due to social distancing, runners were spread-out all-over downtown, and that required me to walk a mile before even reaching the start line. I finally crossed the start line at 7:45. By the time I reached mile 3, the elites were coming down the second mountain and approaching mile 15.

Reading about the course was one thing. Running it was another. It didn't take long to realize this would be the toughest course I faced during the entire challenge. At least at this point, I couldn't imagine anything more demanding.

The first mile was easy and flat. Then, as we approached the first mountain. We entered the park and began the assent. Knowing my glute's limitation, I devised a plan to speed walk up the mountain and then enjoy running downhill. My mental motivational plan included a mantra, "Self, what goes up must come down."

The plan worked as I made it to the top without much pain. Enjoying the vista, I turned around and enjoyed running downhill. Or should I say, entered bliss. Reaching a mountaintop, literally and figuratively is exhilarating. Running downhill is even better in my mind. It is a flashback to the world that once was.

Blue Ridge Marathon mile marker 2

As I approached the second mountain, I changed my mantra slightly, "Self, what goes WAY up must come WAY down." The first one was simply a warmup for this beast. It just didn't seem to quit. I trudged up and up, farther, and farther, but I didn't seem to be making any progress. Reaching an aid station, I thought I was the top, but the volunteers said, "Keep going, it is just a little bit more." I couldn't believe it, then another said, "You still have a half mile to go."

Photo: What goes up, must go down. Runners: 566: Erin Breisacher of Roanoke, VA and 242: Greg James of Boones Mill, VA.

I realized I still had a half mile to go to reach the top of this relentless mountain. With a heavy sigh, I left the aid station and felt like I was about to drop. A nauseous feeling hit like a ton of bricks. My vision blurred like it was the week before in St. Louis. The pain in my glute quickly returned with a pulsating wave. But, somehow, I pushed myself through it, first one step, then another, and continued until I made it to the top.

"Half a mile?" I thought to myself. That meant I was only a little over halfway up. While I greatly appreciated the exuberant welcome and encouragement, my right glute was knotting up and screaming, "Why did you do this to me?" I knew I needed relief any way I could get it.

Photo: Looking at the next half mile that continues to go higher and higher.

"Who wants to walk on my back?" I asked. The little kids backed away from me while a dog looked at me and barked repeatedly.

One woman laughed and said, "The dog wants to walk on your back."

"I'll take it." I was serious but she continued.

"Do you seriously need someone to walk on your back?"

"Yes," my tone showed I wasn't kidding around. "But what I need is someone to not necessarily walk on my back but on my glute."

"What are your glutes?"

"The booty," another answered before I could reply.

126

Without hesitating, she volunteered, "Oh, I'll walk on your booty." She liked the sound of that.

So here I am, at the top of a gigantic mountain, laying on the ground with this woman I've never met before taking her shoes off, laughing, and enjoying the moment. I didn't care because I needed the relief from my tight, right glute. By then, I was in serious pain.

The woman didn't stop there, willingly moving up to walk on my back.

Meanwhile, the medics took notice.

"Never mind them," I said, "unless they come and pull you off of me, keep walking."

My glute seemed to smile and moan, "Oh yeah, right there, that's it."

Photo: Julie Roach's Facebook post

Julie Waldron Roach is with **Michelle Nervo Scarfe**.
26m ·

This is Aaron aka Bullet Butt or #therunningservant. He was on the ground with a volunteer standing on his back at the top of Roanoke Mountain when we met him. He looked up at us (he knew he was last at that point and stuck with us sweepers) and said "and the Lord said I'd look up from the ground and see two beautiful women on bikes!!" He was one of our many treats today. What an amazing story he had (there really IS a bullet in his butt) and what a serendipitous day for a couple of marathon sweepers

You and 16 others   3 Comments

Care   Comment

The medics don't like that type of activity primarily because it isn't the proper thing for others to see at an aid station. I didn't care because she was providing relief for my extreme pain. At that moment, I didn't care about polite appearances. I was grateful that the medics turned a blind eye and acted like they didn't see. That impromptu treatment helped the muscle knotting but didn't cure it.

I'm really not sure how I did it. I do know one thing, I stopped to enjoy the panoramic vista at the top. After that much pain and suffering to make it to the top, I was definitely going to enjoy it.

The mountain top experience was both exhilarating and intimidating. You see, there are no guardrails, and the mountain drops off quickly. I remember thinking "If you aren't careful, you will fall off. You don't want to do that." Collecting myself, I turned, and retraced my steps, this time running downhill.

My ascent was hell, but my descent was heaven. I found my downhill form quickly, hitting the quads, flicking my feet, and keeping my form. I was nailing it, staying on top of my feet, carefully and conscious ensuring I didn't point my heels inward. I let my arms swing as fast as they could knowing my legs would keep up. I was moving well and I gotta say, "man did that feel good."

I was also making great time. From mile 7 to 8, coming down that mountain, I ran an 8-minute mile. That used to be my mid mileage rate prior to the shooting, but that didn't matter, it felt great not having my glute kicking my but. My mind flashed back to those early days running. A wave of peace, pleasure, and exhilaration swept over me. Good memories appeared on the movie screen in my mind as I remembered how easy it was to run. I remembered my old practice runs and the potential I was discovering a few years ago. I remembered how that was my highest heaven. No wonder I felt at one with God when I was on the course.

But then, all too suddenly, just as if I was awakened from a delightful dream, the downhill slope flattened, and hell set in as I looked at the next challenge.

If only that rainy night in Houston hadn't happened. If only I hadn't been shot. If only. . .. In the days long past, I would have enjoyed the challenge up the next mountain.

My mind then flashed forward a few months to another opportunity for this euphoria. On August 15 I was scheduled to run a downhill marathon, the Tunnel Light Marathon near Snoqualmie, WA. "Oh Lord, please don't let it be postponed or canceled." I wanted to prolong this joy.

Watching my time and recognizing that the third mountain was almost straight up, voices from the past started to haunt me. I remembered people questioning me when I signed up for the run, knowing it was a difficult race.

"Are you crazy? You haven't done well in your previous runs. Why are you even attempting this?"

They didn't understand. As I mentioned before, this wasn't just some quest to boost my ego. I knew I needed to do it because I had what we call in the spiritual world, an "unction." It was an overwhelming desire and calling to run 50 marathons (not half marathons or cycling or swimming) in 50 states in 50 weeks. I knew it would be difficult and it was proving more difficult than I had originally anticipated. But even then, I still wasn't going to quit. I accepted the challenge and would see it through.

Those doubts brought back other memories. For example, I had a therapist make a snide comment that doubted me. As I explained how I could feel what was going on in my own body, she doubted me. She couldn't believe I could feel the 2mm bullet fragment.

"Have you ever been shot?"

"No."

"I have."

She infuriated me when she referred to an old story about the Princess and the Pea. "I guess if the princess can feel the pea under the stack of mattress, maybe you could feel that."

Basically, she was skeptical and claimed my pain was just a fairy tale. That incensed and infuriated me. I don't like being doubted and disrespected. The tale finds a prince looking for a wife but being frustrated that no one lives up to his or his mother's standards. When a young lady arrives at the door drenched from the rain, they once again doubt she could be the one. So, the mother devises a test, hiding a pea under several mattresses. If the girl, without knowing of the test, could feel the pea while sleeping in the bed that night, she was worthy of marrying the prince. The girl retired but did not sleep well, bothered by something hard in the bed. Arising the next morning, the mother and prince were anxious to learn of the test results. The girl said she didn't sleep well and then showed the bruise on her back from the hard object in the bed. Indeed, she had found the pea and became the bride.

But enough of the fairytale. I was disgusted with the therapist. Despite being a prominent therapist in pain management at Memorial Herman in Houston, she was extremely insensitive. Essentially, she didn't believe me and implied I was fabricating a story of feeling the bullet fragment.

My mind quickly flashed to an even earlier memory, immediately following the shooting. I told the responding medics, "I've been shot" but they doubted me. One checked but found no sign of an entry wound. "I'm telling you; I have been shot. I can feel the hot metal inside my body." Another medic searched my body and found one entry wound. Interestingly enough, the bullet fragment was exactly where I told them it was. Yes, I could feel that pea under several mattresses.

This is to say, I not only have a bullet and bullet fragments in my body, I also have the physical and emotional scars from the shooting. The doubts from those who should have had my best interest in mind, still cause me acute pain. What amazes me the most is that, as the running servant, I work to encourage others. When they tell me they are in pain or share their concerns, I don't doubt them. I serve them. Yet all these people dismissed my pain, doubted my experience, and denied my heart. That hurts, haunts, and horrifies me.

Speaking of hurting, I paused to look at my watch and calculate my time as I reached mile 11. I knew that I was one of the slowest runners and, therefore, fighting to finish in the allotted time. I knew what I was facing the steepest incline of the race and that my glutes were already played out. As much as I didn't want to call it a day, and as much as I would have loved to run that downhill and finished, I knew what I needed to do. I didn't think it was wise to be out on those lonely state park trails with a body that was depleted. I called it a day.

My Reaction

Despite not finishing, the race was physically rewarding. I made it to the top of that first mountain and loved running down. Even after my struggles on the second mountain, knowing I could've made the cutoff at 11.4 miles by 11:00 meant a lot. I only needed to run 2 miles in 35 minutes. I was running a 14-minute mile so I knew I could do that and stop at 15 miles. I felt good even knowing that I wouldn't have been able to traverse that third mountain with the brutal incline. As I mentioned previously, I was measuring my success not in finishing but in how I could push myself each week. Had there been a timing chip to mark the halfway point in the race, I would have officially finished the half. But since the half marathoners ran a different course, I knew I didn't need to go farther. I called it quits at mile 11.

Photo: Runner 744 Gregory, Lauren McMillen. 780: Gonzalez, 326: Ronald Rees, Sandy McMillen and 62: me, the Running Servant

Looking back, I realize it pays to be a little naïve because you do better than you thought you could. Sometimes your perception is wrong. You can exceed your expectations.

Running this monster mountain race, I reconsidered the Las Vegas run. Suddenly, I wished I wouldn't have given up so quickly on the thousand-foot incline. I wished I would have pushed myself harder. I vowed, "The next time I am in that situation, I'm going to do it."

I remember this race, where at the top of the 1910, "thank you" but the downhill was my celebration. Maybe that was my accomplishment for the week, running that hill.

I was also encouraged because I was seeing the results of improving mentally, emotionally, spiritually, and physically. After the previous week in St. Louis, it was a pleasure to run the mountains. I wouldn't trade the feeling of running downhill for anything in the world. It encouraged me so much and I recognized that it was by the grace of God. My pain tolerance is increasing each week. It's like going through a trial to develop your character, and with each small increment of success, I know I have a lot more in me. This was a trial to develop my character and I passed. As Martin Luther King, Jr. says, character is not forged in times of complacency. I won't give up.

Remember how I hated running during training in basketball and football. I especially hated running what we called "suicides" in basketball and hated off-season because they made us run track. Then discovering a love for running twenty years later only to have it threatened is especially frustrating. It would be easy to quit if I didn't have that burning passion. That's why I'm willing to work toward my goals.

By this point in the quest, I was running 2-3 times a week. On rare occasions I run a 5k or 10k before the weekly marathon. I usually run once during the week as well. It all depends on how my body is reacting. That means I need to listen carefully to my body. Right now, it's telling me that I definitely need to drop some weight. I will accomplish that with weight resistance training. I would like to start this week but had to say, "Self, calm down." I pushed myself hard climbing those mountains and will take a cautious approach in starting my new program. Once a week I'll work on the legs and twice a week on the rest of the body. The rest of my schedule looks like this: Return on Sunday, massage on Monday, stretch and doctors' appointments on Wednesday. I'll be adding cycling to the mix as soon as I get my bike fixed. Every day I focus on prayer, meditation, and bible study to complete a holistic approach involving the mental, emotional, physical, and spiritual arenas.

Suffering

One of the most critical elements of my approach is dealing with suffering. When we suffer traumatic pain that persists, at some point we start questioning why things are happening to us. For me, I was a sinful man leading a sinful life. That's when God, the Father, opened my eyes and understood that Jesus took my penalty for me. Because of that, I'll never have to suffer God's wrath, which I justly deserve. Jesus saved me as the Suffering Servant in my place. So that makes me wonder, "Why shouldn't we suffer? Why should we expect to avoid suffering?" I was telling a friend the other day, "Show me somebody that isn't suffering. Please. I want to meet them." Suffering is a part of life, so we just need to admit we are in pain and be willing to help each other.

Unfortunately, how many people deny their pain? How many hide the hurt by distracting themselves with their jobs, activity, booze, men and women, sports, shopping, and partying? How many people are willing to admit being broken, need healing, or embrace the process of being healed? Instead, we play the macho man, refusing to be vulnerable, never letting them see us sweat. And it's not just men. You may think I'm speaking of men alone, but women are just as guilty, sidestepping the serious things in life or begging that someone take their suffering away. We need to reconsider how suffering helps us build character. No, we don't enjoy it and shouldn't purposely seek to suffer. But at the same time, we shouldn't feel like victims when we encounter suffering.

Interesting People

The people at the Foot Levelers Blue Ridge Run Marathon were very, very friendly. One young man, Braxton, was impressive. His dad is a coach, and his mom is very supportive. Even as a young boy, he loves running and is part of a relay team that won the year before, hoping to repeat this year. I was immediately impressed when I learned that, for him, running wasn't a selfish act. One day he asked his mom about fundraising.

Pleased but intrigued, she asked "Why?"

"I want to run for others who cannot run for themselves."

Wow! That is one impressive young man. I learned that he wants to run professionally and had an opportunity to meet a record holder of the New York half marathon. I smiled when I heard him say he was going to break that guy's record. I took a photo with Ryan and his long hair.

Then there was a 10-year-old girl who ran the half marathon in an amazing time of 2:02. There were lots of kids running adult courses that were getting great times. That is refreshing

and encouraging to see so many young kids tackling difficult challenges. (Photo: Braxton and me)

Lastly, the race was run in such a professional manner. I always appreciate when race directors take the time to attend to the small details. I was especially appreciative of the concert following the race in the nearby college amphitheater. That was a nice touch.

Looking Ahead

Next week I travel to Wausau Wisconsin for the Pine Line Marathon. That will be the opposite of the Foot Levelers Marathon because it is run along an old railroad bed. That means it's flatter than a pancake. While I've always hated flat runs because it taxes my glutes, I'm interested in seeing how I will do after the wind in St. Louis and the mountains in Roanoke.

My goal for next week is to not only see how much I can do on a flat course, but also to see if running mountains hurt me at all. I need to know if my glutes can take the pain and still perform the following week.

I will definitely run this race again. I don't want to leave that incomplete.

With that, it's time to board the train for the Pine Line Marathon. I don't know what next week will bring, but like I said, sometimes it pays to be naïve.

Changing My Training

I made an important step by starting to work with a trainer, Marcus McDade, who is a friend from high school. I first talked to him a few months ago when he explained that I wasn't ready to start working with him. My glutes weren't strong enough yet so I needed more intentional exercises to build my core. I did those and have been making good progress.

In my first session, he had me doing a variety of exercises targeting mobility, movement, core, full body, and weight loss. This was laying the foundation for the basic push – pull exercises that I needed because I had gotten progressively slower due to muscle damage.

One thing I learned is that a younger person's legs are closer together and as we age, we need to look at shoulders, hips, diaphragm, and even the belly button. Learning this tidbit helps me assess my own body and tell me what I need to work on.

Marcus started my training some months ago by assigning exercises to do on my own. These exercises helped build my body to a point where he could push me farther with in-person sessions. I was pleased to see early results and be to the point where he will work with me.

My introductory workout session included three major motions using only five-pound dumbbells. No big deal, right? After all, a big guy like me should easily handle this.

Then someone catches my eye. To my side, there was a lady half my age and size working out using twenty-pound dumbbells. She looked at me, seemingly wondering, "Why is he such a big wimp?"

My male ego kicked in. I wanted to grab a bigger weight but then caught myself, "My race - my pace." I had to remind myself. "She doesn't know your story." I returned my focus to working with my itty-bitty weights.

That first workout was extremely challenging. I completed one exercise and felt like I had been working out for 30 minutes.

"You have." Marcus said, "just not on this exercise."

Once again, I was humbled. Suddenly, my ultimate goal seemed so far off, and I was aware of the long road ahead. I also reminded myself "This is important. I want to finish the 50-50-50 challenge. I also am going to run the Tokyo Marathon and earn my sixth star for the world majors. This is what I need. Besides, I want my old body back. I want to run like I used to, or as close to that as I can get."

A funny thing happened when I was at the gym with Marcus. Another trainer, let's call him Joe, looked at me knowing Marcus works with several famous athletes. He asked his workout buddy, "Who is Marcus working with?"

Willing to play along, he responded, "You don't know who that is?"

"No. Who is it?"

"That is Earl Campbell's son."

Joe was instantly impressed. Meanwhile, Marcus and I could hear the conversation. When leaving, I continued the ruse, saying "Did you try my daddy's sausage?" Everyone in Houston knows Earl Campbell has his own sausage company.

"Joe" was thoroughly impressed, looked at me and asked, "Mind if I shake your hand?"

I said, "Have you ever tried my daddy's sausage?"

"No," he said meekly.

"Then you have to try my daddy's sausage."

After I left, Marcus came clean, telling Joe later it wasn't true. At my next session, Marcus and I all had a good laugh later.

What you don't know is that as a teenager, people would ask my mom if Earl Campbell was my daddy. Earl was well known around the neighborhood; he was the NFL Hall of Famer running back for the Houston Oilers. My size and hair style made me look like him.

Photo: Side by side comparison with Earl Campbell. "You buy my Daddy's sausage?"

Week 13: Pine Line Marathon, Wisconsin, Apr. 24

After literally pushing myself to new heights the week before, I looked forward to a nice flat, easy run. Little did I know how my expectations would be shattered.

The marathon, like so many, was canceled in 2020. The year before 2019, only 50 people ran. But this year, the demand was pent up and saw a surge with 250 marathoners and 500 half marathoners.

The Pine Line Marathon is a beautiful run near a small, stereotypical midwestern town. Unfortunately, getting there proved to be more difficult than I imagined. I couldn't rent a car because my ID didn't register with their third-party records. Had it been a corporate location, there wouldn't have been any problem. But as an independent, they used a different system that didn't synchronize with the corporate records. Having no other choice, I hailed a taxi for the 1.5-hour drive to the race. That little trip cost me $155 plus a $20 tip. Then I paid the same amount for the return trip. As expensive as that was, it was cheaper than renting a car.

I stayed at Woodland Inn and Suites, with several other runners. The atmosphere reminded me of college, hanging in the dorm room, congregating in the hallway with our doors open. That made for a great atmosphere, right? Not if you were trying to get some rest, like I was. It didn't take long, and I started to get irritated. I wondered, "Why don't they just go into their own rooms?"

But then I paused and heard something enticing. As I listened carefully, I heard how much fun they were having. That changed my attitude quickly. I told myself, "Aaron shut up and enjoy."

I exited my room, greeted them, and sat down. All runners were killing time the night before a marathon. We told stories and laughed until about 9:00. Then, as if someone had called, "Lights out," we returned to our respective rooms to prepare for tomorrow's run. It turned out to be a great evening.

The Race

The sun rose about 6:30 and so did I. Preparing for the 8:00 start, my plan was to walk the 1.5 miles to the start. But as I was ready to leave the hotel, I connected with some Texas people who invited me to join them on the bus at 7:00. The picturesque ride took us through farm country houses, barns, and cattle that reminded me of puzzles my grandmas put together. Since this was a point-to-point race rather than an out and back, they dropped us off at the farthest point. We would return by running on the former Pine Line Railroad line. Cleared of the track and ties, the bed is a gentle but steady up and down with some flat stretches. After a few difficult and disappointing finishes, I was hoping this race would be my breakthrough.

That wasn't to be. By mile two, I was ready to quit. I knew something was amiss when I was hurting after my warmup, but I couldn't figure it out. I was well rested, mentally relaxed, and physically ready to run. But now I was hurting so much I stopped, crouched

140

down, and stretched. My muscles were tight and stretching felt like ringing out a wet rag. "What is going on?" I wondered.

The answer came quickly as I listened carefully to my body. The previous week's run had left my glutes in rough shape. My gluteus maximus was pulling on gluteus medius, straining my left side lat (latissimus dorsi) muscles, which caused my hamstrings to overwork. Instead of a fine-tuned machine, my body was out of sync to the point I started sweating profusely. I didn't know if I was sweating or crying, until I realized the weather was at 42 degrees and dropping before the rain began to fall.

But even with the pain, I knew I couldn't quit. Gabby and Aiden don't have that luxury. As was becoming my pattern, I kept my quiet vow to press through and at least complete the half.

Sometimes life seems to kick us when we are down. In the middle of this muscle maze of misery, I noticed gun shots.

"Is that a farmer shooting?"

But then the shots increased to volley after volley.

"Are they having a shootout over there?" It almost sounded like a gang shootout. Knowing I was in an idyllic farm country, I knew that wouldn't be the case. I came to the logical, and correct answer.

"Could that be a shooting range?"

I had no clue that the Pine Line Trap House was a shooting range just 100-120 yards off the marathon course. It was so close that we could see and hear the competitive shooters talking clearly. I took out my phone, turned on the video as a selfie so I could see and focus on myself. My challenge was to narrow my focus and prevent my PTSD from kicking in.

Then I noticed other runners, like a Vietnam vet who was also affected. Looking farther, I noticed it was affecting all of the runners. We were all surprised, unaware of a neighboring shooting range with activity. Some were fearing they would get hit. We learned later that we were safe because they were shooting in the opposite direction.

A few miles later one of the volunteers tried to lighten the mood. Hearing a gunshot, he acted as if he was hit. The joke didn't go over as one runner believed his stunt to be real and rushed to assist him. The volunteer quickly apologized. Fortunately, I only heard about this later. That would have further triggered my PTSD.

Certain sounds trigger my PTSD. It isn't all gunshots, just certain caliber of weapons. Even though the trap shooters were using shotguns and the robbers in Houston used a handgun, the frequency was similar enough to trigger my PTSD. Over the years, I have purposely worked to assimilate myself so I can hear shots without being triggered. Knowing there is a gun range near my favorite running ground of Terry Hershey Park, I purposely ran the trail between the Army Corp and the gun range.

Photo: My PTSD was triggered near the Trap House Shooting Range

So why did this trigger me? First, I was surprised. Had I known about the range, I would have either avoided the race or mentally prepared for it. I was frustrated when I learned later that the half marathoners were made aware of it but not the marathoners. Second, it was only 100 yards away. Third, I couldn't tell which way they were shooting. Fourth, I could hear the shots for over a mile.

I tried to counter it, literally stopping to take my focus off of it. However, it was so traumatic that I looked over, and thought, "I'm not going any further. I'm turning around."

But a wiser voice countered, "Self, no, you need to work through this." That's when I took out my phone to put the video on. I wasn't trying to talk, just focusing on my breathing, and working to prevent it from affecting me.

These episodes not only revisit the shooting trauma, but also remind me of the doubters and accusers who blame me for the shooting. Yes, you read that correctly. Several people, including family and friends, have blamed me for the situation five years previous. They couldn't believe I was there to save lives but rather than I might have been involved in the robbery. Others accused me of making too much out of it. It's bad enough to nearly die but for others to be inconvenienced by my pain is overwhelming.

Then to know that those thugs from the robbery made two additional attempts on my life. They returned to the store looking for me that evening. Days later, they placed stolen goods on my stoop trying to incriminate and intimidate me. Without delving into the dirty details, I learned later that they were part of a national organized crime group. Despite my pleas to the Houston Police Department, I was alone fighting to survive.

On that trail, feeling as if an emotional train had smacked me on that old rail bed, I asked myself, "How can anyone tell me that what I went through wasn't major. They only say that to make their life easier. They haven't been there, having someone standing over them with a gun saying, 'Finish him off.' What did they expect? Did they expect me to simply clock out from that experience, and go home for the day?"

Talking to others after the race, the response was similar. "I've never been shot, but that is scary."

Obviously, this is a sensitive subject. Please forgive me for asking, but how can anyone that knows me and what I have gone through, tell me that I'm exaggerating it. How can they say I'm making too much of it? Would they tell the kids who lived through Columbine, Sandy Hook or Uvalde to "just forget about it?" Would they tell those terrorized by the Washington, D.C. sniper that it was nothing? It ticks me off. I want to say, "Go to these high schools, go to these colleges and workplaces, and tell them this isn't serious." They will find that anyone going through traumatic situations will act the same way. We cannot just forget.

Fortunately, the other runners understood. Runners from Texas and Indiana that have done Carmel with me, understood. One lady who has run 3 marathons with me, (Daufuski, Savannah, and Wisconsin), encouraged me. That meant a lot.

Try as I might, the PTSD, like an ugly stalker that wouldn't be denied, kicked in and I knew it would be a rough ride. I couldn't sleep for two nights. Imagine what that is like. Alone with your haunting thoughts, your body refuses to relax and let you drift off. Instead, the clock ticks, second by second, minute by minute, hour by hour until the sun rises. Then the second night, the torture continues. Imagine how tired you become. You struggle to focus. You have no energy. You don't care about what matters most.

At approximately mile 11, a gentleman on the course, noticing my pain, encouraged me, "It's ok to fight another day." That was hard for me to hear, especially thinking of Gabby and Aiden. So, I tried to dismiss his kind words. But then he continued, "You just continue being a good witness. It's ok to live to fight another day. You don't have to finish this one. Don't hurt yourself so you can't fight another day." I recognized him as a fellow believer in Jesus Christ and appreciated his compassion.

"Thank you. I will get to the half and see how I feel." His kind words touched me, but I already knew by mile 8 that this race would end prematurely for me.

I finished the half marathon but called it a day.

Looking Ahead

Despite the physical and emotional trauma of the race, by midweek I was mentally ready to run the Potomac River Marathon the next weekend. Physically, I knew it depended on how much pain I was willing to tolerate.

I'm excited to work with Marcus because he has me on a good plan to build my core and lose weight. He also has me in the right mental zone and believes in my audacious goals. That is a critical improvement.

My approach to the Potomac River Marathon is to walk and stay in my zone. As I begin running again, I need to focus on my running technique, breathing from my diaphragm, leading with hips, shoulders back, arms swinging, and stay relaxed. One key is to use correct posture while building core back up. By October I should be ready for a month filled with major marathons. Despite my challenges, my goal is to run a five-hour marathon. Right now, I have mental, emotional, and will power, but don't have the core strength to do it. So, I'll follow his plan to walk the next marathon.

Week 14: Potomac River Run Marathon, Washington, D.C., May 2

After several weeks of running hell, I was ready for a piece of heaven. I would find it along the Potomac River, in part because I finally got a full eight hours of sleep a few nights before. After just three sessions with Marcus, having worked on my torso muscles, I was feeling much stronger. Also, I've dedicated an hour each evening to cycling. One exercise I do, while cycling, is to go uphill and let go of the handlebars. That is strengthening my back. Naturally, I'm excited about my progress but also cautious not to exceed my limits.

The scene was very relaxing for this charity run. Arriving in D.C., the weather was beautiful, and the course offered plenty of shade. The course ran through Turkey Run Park, along the river, and near a canal, not too far from the Reagan Airport. I stayed at the Keystone Marriott that was so close I could have walked the mile and a half to the start. Listening to Marcus's advice, I took it easy.

The Potomac River Run was really an out and back trail run, and that brought more runners for the marathon than the half. We started on the towpath, which was asphalt, but only six feet wide with a hundred runners. Fortunately, it wasn't a big race and thinned quickly to make for easy running. It was beautiful and interesting, running along a series of locks, with a gradual incline.

I was running with a friend, Lettie, from Houston. Mindful of Marcus' words, I noticed she was struggling on the inclines. I immediately switched into coaching and cautioned her, "Save your energy."

Meanwhile, I was impressed with how some runners were hitting their stride and making good time. That was impressive given that the towpath wasn't closed to non-runners. We contended with bikers and runners who were not registered and not following the same course. That took some awareness and patience, but the entire experience was awesome. I tell anyone who will listen, "If you want to get away and still have something to do, that's the place. You can go fishing, rent a canoe, or even go white water rafting. The run is great because there are plenty of people to keep your mind busy." (Photo: with Leticia Sagdler)

Lettie and I did pretty well, and it was tempting to run the whole marathon. But I kept hearing Marcus' words, "Take it easy." I know I'm on a 50-50-50 quest, but also recognizing that I'm rebuilding my body. I don't want to push it and end up hurting myself. Taking stock at the halfway mark, I was very pleased that I wasn't hurting. My muscles were sore from running but I didn't have the additional and debilitating pain I had in the previous races.

Out of an abundance of caution, and against my strong desire to finish, I called it a day after finishing the half.

I could've finished in 2.5 hours but waited for Lettie and ended up finishing in 3.20 after waiting for her. At this point, the time doesn't matter. I'm focused on what I can do, not what the official time says.

A Chinese runner led a marathon, doing the first half in just 1.5 hours. I'm always impressed by what the elite runners do. I admire their abilities but also take me back to my best accomplishments. In some ways, my mind is still at the front of the pack, despite being at the back.

As with other charity races, the bling was limited to a shirt, bag, mask, and a rather plain medal. It was simply a small plastic emblem of the run with an equally plain ribbon. Even though the race was beautiful, I've seen better medals for a kid's one miler. This medal was so small and plain, I thought it belonged in a happy meal. Please don't misunderstand me. I realize that charities want to funnel more money to their charity, so they don't dedicate much for medals. Yet, in this age of runners that appreciate great medals, they might raise more money by improving their medals.

Jay Wind has been the race director for a few decades. He is very hands on and runs a good race. Everyone knows that he is very hospitable and personable but if you try to distract him during the race, he snaps. Although that doesn't come across well with the general public, runners appreciate how well the race is run. I will say that Jay has to be the most caring Race Director ever, and the overwhelming support by the running community proves it — See you soon Jay.

Photo: Mike Mebrahtu and Jay Jacobs, Race Director

Recap and Recovery

To give you an idea of how much better I felt during this run and recovery, my massage therapist said, "You didn't even text me."

"I felt so good."

"Usually, you are begging for help."

"That's because I wasn't in pain."

I did find that my right hip flexor, hamstring, and I.T. bands were tighter. Marcus noticed my right leg is still a bit weaker and explained that my muscles shake because they aren't connected to my mind. But once I focus, my body responds. He noted my form and adjustment are good and I can control my body. I began to notice how good I feel when I wake up. I'm now invigorated mentally and physically. At first, I had doubts, but not anymore.

What's Next?

I was supposed to be running in New Jersey. Remember, I had to postpone that one after running Pennsylvania. Unfortunately, I received news this week that my nephew died by suicide. That means I'll be attending to family issues in Ohio. Naturally I didn't foresee that trauma when creating this challenge. So, the next race will be May 16 when I run the North Carolina Tobacco Road Marathon. That is just before the New England Challenge. I was supposed to go to New Jersey for 3 days on the 13th. Instead, I've given my spot away for New Jersey to Bruce in the Marathon Maniacs. I will also switch up the New England Challenge, running Rhode Island on Monday.

The quest continues, as do the challenges.

Week 15: Allscripts Tobacco Road Marathon, North Carolina, May 16

Progress is critical with any challenge. For me, progress is seeing the body being rebuilt to be stronger and faster. Marcus is helping me focus on my form, using complementary muscles to compensate for my weak glutes. That means using a traditional runner's form to engage specific muscles, such as my left core stomach muscles between six pack and oblique. They were squashing me while I was running. I am learning to develop them, breathe differently, and engage other muscles. That has been the most difficult. It is a fascinating, challenging, and rewarding process that requires fueling those muscles differently, so my lower back or hamstrings aren't pulled.

While the work in the gym is great, the test is on the trail. This week brought me back to my beloved trail runs, this one near the Research Triangle in North Carolina. The Allscripts Tobacco Road Marathon follows much of the American Tobacco Trail (ATT) near Durham. Like the Pine Line Marathon, the ATT follows an abandoned rail bed, which gives runners a fast, flat course that many use to qualify for Boston. This was the type of run that I needed.

The day started with a perfect running temperature of 45 degrees and the course was absolutely beautiful. They used a staggered start to maintain proper distancing. I settled into my stride, maintained my form, and could quickly tell my body was responding well to Marcus' training. The work on my torso, core, and glutes were paying off as I felt stronger and was running faster. As tempting as it was, I didn't want to overdo it.

My strategy continues to be walking up hills to save my glutes and then run down and continue running on the flat sections. I was especially pleased with my pace as I was running a 12:48 minute and as fast as a 10-minute mile. The first half marathon was exhausting but nowhere near the pain in my core that I had experienced in previous races. It felt great,

At that pace, I would have been ahead of many people at that point in the race. But not today. I saw two people behind me, a blind guy, and a runner behind him. Maybe that is why my glutes looked at the 13.1 marker and said, "I'm tapping out." I felt like I was running a 10-minute mile, in perfect form, making good progress but when I looked around, it was like I'm running in place. I knew I was in trouble when the blind guy passed me. "Really?" I thought to myself, "Is this really happening?" It was so surreal to feel so good inside but to look at my speed and find it so slow.

For me to feel that good was a big step in my progress. But even so, I knew when to stop. I didn't want to push too hard and put any more obstacles in my way. I knew at this point, the second half of the race required a five mile out and back loop before leaving the trail to run through the park on a paved path. That was simply too much for my body at that point, so I cashed it in, walking the last 2.5 miles to finish. I didn't want to do any damage, as Marcus warned.

My official time was 3:11 for the half. But that wasn't accurate because in my efforts to cheer others on, I didn't notice I was going back and forth across the timer. The actual time was below 2:50, possibly even 2:45. That told me that running a 2:30 is within reason if I were focused on a half instead of the full marathon. That is progress that I'm thrilled to report. I am feeling so much better.

That's the longest I've run since working with my trainer. I am learning patience and discipline to run beyond the race itself to rebuild my form. That will play well as I look ahead to both Boston and Tokyo in the same week in October.

As I continue to focus on my quest, I'm realizing that measuring my progress is a big part of my quest. Before I felt like my lower back and hamstrings were trying to kiss each other and my butt got in the way. That caused a lot of pain that ran from my lower back to my shoulder. My right side, mid back, and right hamstring were so tight it threw the rest of my body off balance. No wonder I hurt. Now, with the muscles strengthened and working together, I'm running better because I'm balanced.

Interesting People

This race reversed the pattern of many runs, with the marathon being on Saturday and the other races on Sunday. On Saturday, one runner was dressed as Buzz Lightyear. I kept thinking, "To infinity and beyond." Buzz loves running and is an awesome marathoner. The next day he ran as Woody, the Sheriff in the same show. He definitely looked and played the part well, as illustrated by his Woody arresting me for failing to finish the marathon.

Photo: The Running Servant arrested by Woody (Brian Rice).

Then there was the blind gentleman with a walking stick who kept a very good pace. In my mind, he is Speedy Gonzales.

Shawanna White from Atlanta is the current female world record holder with 14 sub-3-hour marathons in a row. I enjoyed seeing her run. You may learn more about her record-breaking story in the premiere documentary by the National Black Marathoners Association (NBMA) "Breaking Three Hours: Trailblazing African-American Women Marathoners.".

Take Away

While this race was beautiful and run well, there is one thing that happened that is my pet peeve. I love to drink chocolate milk for recovery. So, when I cross the finish line, I'm looking for a nice, cold drink to refresh me. Today, however, that wasn't the case. Oh, they had the chocolate milk, but they had it sitting out on the table. I knew when I saw it, it was going to be warm, not cold. They told me that they never get rid of the chocolate milk. "Of course, you don't, no one wants it when it is warm."

The next day I volunteered and made sure that chocolate milk was cold. I was giving it out, encouraging people, "Take two, you need one for each leg." The only ones who didn't take it were lactose intolerant. We gave away all the chocolate milk that day. Photo: Shawna White

When I volunteer, I make sure to bring plenty of energy to the entire area. I love to sing and often sing songs that I make up on the spot. That always entertains and lifts people's spirits. After all, I know as a runner, that extra boost of energy is welcomed when running long distances. One lady told me, "Everyone needs to be like you." It is good to be appreciated.

After feeling the difference, I wanted to increase my time with Marcus to three times a week. But Marcus was wise, telling me I need my rest more than I need an extra workout. I knew he was right because I am tired and haven't been sleeping well. Still, I'm anxious to get better, run faster, and finish strong in both Boston and Tokyo as well as finish the 50-50-50 quest. If that was all behind me, I would be looking at a different goal.

I met a lady in North Carolina who told me her goal was to run a marathon in 5:05. Does that sound familiar? That told me that God was speaking to me and telling me I'm on the right path. I mean, who has that exact same goal? Having that reassurance helped settle me.

Looking Ahead

The New England challenge is this week. That is six marathons in six states. Two of those marathons would have counted toward the quest. But I've decided that the money reserved for my travel has a better purpose. I gave it to my sister to bury her son. The "Crazy Race Director," JC Santa Teresa, offered me a chance to do the run in New Jersey and defer the entry to next year. I'm finding that accepting any challenge requires flexibility because there will be several unexpected obstacles.

October is daunting because of Boston and Tokyo in the same week — Tokyo would later cancel runners from outside the country except elites. The travel time alone is overwhelming, much less the runs and time allowed. I know that Tokyo pulls you out of the race quickly, like a bad act pulled off the stage at the Apollo Theater. The first cutoff is at 10K. There is no mercy if you don't make that 90-minute time. You have six hours total, just like Boston but Boston doesn't cut-off until the 18K (20 miles). Knowing that puts pressure on me to get in shape as fast as I can.

I mention October because of so many marathons being rescheduled to that month. So many, I have officially renamed it Runtober. I also mention Boston and Tokyo because that will complete my six world majors that God told me to run. That doesn't mean I'm overlooking the 50-50-50 challenge. It is all part of looking ahead.

I learned this week that the Marine Marathon is now a live race in D.C. on October 31 — It was canceled due to the political atmosphere with the Presidential election. . I plan to run that one. I also learned that the New York Marathon is officially on Nov 7. I won't feel pressured like Boston and Tokyo since they leave no runner behind. I can also relax a bit as I know the logistics and the course, having run New York in 2019.

But my first task is to run the New Jersey Zip Code Run as part of the Bi-state challenge.

Week 16: Rochelle Park, New Jersey, May 23

It seems like I'm either flying home or flying to the next race, the time flies in between. My time at home quickly passes with massages, training, and doctor appointments. Included each week, I have a zoom session with my author and mentor as well as an occasional media interview. This week I interviewed with a Canadian newspaper. Then there comes the reshuffling of my schedule, complete with rebooking flights and hotels. This week I realized that I had forgotten to reserve my hotel in Coeur d'Alene, Idaho the next week. The closest one I could get was two miles away. I'm starting to see how much I need a personal assistant.

This week in my workouts with Marcus, I was using a forward-facing weight machine without weights to work on posture and form. We use a combination of movements to engage muscles. After doing five, I was tired, paused, and did three more. Even without weight it was a workout. I didn't even remove the safety latch and I was sweating. Others around me were looking at me wondering how a big guy like that could be so out of shape. If they only knew.

New Jersey Zip Code 07662
The New Jersey run was different from the abandoned railroad beds of the previous weeks. This course was a two-mile loop on a paved path, taking us out and back. We were to complete twelve loops. Everyone, half-marathoners, marathoners, and ultramarathoners all shared the same path. Meanwhile, the park was filled with adults and babies enjoying the wild geese. Unfortunately, we had to share the

course with those not registered for the race while also navigating around the geese or wait for them to pass.

Marcus and I built a strategy to focus on form and engage certain muscle groups. Once again, he cautioned me, "Don't push it." As I started and found my stride, I could tell I was doing it right because all the right things were hurting. I was pleased that my glutes and psoas muscles were firing. They were sensitive, but that is good. I could feel my core, belt, and waist muscles were engaged. I concentrated on breathing with my diaphragm. I found it harder to run that way because it demanded I change paradigms. Throughout all this, I view my body as a watch that needs to be synchronized.

I completed the half and felt good. If I hadn't been taking photos with my friends from the Marathon Maniacs, I could have run it in 2.5 hours. But time wasn't as important as refreshing relationships with this group of runners who run marathons and ultras. It is like old home week when I see several each week at various runs. We like to stop and take photos together.

The runner who placed first started at the same time but lapped me four times and finished at the same time. As slow as that sounds, I said to myself,
"That's progress" because it was faster than what I used to do. I'm delighted to feel muscles work that I haven't felt in a while. I am definitely stronger and faster.

I finished 6 laps and decided not to push it, knowing I will be better for it. Meanwhile, I'm watching other runners and see several whose form is breaking down. No wonder they are sore afterwards. They got it done and finished, but at what cost. Like me, they needed to take a break, unlearn bad habits, and retrain to strengthen and heal. That takes more time than many are willing to spend.

My physical therapists at Concentra said I would be a better runner in the long run, maybe three to four years later. I'm finding that day is today, and their words proved true.

I met Ronita Bland, a member of the Marathon Maniacs, who only had two marathons left to finish her 50-state challenge. She ran the New England Challenge but not the New York run. Her last state is scheduled to be Anchorage, Alaska in August where I will join her to celebrate. By then I will have done 8 of her last 9 marathons with her. That is, if all goes according to my schedule. I talked to her briefly on every loop as she passed me.

156

Ronita Bland completed the New England Challenge in her quest of completing the 50 States Marathon Challenge. (Photo: Ronita Bland)

There was a young kid, 15 or 16 years old that was hitting it running an ultra. I watched him and appreciated that his form was good. Meanwhile, I was watching elite marathoners whose form was breaking down. I was reminded that it is better to finish the mile the right way, mastering that mile, to ultimately cross the finish line.

As you can tell, working with Marcus has opened my eyes to not just running but learning to run with my body in tune with itself. Focusing on my form has helped me, and also intrigues me as I watch other runners. I'm fascinated with the process and my progress.

My Nightmare

I wear my Garmin watch when running but also when I sleep because it reports how well I slept. My Garmin registered that I woke up four times that night. It turns out, they matched the four times that night where I heard gunshots. I wouldn't sleep well until I returned home for a good Sunday night's sleep.

As with other episodes, the negative effect isn't realized until a few days later when I had two restless nights. The Sunday following the race I slept well but struggled a couple nights after that. Seeking to find my most comfortable position, I've taken to sleeping on the floor. Believe it or not, this has worked well for me. I have an air mattress that stands two feet tall and often where I set my marathon medal, shirt, and bib.

One night following the New Jersey run, I dreamt that, once again, I was fighting for my life. The gunshots triggered me once again and I'm wrestling with a would-be assailant. I woke to find my arms wrapped around that air mattress. I know, rather bizarre and a bit funny, but also disturbing.

The following night's sleep was once again disturbed, but I didn't know until I woke up. Stepping up to the double vanity to brush my teeth, I noticed my pillow by the sink. "Did I sleep on the vanity?" It turns out, the answer was, "yes." All I knew was that this disturbed sleep has to get better. My body is going through too much right now.

Although London had been my lowest point, I was still feeling depleted mentally and physically. I hadn't realized how much I was deteriorating until I saw photos that showed the difference from what he once was and what I am now. It is very stunning, yet I tell myself, "I have to continue."

My Love of Running

I mentioned before that I used to hate running but developed a love after calling out to God for help. Compared to now, when I first ran, it was easy.

Now, I experience God in the physical act of running. Before the shooting, it was easy to run, yet mentally, running has become my way of handling stress. It is my time alone with God.

But this didn't come automatically. I tried headphones and listened to preachers and teachers. But I didn't like the other voices crowding the space inside my head. Instead, I find my connection that allows God to speak to me through my spirit. I use that time for meditation on his word, prayer, and thanksgiving. He also speaks to me through nature. I see his handiwork in the birds and animals. I even see him in the less desirable critters like the hornets, turkey vultures, who serve as God's garbage collectors. I am in awe as I watch squirrels protecting their den.

Running puts me into a spiritual high, then after cooling down, and cleaning up, I'm in bliss. In the end, I look forward to running three hours lost in God, his ways, and prayers. Because of this, once I get past about three miles, my breathing becomes involuntary. My body is trusting the process.

With New Jersey finally checked off my list, it was time to focus on Idaho. At first, I didn't even know how to pronounce Coeur d'Alene. But now I'm going to run the marathon.

Week 17: Coeur d'Alene Marathon, Idaho, May 30

Many don't realize the beauty of this northern Idaho city. It was just as the race site promised. "Resting on the shores of spectacular Lake Coeur d'Alene, welcomes visitors to one of the most breathtaking races in North America." Add to this scene a busy Memorial Day weekend with plenty of activities apart from the marathon attracting families, kids, and seniors. What a wonderful scene.

Unfortunately, the previous week's difficulty sleeping continued the night before the race. It was so bad I had to take medicine for fever blisters. My Garmin told me my stress levels were at 99 from the two shooting incidents the week before. Then, the night before the race, thunderstorms came through and brought not only lightning and thunder, but more nightmares.

The Marathon

Set along the lake with mountains as a backdrop the course ran south and east, with Lake Coeur d'Alene on the southwest and Interstate 90 on the other side. We ran mostly through a park and very few roads needed to be closed. With fewer runners, due to the covid pandemic, and lighter traffic, running was figuratively and literally a run in the park. Add to that the presence of flush bathrooms instead of port-a-potties, and it makes for a great setting.

Then add beautiful weather, starting at a cool 45 degrees. Given how far north we were the sun rose at 4:15 and the race started at 6:16.

159

We ran out to the turnaround at mile 8.5 where we climbed a quarter mile in the park to the highest elevation of the run. It was nothing like the Foot Levelers mountains, with only one significant hill that rose approximately 100 feet. We ran back to the start, continued on for another out and back, then on the other side of centennial trail, before finishing.

Photo: The first quarter marathon turnaround.

I ran well. My body felt great, and I was in good form. The first 10k was flat, which taxes my glutes more than rolling hills, but I progressed by getting other muscles going, keeping the glutes firing, and feel them working during the hills. I was very pleased with how I ran 17.5 miles, ran for 6 hours, and completed just shy of 20 miles. My fastest mile was 9:51, which was much faster than normal. I felt great knowing that at this pace, I can finish a marathon in 5.5 hours. My ultimate goal is 5:05, an 11:37 pace but I'll take this. As a runner, especially a trail runner, we take any course. But if that last 10k would've been flat, it might have been ok. Hills were smaller than the first half but still too difficult for my limitations.

That's when my glutes flared up. Although I tried to get to the second turn around to go back in and finish, my body wouldn't cooperate. The pain was too great. I was walking and it took me 20 minutes to complete just one mile. I saw one guy on a golf cart and asked him to report that I was done. I was going back to my hotel. I kept going to 19.5. Although I was only 10k from finishing, Marcus' voice rang in my ears. "Don't push it."

My right-side body kinetic chain was so off that my Achilles heel felt like it would snap. I was very concerned that I was going to need surgery and didn't want that. As Marcus said, "Don't push it or you will hurt yourself to the point you can't run." Fortunately, a few days later, it was nice and pliable. But that day, even when I was relaxed, the tendon was as tight as a guitar string. My right calf muscle was also hard and my lower back, around the kidney area, was hurting. I was pleased that my psoas muscles were engaged. But all that meant it was time to quit.

Interesting People

As usual, the Marathon Maniacs and 50 Staters were present. I met Monte who completed his 705 marathon that day. Monte, along with his partner on the pavement Kendra Hensley, was pleased to take a photo. I met Shawn, a runner from San Antonio who has Type 1 diabetes, as he joined us for the ride from the airport.

Photo: Monte Pascual and Kendra Hensley

Volunteers along the course were very, very good and encouraging. Also, the other runners were enjoying the race and it was pleasant. Even after the race, sitting at Starbucks, I met wonderful people. I stayed for 5 hours, sharing the gospel of Jesus Christ, with both unbelievers and believers. I enjoyed a conversation with a man and his wife, during which she donated. She used to be a runner but was forced to quit due to disability. Seeking a deeper connection, she asked for my information. Over the course of that afternoon, I spoke with many families and felt very blessed.

When I say that people donated, please understand I'm not selling. I'm simply sharing what I am doing and why. There is no sales pitch so, when they donate, it is simply their appreciation.

Terrified

I always try to book a room on the top floor of the hotel. Relaxing before the race, I was on a phone call when all of a sudden, someone started pounding on the wall and door.

"We know you are in there. We hear you talking."

Immediately, I flashed back to the shooting. I paused my call, went to the door, but no one was there. Knowing this couldn't happen again without my PTSD being triggered, I called the front desk.

"Could you check your security cameras?"

When that yielded nothing, I asked if it was housekeeping. I could sense that I was on edge when I responded, "Listen, if housekeeping is that rude, and they are pounding that hard, you need to get rid of them." That is not my usual servant spirit so when I'm agitated, I know something else is going on. In this case, it was fear. Remember, the thugs that shot me are part of a nationwide gang. I never know where they are or what they look like. I also never know if or when they will strike. Therefore, I'm always conscious of a threat on my life.

"I would like to be moved to a different room."

"Sorry, we are sold out. There are no rooms available."

"I can't have this happen again," I pressed, knowing they needed to understand the seriousness of this event.

As much as I fought back and tried to not let it bother me, the PTSD kicked in. I walked out in the hall and could hear the same voice in the adjoining rooms of 505 and 502. One door was shut, the other was propped open. With the source of the voice identified, I called down to the desk again.

"The shouting and banging I heard is coming from room 502. That cannot happen again or I'm calling police." Listen and you can hear in my words how the PTSD was on full blast. My panic set in and felt like the thieves had found me and were going to kill me. "Was this evening going to be my end?"

I felt exactly like I did on that fateful morning, shortly after the shooting, when I walked out of my apartment to find bloody threats written on the stoop. Since I didn't know everyone in that gang, I never know who they are or if they are tracking me. I do know they are traveling all over the country, and that I am never safe. It makes me so fearful for my life that I'm considering having a discussion with my doctors about carrying a weapon again. They understand but don't think it is the best idea.

For anyone who thinks I'm making more out of this than necessary, please realize that these killers have made three attempts on my life. I never know where they are or when they would attack. This isn't a fabricated fear but a matter of survival. What appears to be an inconvenience to others appears as a viable and lethal threat to me.

That is the world I live in every day.

Not Again

As I was running the race, after the turnaround and near the water treatment plant, I was very relaxed. That is, until I heard what sounded like a gunshot. I jumped into the air as it scared the living daylights out of me. Again, I struggled to keep my wits about me and fend off the PTSD. Checking my trusty Garmin, I saw my stress level was 99 out of 100 and didn't drop for days. Felt fever blisters broke out on my lips a day later so I started taking the medicine my doctor prescribed for it.

That was the beginning of a very challenging week. In retrospect, the second event might not have been a problem if the first event hadn't happened. Already on edge, when I heard the shots, my body automatically went into self-preservation. In the aftermath of the two events, I cried twice the week following.

Please realize what is happening. Days after the incident, I suddenly start crying, sometimes uncontrollably. Now realize I'm a big guy that doesn't want to be dependent on others or seen as a wimp. Yet there I am, tears rolling down my cheeks. That is humbling if not embarrassing.

Recovery

I'm getting stronger but so is the pain. I was so disturbed by the hotel incident that I started to call my doctor on Saturday night. But then I paused and reconsidered. I already knew what I had to do. That showed I was getting stronger one small step at a time. I am able to handle it better.

But that doesn't mean I handle it well. The sadness of the situation still deeply hurts my soul and sends me into a profound depression. That is humbling because it tells me I'm stronger, but not as strong as I want to be.

One way I compensate is to cheer and encourage others. That helps me take the attention off of my problems and focus it on others. When they look at me, they see a smiling, encouraging, big, strong guy with even bigger hair. They don't see the bullet wounds, emotional pain, or fragile sensitivity.

A few do notice and offer encouragement. They are often individuals who have suffered their own trauma. For example, a friend of mine was a domestic abuse victim. Her boyfriend put a pillow over her and shot her through the shoulder with a 9mm handgun. She survived and used the trauma to make the world better. First, she got a good job with a private flight company, and then was selected to serve on the mayor's council for domestic violence. Her role is to update the laws for abuse. She understands trauma and reaches out to

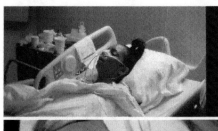
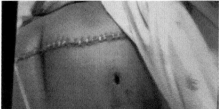

encourage me. It turns out that her shooting happened the same year as mine, 2015. She was shot in the spring, me in the fall. Her wounds are visible while mine are not.

Photo: Victorious Joneen Mirrors (top) Her 9-millimeter bullet wound (bottom)

I remember one runner who only had 2.5 miles to go in the marathon. I was cheering him on while asking, "Are you hurting from running or something else?" My point was that if you are just hurting from running, you can continue. If it is something more, then we need to find help. The runner, realizing the source of his pain was not serious, responded enthusiastically, and ran to the finish with an extra dose of energy.

Looking Ahead

I learned this week that the Delaware Marathon Running Festival was canceled. Unlike the other races canceled in this world of covid, this race was canceled due to lack of police available to close the streets. Just when I think I have seen it all, something else pops up. Life is definitely interesting.

My next stop takes me to another out of the way place, Havre, Montana.

Week 18: Bear Paw Marathon, Montana, June 5

Flying east or west is pretty easy to make connections. Flying south to north is another matter. Connecting to a small town like Havre, Montana, just a stone's throw from the Canadian border with a population of only 9000 people, limits daily flights. You have very few choices of how you can get there. Flying United, I flew from Houston and connected in Billings and then to Havre on a commuter airline.

Photo: Near Hill Country Montana

The Bear Paw Marathon is a point-to-point marathon where they bus you out into the beautiful Bear Paws Mountains and you run back to town. They are named the Bear Paw Mountains because each mountain seems to stand alone and together look like a bear paw. Mix in the lakes and the trees and it makes for a beautiful run through the largest county park in the nation.

The course was definitely flatter than Foot Levelers but not as flat as Pine Line. There is some elevation so I was a bit concerned whether I would achieve my goal of running twenty miles. I knew I was getting stronger each week but didn't think I was strong enough to finish.

Unfortunately, I was still discombobulated from the week before. The fever blisters persisted on my bottom lip, which was unusual because they usually develop on my top lip. It's hard to explain to someone who hasn't experienced life-threatening trauma how the PTSD sets root in your body and brain. Then it is quickly triggered in a variety of ways. I never know when it's coming. I'm never sure how long it will last. When that happens, no matter how hard I try, I just cannot function well. I can't sleep and cannot push myself to get up and get moving.

The morning of the race, something strange happened. I couldn't get up. I tried and tired and then finally stood on my feet, got ready, but not in time to catch the only shuttle to the start line. "Now what do I do?" The marathon started at 6:00 a.m. 26.2 miles east of the city.

My hotel was about three miles from the finish line. I didn't see any other choice, so I simply ran to the finish line. I learned later that the bus station was between the hotel and finish line so I could've taken a bus.

By the time I arrived at the finish line, it was already 7:21. Considering my options, I thought, "I could run the 5K that was going to start at 9:00, or I could volunteer at the finish line to cheer people on."

That latter sounded good but once I arrived, the race director informed me I could just run the course in reverse. That sounded great, and different so, I started running. I met the two lead runners when they only had four miles to go. They were relaxed, talking to each other and not even sweating. They both finished under 3:15. I continued to run until I met the last runner who was on mile 18. With the run from the hotel, I had run 12 miles to that point. Knowing I was the last one, I turned around and ran the eight miles back to the finish. Although it wasn't the way I wanted to do it or the way it was supposed to happen, I met my goal of running 20 miles that day. Sometimes, to reach our goal, we must be willing to be flexible.

Photo: Brandelle McIntosh and the Lions Club (top) and the Sweeper Crew (bottom).

The scenery was beautiful, making me feel like I was back in the wild, wild west. Running through this huge country park, I kept thinking about what it would have been like back in the stagecoach days. Running on those gravel and dirt roads was very easy and relaxing, feeling like I was on a long run on a Saturday back in Houston. The only problem was the wind that blew hard for three days. Fortunately, it was very gentle in the mountains. The overall drop in elevation made for a very easy run. There was just enough hill play that you do have to run but not hard. All of this created a great atmosphere.

Fortunately, the mountains cool off at night, making for a refreshing start in the 50s before heating to temps topping out at 93. Fortunately, the humidity was low. Even with a high of 93, it was still gorgeous at 3 p.m.

Despite all that happened earlier that morning, I felt great running. My muscles were engaged, I was encouraged, and felt a bit like my old running self. After I finished and was relaxing and talking with my new friends, I felts a new sensation. It was like I sat on a device emitting a pulsing electrical current. My glutes were firing. The sensation continued for the rest of the evening. As it dissipated, my glutes itched, and I wanted to scratch like a dog with fleas. Marcus later told me that my glutes were forced to work and that meant the training was working as promised.

I did feel my glutes shut down twice on the run. But this time, when they shut down, they didn't pull on my lower back. Neither did the rest of my muscles overcompensate. My hamstrings didn't tighten, nor did my spinal muscles hurt. Normally I felt pain under my shoulder, but not today. Instead, with my psoas muscles and hip flexors engaged, they balanced the load and helped my right calf muscle stay loose. Even when my glutes quit briefly, they kicked back in within a mile. Even better, when they shut down a mile later, once again they kicked back in. That meant my core is picking up slack.

This was the best I felt running 20 miles since London in 2019. This race proved that my body was responding well to the training. That gave me hope and confidence.

As I was running, a dog showed up and ran with me for the last five miles. Or should I say, he ran with me when he wasn't chasing moles in the field. I learned later his owner's name was Richard.

Photo: Richard (Top)
Finish Line Crowd (Bottom)

When I finished, I was pleased to find everyone gathered at the finish line cheering me on like I had just set a world record. Because I had cheered each one of them on, they came to return the favor. That felt great!

In the aftermath, as usual, I had them laughing. especially the guy running the barbeque. I teased him that he is the only one with dark meat. "People want lean protein, not just the dark meat. Next year, put some lean on."

We had a great time together.

Interesting People

One lady was hoping to finish in 6 hours, but the course was so forgiving that she finished in 5.5. That's a very forgiving course. Then there were two 19-year-olds who started walking at mile 20. They finished in under 4 hours.

Being an outgoing guy, I met every single runner except the 5K runners. I even took photos of all the runners. There were 84 full marathoners and even more in the half marathon.

One family had kids run the half with them. The lady I was running with as we finished traveled from California in part because she grew up in Montana. Her name was Brandale, which turns out to be a combination of my son's name, Brandon, and my mom's, Shandale. That was cool.

The Race Operations

The race director did an excellent job. If they hadn't told me I wouldn't have known this was their inaugural marathon. Usually there are plenty of hiccups for the first race, but not on this one. The planning was executed well, the volunteers were where they needed to be and performed well. They had plenty of well stocked hydration stations along the course. Then the finish provided entertainment and food with a live country band and two food trucks. I'm telling you, they did it right.

The only suggestion I have is to add a 50k and 50 miler to it. The race director would attract more runners with the Ultramarathons. This course is fantastic training with the elevation change, nature, wind, and other factors. Being that close to Canada, they would also attract a number from north of the border. It is also just east of Glacier National Park which makes for a great before or after trip.

I would love to come back and be able to enjoy the course. I feel like a wild horse begging for someone to open the gate and me run in these mountains.

Return Flight

The only thing left was to return to Houston and prepare for the next race. Unfortunately, United Airlines isn't as well run as the Bear Paw Marathon. I double checked my flight schedule and made plans to be at the airport in plenty of time. But upon arrival, one hour before my flight, there was no one there. As another flight arrived, a lady showed up and gave me the bad news.

"The last flight of the day left this morning."

In reality, it was the only flight of the day. That meant I had to wait until the next day.

But that led to another problem. My hotel was sold out due to a car show, little league baseball tournament, and yet another event that brought more people to town.

After finding another hotel, spending the night, double checking the flight time, and making it to the airport on time, I finally climbed on board the plane home. This plane only seats 6-8 people, most from other parts of Montana. We flew to Billings where I waited for my flight to Houston.

Photo: Cape Air's New Plane (Top) Welcome Sign (Bottom)

But that wasn't to happen. For the in-bound flight, we were on a beautiful, new plane. On the return trip, however, we had an old plane that proved unreliable. As we boarded and began to taxi, we slowed, turned around, and returned to the airport for a mechanical problem. That meant a change in planes.

That delay changed our plans. We would now be diverted through Dallas. I hate flying through Dallas which is known to have thunderstorms that shut down the airport. But now that is the only option. To add insult to injury, had I caught the flight the day before from Havre, I would have connected through Denver to Houston. But now, I'm diverted through Dallas, and won't get home until 8:30 p.m. My week is already off to a late start. Fortunately, I don't check luggage, so I don't need to wait at the baggage check or fear that it has been lost.

I was pleased that everything went smoothly from there. It felt great to finally be home.

Looking Ahead

Next up is the Hatfield and McCoy run in Kentucky where runners divide and choose which clan they want to represent. From there times are compiled, and the winner of the feud is named. All I know is that it will be good to settle this feud.

I begin by flying into Parkersburg, West Virginia.

The week after I ran Grandma's Marathon in Duluth, Minnesota. Had to finagle to get a good price. My game plan is to fly Spirit to Minneapolis on Wednesday and then Delta to Duluth on Thursday.

Leaving Wednesday, I won't have much time in Houston. I'm hoping to hang with my brother in Minneapolis on my layover.

Meanwhile, I talked to Chicago about deferring. Depending on how I feel, if my body responds well, I may run Chicago and then jump on a plane and run Boston the next day. Mentally, I'm looking at the two races in two days as 100k with a 12-hour break. Then I'll fly out Wednesday directly from Boston to Tokyo, a 14-hour flight. Fortunately, I don't have much trouble with jet lag. If the sun is up, I'm good. When the sun sets, I shut down.

That is an aggressive plan, running three world majors in one week with a body that hasn't delivered. But that is part of the quest. Mentally, I'm not giving up.

But first things first, it's time to join the Hatfield's and the McCoy's. But which side should I join?

Week 19: Hatfield – Mccoy Marathon, Kentucky, June 12

The Hatfield-McCoy Marathon is a mind-blowing, amazing, encouraging, fun, exciting race. From the packet pickup to the run to the after party, it was a phenomenal experience. Everyone I met was cool. Shawn was the Vice President of the race, and his wife Tanya, showed me great hospitality.

My challenge for this race is that I will be pacing the 14-minute mile group. I feel like I am ready, and my strategy is to run ¼ of a mile, and then walk ¾. I will increase my time in the last 10k to get to 14-minute average.

Photo: Hatfield and McCoy fire a shotgun to signal the start of the race.

This is yet another run that crosses state lines. It starts and finishes in Kentucky but enters into West Virginia for a short time. It is such a popular race that it has already sold out.

175

As is their tradition, they start with a skit featuring the Hatfield's and the McCoy's at packet pickup. Normally, an older man plays a central role but for some reason he couldn't do it. With the DJ playing lively music, I purchased a hand carved walking stick from SD Redneck, one of the vendors. Using it as a microphone, I took the stage and started singing. The audience was happy to join in. Everyone was singing and shouting, having so much fun and making such a noise that even those outside the building heard us. Shawn heard the commotion from outside and entered the cafeteria to see me in my glory.

Photo: State lines of Kentucky and West Virginia.

Later, I was enjoying a moment of solitude when Shawn approached me. He appreciated my spontaneous entertainment so much that he reciprocated by introducing me to everyone. Later he took me to lunch at a restaurant to continue the conversation. What a phenomenal experience.

The race had about 325 marathoners plus those running the half, 5k and the kids 1k. You can choose to run one of two courses, one from Kentucky to West Virginia or from West Virginia to Kentucky, depending on your allegiance to either the Hatfield's or McCoy's. They also offer a relay with four runners total, two for each half. Meeting in the middle, we enjoy a big celebration in the small town of Williamson, West Virginia.

While we are supposed to declare our clan allegiance to either the Hatfield's or the McCoy's, I chose neither. Instead, my focus is a ministry of reconciliation.

I was so impressed with the people in this run, that my run itself was rather anticlimactic. For example, for those returning runners, they hang handmade signs with their names written along the course. That means you run looking for your sign. Not only is that very unique, but it is also very impressive. To do that for hundreds of people requires community participation, time, and effort. The community was involved in several ways, more than any other race I have run. I found it very moving.

Photo: Choose your side: Hatfield or McCoy? Make it quickly because there is a race to be run.

But it didn't end there. Everyone who finished received a mason jar. Who does that? The Hatfield and McCoy Marathon does. Also, they dressed the part. Two guys dressed up as brothers for Hatfield and McCoy's at the finish, adding to the enjoyment.

The course, however, was challenging. The hills were difficult, especially one hill between miles 8 and 9. It was a small hill that became a steady incline to a big hill. About three quarters up, I handed my pacer sign to another pacer, knowing I couldn't keep my pace. Funny though, I caught up to them going down the other side. At one point they were a mile and a half to two miles ahead of me. But going down that very steep hill, I almost took flight with a pace of 9:48. I was definitely pleased with that but knew I was pushing it. I do love that feeling of running downhill.

It wasn't like Foot Levelers but still taxing. I ran pretty well, although I quit at mile 15. I was in some pain and could have gone on, however, I am always looking ahead. My goal was to run 20 miles but by mile 15, I asked a woman, and she told me of an upcoming swinging bridge. She also said there was nobody available to help for the next 5 miles. Always aware of my surroundings, I didn't want to put myself in a place where I couldn't get help. So, I humbled myself and asked for help.

The downhill thrill after the uphill drill, mile 8.

I noticed a man outside his home. It turns out his wife runs a retreat camp. I stopped and he quickly called for his wife. "This guy is in some pain and needs a ride back." It was good of him to notice my pain without having to say anything. He didn't hesitate in asking if I needed a ride. I was happy to accept.

The gentleman gave me a ride back to the finish. Disappointed, I still was overwhelmed and could not even begin to tell each person's story. I met so many, and each story moved me.

I loved how the community came together to have a great time. Many shared a family lineage and had one family autograph my medal.

They live in Pikeville but have roots in Ohio where I'm from. These were very down to earth people, authentic people.

Had so much fun along the course sitting outside, looking at the miniature horses. I guess you could ride them if you wanted. I'm not sure how a big guy like me could do that.

The only complaint I have involves my favorite post-race drink. You have already read how much I love and need chocolate milk after a run. Well, they didn't have any. I looked everywhere, at the finish line and then around town to other stores. I was shutout. Next year I will bring my own.

They did have a lot of energizing snacks along the course such as drinks, fruit, and oranges that tasted great. But no chocolate milk.

I stayed at Hampton Inn in Pikesville where the people were very hospitable. There was one guy playing guitar that made it very enjoyable. As we talked, I mentioned that I needed a ride back to West Virginia. The guy replied that he has a friend, "Pookey" who just graduated and is going to be teaching history. He called him, announcing it was Cousin Cuddy, using his local accent. Then he posed the transportation question to Pookey, who quickly declined, but asked to talk to me. We quickly found a personal connection, and all of a sudden, the conversation led to an opportunity to share about my Lord. Pookey suggested I talk to a friend who drove a taxi. That guy would have charged the going rate of 150 dollars to go 1 hour and 45 minutes. That's when Pookey reconsidered and agreed to drive me.

On the ride we realized our similar backgrounds. Both of us were involved in drugs at one point. He was once an addict but now, runs 5Ks and 10Ks and wants to run a half. He is a large guy who had bypass. Pookey moved to Lexington to teach history at the collegiate level. What an amazing connection, one where we will definitely keep in touch

I met several who had tough backgrounds of addictions and struggles but found that running helps them break free. That is my story.

Shawn was incredibly generous in connecting me with everyone. Then, as I was leaving, he invited me to come back next year and stay at his house. That is unbelievable hospitality. Unlike its name, I didn't find any feud in running the Hatfield and McCoy Marathon.

Meanwhile, I saw many old friends and acquaintances from the 50 States and Maniacs Double Agents. Mary ran with me at Daufuskie and Penny in many other races. I met Robert who I stayed with and split the rental car fee from Kentucky. Last week there was only one 50 States in Montana but this week there were over fifty.

Various Runners

The only complaint about race was a very odd one. Some said there were too many aid stations. What marathoner says that? Yes, there was one every mile. I think that is great but if you don't like it, you don't have to stop. Duh. Given there were multiple runs taking place at the same time, they needed several stations. Evidently a few people felt compelled to stop and take something at every stop. I talked with a couple of these complainers after the race and learned that the only one they didn't complain about was at the top of the big hill. I noticed they didn't complain about there being plenty of port-a-potties, at least one at every aid station. Unfortunately, too many believe the race should be built for them and them alone.

Hatfield and McCoy Marathon:
The race is over, but the fun is never-ending.

Looking Ahead

I know this will be a short week before I leave for Minneapolis. My brother is going to pick me up and then I'll fly to Duluth the next day. I'm looking forward to seeing 50 Staters and Marathon Maniacs. I'm also looking forward to my hotel where I will be able to watch the big concert. Hopefully I can see the race celebration concert from the balcony before returning Tuesday.

I have until July 1 to defer Chicago to next year. I know the best thing is to rest but that means I will need to reschedule my Illinois run. The only other time is in August or September.

Searching for races is very exhausting at this point. I've scheduled and rescheduled so many times I'm feeling like, "I can't do this right now." It isn't just rescheduling races, but also the flights, hotels, and ground transportation. Fortunately, in 2021, the airlines are getting money from the government, so they aren't charging to reschedule airfare.

Many of these races require flying on small planes. I'm finding that United planes are old but American has nice ones. Because of connections, I like to fly Spirit Airlines going west, American going east, and United in the middle.

I need to continue my training and increase my ability to tolerate pain.

Meanwhile, I'm learning how much fun it is to run with the "Back of the Pack". Before the shooting, I enjoyed the mindset of running with the local elites (those that finish in 1:35 or less for the race) or the pack (2:25 to 2:45). My pace was about 2:10. The elite runners are in their own worlds and don't connect with each other during the race. They come, run, take photos, and go home. But the "Back of the Pack" is far friendlier, showing more passion, and showing more desire. They show more hope, and everyone has a story. The front of the pack is focused on "I - I - I" and while the back it is "Us – us – us." Camaraderie is the norm at the back. I feel very privileged meeting each of these individuals at the back. I've made it my mission for all runners under that finish over four hours to know me. Meanwhile, none of the elite seem to know me. Before I was shot, I wouldn't appreciate the "Back of the Pack". But now I shake my head at that thought. I want to go back and tell myself that, "You don't know their story." The stories at the back are far more compelling than what the front of the packers realize.

With that, I'm looking forward to Grandma's Marathon.

Week 20: Grandma's Marathon Duluth, Minnesota, June 19

I liked the name of this race as it brought back memories of my grandmothers, Winnel Burros, maternal, and Emma Templeton, paternal. It seemed appropriate that I dedicate the race to them. To honor their memory, I asked the marathon for two extra medals so I could put one in the shadow box and give another one to my dad for his mother. That made finishing that much more important.

Photo: Dedicating this race for y'all Grandmas.

Running this 50-50-50 challenge has brought a benefit that I didn't expect. I'm learning my U.S. geography. For example, as I started planning my trip to Duluth, I learned it was right across the river from Wisconsin. I did not know that but now I do.

As you have noticed, I am attracted to smaller races. The big events like Boston and New York are exhilarating, but the smaller races provide an opportunity to meet the Race Director and many of the runners. Grandma's Marathon attracted about 4000 runners for all of the races, 5k, Half and Full

Marathon. Most of them were running the full marathon, which is different. Often the majority run the shorter race. There were 1546 for half.

The important point is that out of those running the full marathon, I finished 2764 out of 2771. Notice I said I finished. After the problems I had been enduring, finishing was a major accomplishment. I averaged 16:38 per mile for the entire race I started strong with a time of 13:40 at the 10k, 13:40 at the half, 15:11 at the 20-mile post, 17:32 at the 23.9 point, 18:40 at the 25.2 mark and then 22.55 for the last mile. My fastest split was 8:40 for a quarter mile going downhill.

My strategy is shifting as I'm getting stronger working with Marcus. For this race, my strategy was to run/walk for 15 miles. Then I would shift to mostly walking with intermittent running.

The first 15 miles were great. I enjoyed walking up the hills and running down. Like the Foot Levelers Marathon, running downhill brought back great memories. Up and down, the course was composed of country roads with beautiful homes along the way. The setting was peaceful and simply gorgeous. Even though I was running a marathon, I found this course very relaxing.

By mile 15, my old nemesis "Pain" returned. My glutes started to hurt and by 23.57 on my Garmin watch, they stopped firing and caused my whole body to hurt. Walking was the only option at that point. Being that close, I wasn't going to quit. But yet to come was "the lemon drop" hill. It almost broke my spirit and my body, causing my legs to buckle. I definitely didn't want to hurt myself, so I slowed my pace and took 52 minutes to cover the last 2.7 miles. That stretch was brutal. At one point, I was in so much pain I didn't want to finish. I hit the wall physically and emotionally. The pain pierced my previous resolve. Then watching, and counting, nine people passed me in that last section of the race, nearly shattering my resolve. However, I was coherent enough to piece just enough of that resolve together to continue and finish. As I looked back, there were only six runners who finished after me. It was a bittersweet moment. I finished but nearly in last place. In one moment, I felt exhilarated and another, embarrassed. Letting go of the old memories and pride of excelling haunted me. But more recent memories pushed to the forefront of my mind. I remembered the wind at St. Louis and the PTSD that followed. The shooting range at the Pine Line Marathon and the torture that took me off the course. Then my legs buckled in this race. Suddenly, I was grateful for the finish. I did it! That felt great!

Interesting People

I like to attend the shorter races to cheer them on. The advantage is that I get to meet a ton of people at 5k and hear incredible stories. Remember how I mentioned earlier that the back of the pack runners had the best stories? I can't think of a better story than Father Ben. Despite a stroke and the need for a cane, he was determined to start and finish this race. Surrounded by his wife, daughter, friends, and other ministers, he rounded the last corner. I knew I had to join his entourage. How could I stand by and just watch? No, I needed to celebrate this man. So, in my usual, boisterous manner, I sprinted across the start line to cheer him on. Joining him on the course, I used all my creativity and humor to show my appreciation for his resolve. Ben broke out a big smile, laughing, and loving every minute of it.

Photo: Brett Hauer (from left), Father Ben Hadrich of Duluth and his dad John "Hondo" Hadrich celebrate at the finish line of the William A. Irvin 5K on Friday, June 18, 2021, in Duluth. Father Ben is a stroke survivor that ran marathons before his stroke and this is the first event he has participated in. (Clint Austin / caustin@duluthnews.com)

Ben's story helps reinforce an important lesson. Racing isn't just about winning. Winning isn't just about finishing first. Sometimes simply finishing is the victory and that begins with having the courage to register for a race. Daring to do what others never imagined is the beginning of the challenge.

As I've mentioned before but want to reinforce, I love to encourage and celebrate others. That's the way I was before the shooting, but now, it also provides a distraction from my own pain. By focusing on others, I focus less on myself. In many ways, I just can't be silent. It's not about ego or pride. Sure, it is fun to get attention but that doesn't make me any more important or better than anyone else. It's all about raising the energy level to lift the spirits of everyone.

After I finished the marathon, I was cheering the last few people on and one woman looked at me and said, "You just have too much energy." She then looked at her husband and said with amazement, "He was doing this the whole race."

People appreciate how I celebrate others but also enjoy my creativity and humor. After what I've been through, I see the value in focusing on the positive. That's where celebration becomes critical. When we purposely choose to focus on helping others, cheering them on in their race of life, we take the focus off our own pain. I ask you, the reader, to challenge yourself, focus on others, and celebrate them.

That is one of the reasons I include interesting people in every race. I had just hailed a cab when I met my first interesting person. Jeff, the driver, mentioned that his brother is training for his first ultra, a 50 miler. I shared my story including injuries, weight loss, and #RunningServant. "I've heard of you." He went on to detail how he heard my name on national news and said that I was doing a 50-50-50 challenge. Jeff is a big guy, weighing in at 390 pounds. To make matters worse, he smokes. He knows he needs to lose some weight and quit smoking. Amidst all that, he is committed to running the half marathon next year. That story reflects mine and so I promised that I would come back and run it with him. That is a story that I must celebrate and assured him that he will have a host of people cheering him on. He is a man that knows what he needs to do, and with a little encouragement, will do it. Jeff sent a friend request before I even got checked into the hotel. I quickly connected and knew who I was going to call for the return trip to the airport. On the return, Jeff informed me he had downloaded the coaching program to train for the 13.1. He was hoping to keep up with the app schedule. He laughed as he recounted being on the side of the road throwing up after his first run/walk cycle. I told him it was better to speed walk than trot. I'll keep in touch and coach him in the process.

Every race has an expo, some larger than others. There I met people at Orthotic Foot, Cold Stone, and Caribou Coffee among others. I also met Stephanie who recounted a horrifying story where she fell in a marathon and was trampled by other runners who couldn't avoid her. She managed to get up but had to stop at the halfway point because her knee was so swollen. Sitting with her mother and aunt, they invited me to sit with them as I shared my story. Stephanie was moved and asked for my donation information. Fortunately, I have abbreviated both of my articles by Loren Murfield to make a quick read on my fundraising page. Stephanie helped others raise $28,000 for charity and promised to help me. She offered, and I quickly accepted constructive criticism for fundraising. I'm grateful that more people are hearing the story and connecting.

The fun part about connecting at the expo and the 5k is that people love to reciprocate the joy I shared. Walking around town the day or two before the marathon, people saw me and shouted out, "The Running Servant." I'm happy to have made a difference.

Looking Ahead

Next up, is the Morgan Utah Marathon, a trail run. To run the projected hills, I'll need to dial back my enthusiasm for trails. Running trails always generates a lot of adrenaline in me, engaging different muscles because of the uneven running surface. I just need to bridle that energy and use it properly. Street runs, however, feel like a rehab session compared to the old glory days of running Terry Hershey, Bush, Bear Creek, and Cullen Parks in Houston. Trail runs demand your best or you will end up on your face. You must pay attention and maintain your form by picking up your knees and swinging your arms. It's easy to get lazy and relax your technique on a road race. I've got my trail shoes so I'm ready to run the Utah trails. All I need is a country music dude to play a country song about running trails.

My recovery from finishing this race was also better. The pain was there but everything was hurting that was supposed to. I didn't experience the electricity feeling as I did in Montana and that meant I was making progress.

I'm also taking diuretic medicine to reduce some of the fluids in my legs. That is another change in my newly adopted practice of running with compression sleeves on my legs. A sales guy at Robert's Clothing and Running Shop in Charleston, West Virginia, a place I visited during the Hatfield McCoy Marathon, recommended the CEP brand, so I bought five pairs. To my pleasure, they worked great. My legs didn't swell nearly like they had previously. Another guy recommended a brand for compression socks and sleeves. I'm also going to the vein doctor this Friday before leaving for the airport to explore a potential surgery.

Since losing those 180 pounds several years ago, I've put some back on. I'm determined to lose at least 30 pounds through training, cross training, and cycling. I'm particularly interested in HIT (High Intensity Training) for runners, weightlifting, lunges, kettlebells, and planks.

I'm mindful of my progress in the Grandma's Marathon. By making it to mile 23 by the 6:00 mark in the race, I'm not that far off my goal for Tokyo. But in typical 2021 reshuffle style, they just announced this last Wednesday to restrict the race to Japanese citizens. They won't allow any foreigners to run so Tokyo is scratched from my 2021 schedule.

That will ease up a very hectic October. I'm still considering opting out of Chicago since Boston is the next day. The other option would be to walk Chicago and then fly out to Boston. I'm not sure what I will do but know I have until July1 to make that decision. I keep reminding myself that Boston has a strict 6-hour limit. They pull you and there will be no medal or finish time. Worse yet, the race won't count towards the six world majors. Fortunately, I have run those Boston hills before and know how to take advantage of the elevation drops. Meanwhile, Chicago has a 6:30 limit and won't pull you off the course. I have some critical decisions to make to reach my goal. My immediate priority is to get to Utah and run that race.

Week 21: Morgan City Marathon, Utah, June 26

As I approach the halfway point in the quest, you can see that each week brought a unique experience in the race itself but also in the people I met, and the challenges I faced.

I flew to Salt Lake City and headed to Morgan, which sits north and a little east of the capital city. As I approached Deb's Spicy Pie Pizza, I noticed a group of young ladies from nearby Ogden. I learned they were on a girl's trip to Morgan as part of a youth group from a Mormon church; and making the most of it by wearing matching pajamas. To my amazement, they greeted me with a wave — literally they did the wave as they sat lined up on both sides of three six foot picnic tables in front of Deb's. They were having a lot of fun. The pizza place wasn't  very big so I couldn't help noticing and couldn't resist commenting. "I didn't get the memo about the pajamas. I would have loved to join you." That brought even bigger smiles to their faces and broke the ice. From there we enjoyed a lot of laughs.

As I prepared to leave, I asked them to sign my prayer mug (a finisher's mug from the race that I have memorable people sign so I can remember to pray for them.) I noted one gal's funky hairdo and then propositioned them.,

"y'all can run the 5k with me?"

"We aren't runners."

"Then you can walk."

"If you run the 5k next year, I'll come back and run it with you."

I didn't know if they would or not but wanted to plant the seed.

As they left, one gal said, "You made our evening."

"Thank you but you ladies were the ones who wore the matching pajamas and did the wave. You made my evening."

Photo: My autographed Prayer Mug. I keep this on my bathroom vanity as a reminder to pray for these young ladies and their adult mentors.

Often races hold a spaghetti dinner so runners can gather the night before the race for a carb up meal, meet old friends, and make new ones. It was there that I met the Jacksons who were traveling through Morgan on their way to Seattle. Unfortunately, their hearts were heavy as their teenage son was recently killed going the wrong way into traffic. They only stopped in Morgan because they were taken by the street filled with old west storefronts. As we shared our stories, I learned they were already supporters of St. Jude's. After hearing my story, the guy gave me a $20 bill and paid for my spaghetti. Unfortunately, by the time we went to get our meal, they ran out of spaghetti. I took the $10 that I would have paid for the meal, added another $20 of my own, and sent it to St. Jude's. I appreciate the generosity of others and use it to donate myself. I won't insult someone by refusing their gift of a meal but I'm also not a freeloader. When they give to me, I take that money and give it to St. Jude's.

As much as I appreciated meeting new friends, I was in Morgan City to run a marathon. The Morgan City Marathon was started by a group of six ladies in 2011. They wanted a race that was for runners that was run by runners. In 2020, they decided it was time to hand it over to a professional management company, SKOL.

The Race

The course was beautiful, winding through the back side of the Wasatch Mountains in the Morgan Valley. Run at approximately 5000-foot level, the elevation gain was only about 484 feet.

We started at 5:30 a.m. with temps hovering around 50 degrees. The half marathon followed at 6:00 and the 5k and 10k at 7:00. While this was a trail run, it was run on roads with open traffic. Police were stationed at the bottom of the hill, stopping traffic to momentarily warn them of the runners on the road. This was critical because this is where traffic exited a canyon and entered the valley. There was no room for signs going down into that valley.

Photo: Start of the Marathon

The race required two loops. The first time around there was no traffic so we could run on the road. That was nice. The second time, however, there was too much traffic for me to run on the road. Running on the side and at times on the road forced me to run awkwardly. I couldn't use my quad and that taxed my glutes. You know that isn't going to end well and it didn't. On the second lap, I could see the aid station when the pain intensified. I slowed to a walk and had difficulty doing that. Like a parched man headed for water in the desert, that last quarter mile was brutal.

Finally, arriving at the aid station managed by two teenage boys. Their mother was running the race. The older one was very outgoing and engaging and together, they ran that aid station as well as any I've seen. They engaged runners and helped them get what they needed to run the race.

Having engaged them on the first lap, they anticipated my return with a request.

"Sing us a song."

I like to spontaneously create songs, often in a rap. This one was "Any Given Sunday." Despite my pain, I sang, danced, and together, we smiled and laughed. To say that they enjoyed it is an understatement because they told everyone. By the time I got to the finish, everyone was talking about how I had rapped for those two boys.

Knowing that would be the last time I stopped at that aid station, I offered a complement. "You will make great adults."

I ran the race with two women I called "the Jennifers." The first Jennifer got a late start for the half marathon. I ran with her from mile 5 to 10. As we got to know each other, she shared how she had recently enjoyed seeing one of her friends win the competition on the TV show *Cake Wars*. We ran together for the last 4 miles of the half marathon and were walking the last mile when I suggested that she get your time for the half and run the last 5k. **???**

Jenn #2, the baker who won Cake Wars, was running the marathon. From nearby Ogden, she lost a bunch of weight, but put some back during covid. She struggled with a messed-up sciatica. For a time, we also ran with Mary, from Portland, who had a slipped disc. I listened as Jenn #2 and Mary shared their pain stories. But those stories were just from the past. As we ran, they were both in pain, especially Jenn #2. Doing what I do best, I cheered her on with songs and boisterous cheers. It wasn't pretty but she finished in 3:45.

Photo: Jen #1, Jennifer Skidmore (left 158) and Jen #2, Jennifer Vesper (right 142)

I finished the first loop at 3:34 and knew I had to pick up the pace. Looking ahead, I could see the 5.5-hour pacer a quarter mile ahead. Fortunately, I was at the top of the hill and headed down. "Perfect" I said as I went into my Foot Levelers "down the mountain stride" and engaged in the euphoria of running. The scenery matched my mood as it was gorgeous. I was in heaven as I caught the pacer and was determined to stick with him.

Interestingly enough, the pacer was running alone. But having paced many races, I knew that didn't matter because he was there for me to gauge my run. As we began our next incline, my glutes said, "That's enough." Sure, they did. They were freeloaders on the downhill run but when it's time for them to take over for the quads, they chickened out. Part of the problem was the competition with the traffic. With only a single track, there was only room for one foot on the road and semi-trucks screaming by. That made for very treacherous running. Although there were signs and truckers did slow down, that was too close for comfort.

Meanwhile, the winner was already finished with a 3:15 time. While I can no longer run with the local elites, this race reminded me of the added benefits granted to the front of the pack. They held the traffic, so he didn't have to worry about being taken out by a truck.

When I ran to catch up to the pacer, I came across a fellow runner, Marie, who I would later run with in Portland.

I ran three more miles but called it quits at mile 20. A guy picked me up in a truck and took me to the finish. When people who don't run can see your pain and offer you a chair, you know you are done. I wanted to tell the sweeper guy to pick me up at mile 20 but only made it another 100 yards. I really wanted to finish, or at least get to 20. But when I couldn't even go down the hill, I knew that was too much. I was in so much pain I could hardly walk in a gravel parking lot.

To add insult to injury, someone broke into a race trailer and stole the medals. What would someone want with them? It's not like you can resell them since they are race specific. But the Race Director was good and promised to mail the medals.

I did enjoy the unique flavors of ice cream, including banana, chocolate, vanilla, and coconut. They even had a fudge popsicle.

Recap

That narrow track with traffic screaming by took too much attention and put too much stress on my glutes. Add to that the stress of going uphill and that adds up to pain. I know this sounds obvious, but had I been able to run down the hill it would've been different. "Of course, it would" you might think. "Running downhill is always easier." That's not quite right. Running downhill requires different muscles and especially taxes your quads and ankles. But for me, I can deal with that because the bullet is in my glute, which isn't needed for running downhill.

Unlike the week before, even though I was hurting in a good way, this race wiped me out for a week. Despite taking my sleep medication, my Garmin watch recorded that I only got a total of 3:27 of sleep with no deep or R.E.M sleep. That left me totally exhausted and unable to prepare properly for the next week. That was yet another factor to this challenge. I knew it would be difficult but didn't imagine that it would lead to a week of sleeplessness.

Looking Ahead

After a short week, I was headed back out west, this time to Portland.

Week 22: Foot Traffic Flat, Oregon, July 4

Landing in Portland, I found my hotel in the city but was looking forward to time in the country. Once again, I would be running a trail run, this time on an island in the Columbia River. Sandwiched between Oregon and Washington, this run reminded me of my early runs on Daufuskie and Skidaway Islands.

Sauvie Island

Driving out of Portland, the scene quickly transformed from urban to the "Sleepless in Seattle" views of boat houses along the river. Very quickly we left the city behind to find the tranquility of a beautiful sunrise dotted with eagles soaring and mist rising off the river. Entering Sauvie Island revealed peaceful farmland featuring cows,

199

FINISHER CERTIFICATE

TYLER BYERS

FINISHED THE 2021 SAUIVE ISLAND FLAT MARATHON WHEELCHAIR IN

1:44:06

PRESENTED BY *Foot Traffic*

ON THIS DAY: *July 04, 2021*

horses, lambs, and goats. The purple flowers blended with the nearby river to create a masterpiece deserving to be painted.

The course involved first running a loop with the half marathoners before splitting to run an out and back segment before rejoining the half marathon loop.

One hand cyclist found his stride on the flat terrain, as did the elite runners enjoying the fast course. Behind them was a diverse group of racers that included high school kids, those out for a rare run, and several of us who are more serious but not elites.

The course was fairly level with some up and down requirements. The last hill of the out and back was a bit steep. That is where I was trying to catch up with Marie after a bathroom break. Evidently that pushed me too much, because as I got closer, she pulled away. That tells me my glutes aren't working.

Carrie and I started together. We quickly found ourselves at the back of the pack but not the very last. At about the halfway point, a couple people who had been trailing us passed us. At that point, I was in a familiar position, as the very last runner.

At one point I slowed, and Marie continued. That was when I needed to stop and use the bathroom and she increased her lead over me. Finishing my business and getting back on the course, I felt great, so I decided to push it. I could see Marie and decided to catch her, like I had tried to catch the pacer the week before. But by the time I made it to where we rejoined the half marathon loop at mile 17, I was spent. I pushed too hard.

While that was disappointing, it tells me two things. First, I am getting stronger and can push myself. Second, it tells me that I need to save any pushing for those last two miles. It seems that my glutes will only tolerate pushing for two and maybe three miles. In other words, I need to save that for the finish. Otherwise, like today, I can only make it to mile 17.

Last week, I had 2:45 miles to finish but couldn't move. Again, I had a total of seven hours to run the marathon and had eight miles left. Unfortunately, my glutes immobilized me to the point that I literally couldn't move. The good news is that for part of the race, I can turn in a time between 9.5 and 13 minutes per mile. It is the end of the run that's costing me the time.

10:47 AT&T   🔋 📶 5G⁺ ⊿ 50% 🔋

←   **Carrie Kelley**   🔍

Carrie Kelley   ···
1m · 👥

This week I had the honor of running 16 miles of the Foot Traffic Flat Marathon with Aaron Burros, who is running 50 marathons by his 50th birthday. 🎉 Aaron is like this burst of joy with a positive word for everyone. Even the little old lady in her garden. How did I get so lucky to run with this fella? It turns out we're both injured & struggling in so many ways. You might have read about Aaron a few years ago. He took some bullets deep in his glutes back in 2015 when he jumped in to save his co-workers during a workplace shooting. Real.Life.Hero. 💜 Those bullets are still in his body and causes him unbearable pain yet he keeps on running for 2 reasons. He loves it and he's raising money for St. Jude's Hospital. Sauvie Island was beautimous, those houseboats made me jealous. Too many cows, horses, deer, peregrine falcons and eagle's to list but what really made the race special was running with Aaron. Now I know why I felt so compelled to run this race.

♡ Love   💬 Comment   ↪ Share

⭕⭕ You and Dave Al Paystrup

Dave Al Paystrup
Two of my favorite people on the running community. That's awesome!
1m   Like   Reply

📷   Write a comment..   GIF 😊 ☺

The People

Connecting to people after the race is always fun. Elite runners tend to show up, run, and leave. But those of us in the back of the pack know they aren't going to win so we appreciate the relationships we make.

That is where I met Jill and her husband, she is Asian, and he is Caucasian. They generously asked if they could buy me a drink. The husband went for my desired latte while Jill and I talked. She was on race #8 of her 50-state runs. I knew immediately we had something in common. As we shared stories, I noted that I couldn't finish. That is when she did something very generous. She gave me her medal.

Normally, I wouldn't have taken the medal. It is hers. She earned it. I didn't earn a medal because I didn't finish. But she insisted.

Then made me another offer.

"This is a special sign that I made to encourage the leader of the race. I want you to have it."

"I don't want to take your special sign. Besides, you just gave me your medal."

"Please, I want you to have it."

"Ok, but only if you autograph it."

"Ok"

"Could you also date it?"

Hearing that I was raising funds for St. Jude's, she quickly donated. We continued to chat, and she asked more questions about my story. It wasn't long and we were both in tears, hugging each other.

That conversation was more important than you might imagine. It wasn't just receiving the sign or the medal, but rather the healing. She encouraged me and took time to listen. That is a very rare experience these days. Usually, it seems we trade stories by exchanging opportunities to speak. But she listened from her heart before encouraging me. That attention, empathy, and compassion helped me heal. Shortly after the race, she reached out to me on messenger. That told me this wasn't just a friendly conversation, but the beginning of a relationship.

I'm looking forward to meeting her again, this time in Tokyo in 2023 when we will both be running the marathon. By then I expect to be receiving my sixth star celebrating the completion of all six World Majors.

The swag was great for this race, beginning with the beautiful, custom cloth bags with a rope handle. As we finished the race, we entered the marketplace filled with fresh produce. Normally races have pizza, brownies, and bananas, but the fresh fruit here was fantastic. I chose a big juicy orange and enjoyed every bite.

Photo: The Hubby and Jill

There were also plenty of gift shops along with food tents offering great burgers. One added feature that made a big difference was having plenty of tables and chairs to sit on. Normally runners don't have a nice picnic area to relax so we sit on the ground and juggle our food and drink. Not here. Portland knew how to do this right.

I was in heaven before but then I saw the coffee. You remember how I have my "office" at Starbucks in Houston and spend most of my days there. So, you can imagine when I landed in the northwest with Starbucks in Seattle just up the road a few hours. But you don't have to take that drive, the entire northwest is known for great coffee. I quickly made my way over to the Portland Roast Coffee booth and asked for the Americano blend. It was so good I was almost speechless. You know that has to be good. I can honestly say that was the best Americano I've ever had.

I had already decided this finish line was worth a repeat visit when I remembered "Ice Cream." The Uber driver who dropped him off made sure he told me, "Whatever you do, go get your ice cream sandwich." He was insistent and I'm glad I remembered because the ice cream was almost as good as the coffee. They had ice cream sandwiches in a variety of flavors including strawberry, vanilla cookie, and chocolate, just to name a few. That guy was right. If you run this race, make sure you get your ice cream.

This race was run so well, set in such a pristine area, and they were so generous with the food, I will definitely do this race again. And I will definitely come back for the coffee.

I hated to leave but knew I needed to get back to Houston to prepare for the next race. It was originally going to be Detroit, but I decided not to run that one. Now it will be Kansas.

Missed Iowa Flight

The challenges for running this quest make life interesting, but at times, are downright demoralizing. After returning to Houston from Portland, I was ready to run my next race in Iowa. I'm finding that the quest has already accomplished one of the goals in that my mind is on something other than worrying about the thugs. I'm immersed in the challenge of running, the task of traveling, and the joy of meeting new and old friends. Unfortunately, United Airlines doesn't prioritize my quest. Not that they should, but when they rear their ugly head, it costs the rest of us problems.

I was looking forward to running with my friend Petra Montgomery (aka "Push Thru") and a couple others in their quest to run all 50 states. Petra had friends traveling from Louisiana and we were coming from Houston, all headed to Moline, Iowa. Although there was no canceled flight due to lack of a crew, we still ran into other problems.

Petra was in line 30 minutes before the flight. Like me, she didn't have a bag to check. But United disagreed, claiming she wasn't in line in time and bumped her from the flight.

She called me as I was ready to board in Houston. Quickly rescheduling, she was flying into Chicago and renting a car for the three-hour drive to Moline. That wouldn't work for me because I knew I couldn't sit that long the day before a race. My glute wasn't doing well as it was, much less put it under that type of pressure.

I wanted to be there and cheer on Petra and other friends in their quest, but I didn't see any other choice but to cancel. (Why couldn't you just fly to Moline?) I was also angry because it seems that United picks and chooses to make sure they are not taking roller bags on the planes.

I will use the time to stay home, rest, plan, and recoup. Now I need to find a race for Iowa.

Meanwhile, California and Hawaii keep canceling, not just for the pandemic but now for wildfires.

As I look ahead, I'm finding it difficult to find races for the last seven states that are not currently scheduled. I'm hoping no additional ones cancel. I had a run in New Hampshire, but it was moved from 17th to 24th, which made me reschedule Michigan. I will now do the Tunnel Marathon in Michigan. I met a guy in Kansas that will be running it and shared that it has a small hill at front then drops 3000 feet and runs through two tunnels at the end. That New Hampshire run bothers me because they only have five races the rest of the year. I hope I can schedule one without shattering the rest of my schedule.

Week 23: Walnut River Gravel Run, Kansas, July 10

I'm a little frustrated preparing for the Kansas race. Nothing has been predictable in this challenge, except the unpredictability. First, I had to change runs in Michigan, rearranging my schedule to now run the Riley Trails Marathon on August 7. It is a trail run but the first 10k goes up 700 feet and then declines 1300 feet. I'm loving the thought of that.

Meanwhile, another run in California was canceled. That was a replacement for the previous run I had scheduled in California. I'm starting to wonder if I'll ever check the Golden State off my list. At the same time, California has many more races than some of the other states, like North Dakota or Kansas. I need to plan ahead because the northern states run very few marathons as we get into October.

Meanwhile I scheduled Iowa and Wyoming and was supposed to go to New Hampshire. But I had the wrong date and was forced to change everything for July 24th. Right now, I still need a race for the 17th of this month. I am serious when I say that nothing is predictable, or stable in this environment.

I decided to run Kansas to take pressure off my body. Kansas will be a short commute after two trips farther west. Another benefit is that the Walnut River Gravel Run is a trail run, and you know I love trail runs.

But then yet another, unexpected problem arose on the return flight home. This should have been a short, uneventful commute but United canceled the flight. They didn't have a crew or a plane. I guess that is a problem. I quickly adjusted and bought a ticket with an American for $300. But United refused to refund a basic economy ticket. How can they do that when the government bailed them out? It proves these corporations simply don't care about anything beyond the money.

As I was landing in Wichita, I saw that they had just finished harvesting grain.

The Course

Like the Pine Line and Tobacco Road marathons, this is run on an old railroad track. That means dirt, gravel, and gentle hills in a point-to-point run where they bus us out to the end, and we run back. As the Race Raves website says, "The Walnut River Gravel Run (nicknamed Hell on Gravel) is dirt roads, rolling hills, and prairie. During the race you will see wheat, soybeans, cotton, hay, sorghum, and corn. Cattle will be your biggest spectators!" To me that sounds great.

I like the generous 7.5-hour limit. Someone suggested that I stop and rest for an hour at the end of the half since I can easily run the marathon in 6.5 hours if my glutes don't give out. Instead, I like the idea of resting after 20 miles. I also considered wearing my new trail shoes, Glycerin GTS, because the race isn't that technical. I used to run in Transcend by Brooks. I ran in the Glycerins in Portland and my feet felt great, even at mile 17. They felt so great that I'll order a pair for Boston and a couple more pairs.

The Race

The Race Director, Brandi is an African American female. She is the first minority race director I have seen of an ultra-marathon run with Oz events. That's impressive.

This race is out in the country, north and east of Wichita, Kansas. The course starts in a park, runs across bridges, and then under bridges on a roadway that was muddy before turning into gravel. Some of the rocks were the size of my fists, needed to provide a solid foundation for the trucks that drove this road. The terrain took us repeatedly up and with big inclines. Trains need a low grade and that meant going out was steading incline. The course was very peaceful but challenging. After missing out on running Iowa, I was super hyped for this trail run. Imagine after fighting to run the narrow path in Utah with trucks screaming by, seeing this 8-foot-wide path with no traffic. There is no doubt, this will be fun.

I watched those running the ultra-marathon and was very impressed. One runner aiming for 50K covered the marathon distance in just 2:58:226, a 6:49 per mile pace. He was cruising and once I noticed his perfect form, I knew why.

Meanwhile, I was again bringing up the rear. I was so far back; I think even the tortoise beat me.

Yet, I was very happy to be out on the trail. No wonder I felt so good, confident, and determined to finish. Unfortunately, between mile four and five, I rolled my ankle. I didn't sprain it and definitely didn't break it, or I wouldn't have kept going.

Somewhere between mile eight and nine, while running on another stretch of big gravel, I rolled my ankle twice. This time I heard a dreaded pop. Knowing that the fourth time wasn't going to be the charm, I called it quits.

I was kind of irritated with myself because I broke my own rule for trail running. "If you injure yourself, stop. If you are going to be babying that injury for the rest of the race, stop." I create that rule knowing that the next injury will be bad, really bad.

Photo: Randy Taylor lead runner for 50K.

The pop came on the second roll. I made it to the aid station where marathon and ultra-marathon split. The ultra-marathon went right, for an eleven-mile loop, while the marathon continued on for 3 miles. I could have used a sag wagon, but there was none. Fortunately, a gentleman's grandson, Kyle, was running his first marathon, an ultra at that. His dad was his crew and ran the last 10 miles with him. Grandpa offered me a ride back to the finish.

That's when I learned that gramps is a believer and does prison ministry. I appreciated that. While I don't believe I rolled my ankle just to meet him, I do take every opportunity to meet, bless, and serve anyone I meet. That brings many new opportunities.

At the finish line, I encouraged everyone else. If I can't run, I'll serve anyway I can. That isn't just for runners, I appreciate and applaud the aid station volunteers.

Grandpa dropped me off and quickly hurried back as his grandson's quads were cramping. Grandpa also believes in encouraging and knew his purpose was to encourage Kyle to finish, even as he had to walk it in.

In many ways this race was both beautiful and bittersweet. On one hand, it was great until I rolled my ankle. I loved running that trail.

Photo: Hell on Gravel.

On the other, it is bittersweet because I know I need to get stronger. The glute keeps pushing back. When I returned to Houston and got my massage, the therapist noted how my muscles were in a knot.

I also need to get into a comfort zone with pain and push out of that comfort zone. Unfortunately, that means the glute will continue to push back. I need to prepare mentally for the physical reaction. The problem is that the point of the pain starts to itch when the scar tissue starts to break up. It itched so bad I told the therapist that I wanted a donkey to kick her in her chin." Naturally I didn't mean it, but it was just an expression of how much pain I was in. It hurt for several days, even with the massage.

Halfway into the challenge.

By now I wasn't sure exactly how far I was in the 50-50-50 challenge. By now I was supposed to be #26 but I wasn't. Despite falling behind due to various obstacles, it was a good time to reflect on my quest.

My emotions have been a constant roller coaster. I feel good and then the pain hits. I get a schedule and then there is a cancellation. I go from being in a good mood to being attacked by PTSD. That instability is incredibly difficult.

I asked myself a tough question, "Knowing what you know now, what would you tell yourself at the beginning of the challenge?"

Gramps, Dad, and son (Kyle)

Logistically – focus on yourself rather than family members. My mom, brother, son, and cousin unfortunately don't fully appreciate what I was doing and why. I would tell Aaron Burros, "Don't focus on them. Focus on your own plans. Raise the funds for St. Jude's and encourage others at each race. That's what's important." As much as I care for my family, they put me in unnecessary struggles.

I knew my schedule would change but had no clue I would run into as many problems. It started with Chevron canceling, then Louisiana and Hawaii. Fortunately, I found Daufuskie Island. This challenge has been very draining emotionally. That is the part of this that I hate the most, rescheduling.

Then there are the little things like parking at the airport. Houston is especially ridiculous. It's hard to find spaces and shuttle service is poor.

Physically – I knew my body had deteriorated since the shooting. But I talked with the surgeon who knew I would be in pain. He told me so. When I asked him if I could still run, he said I would. It just depended on how much pain I could tolerate. At that time, I didn't know exactly how much pain it would be.

I specifically didn't hire a trainer because he didn't want to take my money because he knew I wasn't ready for him. Fortunately, I found an ethical trainer in Marcus. He put me on exercises until I got stronger. He knew I needed to establish a baseline with the exercises. Then, at the end of April, I started working with him.

Surprises – I didn't realize prior to the challenge how many people I would meet and make such a powerful connection. I didn't imagine how much support and encouragement I would receive. I think that is because they see me as a type of pastor who gives and gives but few people give back. For example, one guy gave me his medal from his first Boston Marathon. Are you kidding me? That is his unicorn. Nobody gives that away. Then there was Jill in Portland who gave me her medal from her eighth race in her 50-state run. She humbled me when, knowing I didn't finish, said, "You deserve a medal." While the pain has left me crying uncontrollably at times, the generosity and compassion has also brought tears to my eyes.

Next Week

As usual, I will return to Houston, rest, get stretched, and massaged. I have a bit of a layoff given my next race isn't until the 24th.

I feel like I'm at a tipping point. I need to run. Having a week off after so many consecutive weeks is unnerving. I'm also frustrated that my glute isn't firing. I did a ten-mile run with a friend and cycled, but it's not the same. All I'm concerned at this point is healing the ankle and getting back on the quest

Week 24: Orange Curtain 24-hour Ultra-Marathon, California, July 17

I'm worried that I won't be able to run all fifty states because so many races have been canceled or postponed. Even though it is only July, the clock is ticking on the states where I don't have a race scheduled. Add to that the reality that even the states where I do have them scheduled, they will postpone or cancel at the last minute. That takes some scrambling to find races, register, find a flight, and book a hotel. That's assuming ground transportation is available. With the problem with car rentals and the spike in costs, that has also become a problem.

I registered for the Orange Curtain 24-hour ultra-marathon in February. But then it was postponed. California had strict covid restrictions that made the reality of a race a problem. That meant it was back to the schedule and I held my breath. At this point, I had given up on the race being run. Races in California kept canceling due to covid but now another restriction closed races, fires. The wildfires of California wiped out not only acres of trees but also several races. I had heard that the Orange Curtain was canceled.

Then, a day before the race was to be run, I found out it was indeed going to be run. I quickly emailed the race director who graciously let me run since I was on the wait list since February. Since registration was online and already closed, he asked me to bring cash. That was the first obstacle.

With only one day to get to California, I tackled the next obstacle, finding a flight. Normally a flight from Houston to John Wayne

Airport isn't a problem, but this summer it was unpredictable. The lack of pilots and the canceled flights has already cost me two races. The benefit I had was that this was a 24-hour race, so I didn't have to be at the start line at a specific time. The only choice I had was to fly on the day of the race, run the race, and then hurry to catch the return flight that same day so I could make my next race. Unfortunately, that race was in New Hampshire. As I mentioned earlier, logistics played a major obstacle in running this quest.

Sure enough, my flight was delayed. When we landed, there was no gate available for an hour and 20 minutes. I quickly readjusted my game plan, deciding to run only the first half. I felt like I was a pilot doing a touch and go landing.

The course was a loop that took us out 5k and then back. The aid station was in between. To complete the ultra, ten laps were required. For those running the marathon, we went ¾ of the way out and then started the cycle to do 4-10k loops.

I started late and enjoyed the deceptively flat course to be nothing too difficult. However, there was very little shade which made the sun on asphalt tough. I was pleased that I was maintaining a 12:18-12:30 pace, focused on form with my hips moving forward and activating glutes. I was feeling good.

I came across a 21-year-old man, Dane, (photo) 21 running the marathon. Unfortunately, he hadn't done much since February. Oddly enough, he did a bit in February, then quit until April, when he did a little more before quitting again. As a trainer and a runner, I know that isn't a good plan. I caught up to him at mile 5, his mile 13, where he was ready to give up. Naturally, I started talking to him. Meanwhile, he was complaining about what aches and how he should have trained better. I believed him because he looked like he was 90 years old.

Being the #RunningServant, I couldn't just run past him, so I stopped to help. "If you let me help you, I will help you finish." I stopped and showed him tips to maintain his form. Despite the lack of training, I knew he could help himself by focusing on his form. "Relax, keep your head up or it will hurt even more."

"This is weird," he continued complaining.

"Yes, it is." I continued to listen as he got up and started to run. I kept listening with my ears but also with my eyes, watching how he was maintaining his form.

"This is really helping," he said, reflecting a shift in his mindset that he could finish. The last 10k, the last loop, he was engaged. Having only 5 miles to go, Dane started to struggle, so we stopped at the restroom and hydrated at the aid station before finding some shade. Dane waited until I returned from the restroom.

Dane acted like he wanted to quit, so I started walking to keep him going. Experienced runners know that when you stop and are discouraged, it can be very difficult to start again.

I helped him ice his cramps and encouraged him. That worked and he was soon back into the "I can finish" mindset. We made good progress and only had a half mile left before his finish. I told him, "Go ahead and finish on your own. I don't want to steal your thunder."

"Really?"

"I want to honor you. You need to go across on your own."

He was elated when he finished and quickly told everyone what I had done. We exchanged numbers and met another guy who agreed to help Dane train. I promised him that, from here, it only gets easier.

Meanwhile, I noticed a gal and felt the spirit of God when I saw her. While I'm open and willing to talk to anyone, this was different. I felt a calling to minister to her but didn't know what to do. As I greeted her, she began sharing. She was originally from Texas and went to school not far from my mom. Then came the ugliness. The trauma began as a child when her mother sex trafficked her to family members. As sick as it was, her mother did it for the money. Then she was gang raped in high school. After a car accident as an adult, she could take no more. PTSD set in and imprisoned her in the house. It has been two years since she had been out. The end result was debilitating PTSD that imprisoned her inside her own house for two years. Finally, a day before the race, a friend convinced her to come out and support her brother in the race. Paroled but not freed from her prison, she sat there, speaking to God, crying deeply, and begging God for release.

I spoke to her, using verses from Deuteronomy, that lightened her heart, freeing her from her shame. I'm very pleased that God used me to bless her. Helping her, and Dane, was my assignment for the race.

> 25 "But if in the open country a man meets a young woman who is betrothed, and the man seizes her and lies with her, then only the man who lay with her shall die. 26 But you shall do nothing to the young woman; she has committed no offense punishable by death. For this case is like that of a man attacking and murdering his neighbor, 27 because he met her in the open country, and though the betrothed young woman cried for help there was no one to rescue her. (Deuteronomy 22:25-27, ESV)

Fear the Goat Aid Tent

I continued to run and met a lady at the aid station that hosts an ultra-marathon around her house every year. "That's different but cool" I thought.

When I sat down because my glute was hurting, she asked, "Are you a pastor? Where's your church?"

"Everywhere." I know God is leading me.

The finish line of the race was my goal but, especially after this race, I am realizing the race and the quest is bigger than I can run. The other participants are more than I can count, and the finish line is further than I figured."

I only finished 14 miles in California, in part because I lost over an hour at the beginning, sitting waiting for a gate at the airport. That was the critical part. Yes, I would have finished the marathon if not for that delay and helping Dane. I don't regret stopping to help Dane. Working with him and the gal in need is why I am the #RunningServant.

With California off my list, I rushed back to the airport to catch a return flight to Houston, and then to Boston the next day.

Week 25: Allenstown, New Hampshire Trail Run, July 23

As I boarded the plane to Boston for my race in New Hampshire, I couldn't help but think about the Boston Marathon in October. It will be my fifth star for the six world majors. I have run the course before and love running the city, enjoying the hills, scenery, and history. I'm also excited to be raising funds and running for Hale Reservations, which is renamed to Hale Education. They have partnered with Boston schools and do tremendous work.

Part of the reason I had to leave California so quickly was that I had an appointment set with Hale Education to tour their facilities. On the tour, they expressed a concern as to whether I could finish in the time allowed. I answered honestly. "I will do what I can do but can't guarantee my glute will show up."

I reflected later that I am concerned about the rolling hills. But I have a plan to walk up the hills and run down to prevent blowing out my glutes. I'm not like Dane from California who hasn't trained or thought this through. I estimate it will take 3.5 hours to empty the corrals. Since the elite start at 8:00 and the other qualifiers follow, charity runners will begin at 11:15. Hale is scheduled to start at 11:00. I am used to the hills, have run Heartbreak Hill but not at the end of the marathon, or with a bullet in his glute. However, one of the hardest aspects of running Boston is that I must finish in six hours. As much as I want to help others, this race must be about me finishing. That is difficult for #RunningServant to do. I can offer encouragement and technique to anyone, but I must keep going. But that is for October. I can't get too far ahead of myself.

The questions from hale made me think. In a session with my massage therapist last week, she was trying to compress the glute to relax the knot. I've been using her for two years because she is good. In the process, she has noted how her job has gotten more difficult as I've gotten stronger. That requires her to learn how my body is changing and what she needs to do to activate the glute. Along with Marcus, I'm making progress, but it is one and a half steps forward with one step backward. Slowly I'm progressing but not without continual setbacks.

If that isn't enough, I've been having nightmares and terrors about my old place of work, fighting for his life, and the company exposing me to the dangers. I've found that no one else can help me through those dark moments. I just have to walk myself through it. After the latest barrages, I reached out to my psychologist, in part because it has been two weeks since my last session. In the end, I just "sucked it up buttercup" and talked my way through it. But that doesn't mean it didn't take a week to fight through the depression. Oddly enough, I sleep better during periods of depression, but that brings other problems. In the end, I'm constantly fighting to find the right balance.

To anticipate and develop physically, there is something inside and outside of me that is developing. As I told Aaron Stephens that I met in Boston, God is using the shooting for his purpose. It is an affliction but also a tremendous blessing. It has slowed me down and taken the focus off of me. It has moved me away from a competitive marathoner to a compassionate, #RunningServant. One of his therapists told me early on in the process, "after all this is over with, you will be a better runner." I couldn't believe it but now recognize the vintage Aaron Burros. God has already made his name famous. I thank him for dragging me along.

The Race

Once again, I chose a trail run, this time in north of Nashua, New Hampshire just 31 miles from Allenstown. I am pleased that it has 9 hours to finish because that will give me time to rest my glutes and still finish the race. This race promises all kinds of nature on their website, "rocks, roots, sticks, animals, mud, deer flies, ticks, porcupine, bear, moose, squirrel, chipmunk, turkey, streams, mountain bikers, hikers, horses, horse poop, bobcat, trees, singletrack, double track, and dirt roads."

The weather was a perfect 56 degrees in Fairbrook State Park, where we were running. I immediately met Joe and Zachariah. Joe is older and running a marathon with his girlfriend. Zacharia was running his first marathon. I started at the back and caught up with Joe.

As quick as we started, I realized why I chose this run. It is beautiful to be in a full-fledged tail run. The varied terrain worked to protect my glute even though the trail run demanded more muscles because of the uneven footing. My lower back was hurting, but I can tolerate that. I'm very pleased to say my glute didn't give me any problems.

You might expect it was an easy run and I finished. But by this point in the story, you know that wasn't to happen. So, what was it this week? I got lost.

Trail runs are not like street running where the course is clearly marked with signs, traffic cones, volunteers, and police officers. The race director and his wife marked the course, but in the end, they didn't have enough signs, especially given the rain, that messed up the markers. Then there was another problem. They used the same colors, pink, for three races, the 10K, half, and full marathon. That meant when the courses crossed, we didn't know which way to go. Even when we tried consulting the printed map they provided, we were confused. Imagine one lady's dismay when she was running the half but got lost and ended up completing the full marathon. She had never run more than a half. Yet she completed it in less than five and a half hours. Wow! But before you think it was a blessing in disguise, realize that almost no one knew the course. Only a couple of people who had run the marathon before were familiar with the route. So here we are, almost everyone running around a park totally lost. To an observer, this must have looked like a zany comedy. We definitely needed more volunteers and a better organized event.

But that's not to say the people were anything but great. They were so nice that I'm blaming the poor markings on the black bears. They must have messed with our route and then sat in the bushes and laughed at us.

To make matters worse, my Garmin watch stopped at mile 10. I wished I would have started with my Strava app on my phone and saved the power in my Garmin. Oh well, it adds more drama to the story, as if I needed that.

Photo: Start of Bear Brook (top)
Zachariah, Joe and I (bottom)

Photo: Allenstown, New Hampshire

I ran somewhere between 15 and 18 miles in 5.5 hours. I didn't know exactly since my watch stopped. I would've finished had I not gotten lost and known where I was.

The 6-8 miles that I missed required running through water over my feet, and across a floating bridge with segments tied together. Depending on weight, the bridge dipped into the water. I probably would've gotten my feet wet again. As you can see, there was no room for error in this race. If you weren't careful, you could've killed yourself on the boulders.

By the way, I was looking but never did see any of those black bears messing with the markings. Believe me, I would have had a word with them.

At the cutoff, there

were still 37 full marathoners remaining on the course. Two half marathoners finished after the nine-hour cutoff. It turned out that part of the marking problem was that there were old markings left on the course from the previous race and were, again, the same color, pink.

Despite the confusion, people didn't complain. Instead, everyone laughed it off and enjoyed the run. Maybe that is because the course is a total beast that demands a different mentality. It may also be that the race directors are good people that create a great atmosphere. Everyone was laughing and joking, not getting angry. Those running trails know it isn't exactly 26.2 like in a road race. As the sign at the finish line stated, "Don't worry about it. I won't charge you for the extra mile."

I checked for Zachariah but didn't find him. I learned later he made a wrong turn and went back to where he started. By the time my taxi arrived, he still hadn't finished, wasn't at the cutoff or checked his name off at the last aid station.

As you might imagine from the challenging course, getting lost, and retracing their steps, some were completely exhausted by the time they finished. Ally and Garrett were delirious, but we had a great conversation where I shared my story, and we connected on Facebook. I am pleased they donated and promised to cheer me on in Boston. Others also promised to donate.

The sense of family is overwhelming at the trail races. Maybe it is because we are in nature and kindred spirits that the run becomes a party on the trail. This reminded me of the Hatfield and McCoy race. In the end, I had a great time, and I needed that.

The Aftermath

I could hardly move the next day. Even though I felt great during the run, the pain returned with a vengeance. That was the second worst pain since the shooting, only surpassed by California. I hadn't mentioned it, but I was in pain since California. New Hampshire didn't exacerbate California pain but added to the kinetic pain by moving upward. The pain started in my lower back, climbed up back on right then to left, back and forth. My back locked up with intense pain where my lower back and hip felt like one big, tight muscle. This was all due to different muscles needed for a trail run.

The follow-up massage required two hours just for my back and shoulders. Then add another 45 minutes for the stretching therapist to work my neck, back, shoulders, hips.

The good news was that I had been working to build up my torso, back, and core with a trainer for two months. Marcus said it was loud and demanding, climbing over boulders. But the load was too much in this race. Trail running is great because I don't have time to get bored.

Signs along the Struggle

While watching for rocks and roots, there is no time for my mind to wander. Everything is and must be engaged.

But it is taxing and told me that I still need work on my lower body. Like returning for my blonde roast refill at Starbucks, I needed a second massage that week. While that pain may sound terrible, I have to say it is rewarding pain because it says I'm making progress. It is the pain of growth, and like the old saying goes, no pain – no gain. Yes, it is still painful, and it hurts just sitting at home. In my times of doubt, I wonder whether it will get better or continue to get worse. I find that answer by continuing to go out and do it. In the end, I can see progress and that helps me shift my perspective toward the pain.

Going Forward

Next week I'm headed to North Dakota for the Maah Day Hey Trail run. I am scheduled to leave Friday, fly to Williston, North Dakota, run on Saturday, and back on Monday.

I'm pleased that every race through August 15 is trail runs.

Light at the End of the Tunnel in Washington is less of a challenge because once I get through the tunnel, it is downhill all the way. Unlike the last race, there will be no boulders, roots, or rope bridges on that one. It is an old railroad track with dirt and grass, and pebbles. From what I hear, the view from the bridges is spectacular.

I'm seeing that most races require covid testing to run. They test you when you enter the state and then take your temperature before you start. They also check for any signs of a cold.

With New Hampshire finally checked off, let's move on to North Dakota.

Canceled Flight to North Dakota, Aug. 1

Well, that didn't happen.

My flight on United Airlines was supposed to fly out of Houston on one of the big international jets to Denver. We landed and I walked across the airport to N83 to wait for my flight. On the way I purchased some of their expensive food and finished my trek to the assigned gate.

But there's a problem. There is no plane. It turns out our scheduled plane is not in Denver but rather in Sioux Falls, South Dakota. There wasn't even any pilot or plane even assigned to that gate.

"Someone should've caught it." I said aloud before noting to myself, "This proves it, they don't care about the passengers. Just the money."

Having no other choice, I booked a flight back to Houston. But I had to hurry through the airport to arrive just as they were about to close the door. I asked if I could get on since I noticed on my phone that a storm was coming. I did not want to have to spend the night in the Denver airport. That would have been an insult to my latest injury.

Sitting on the plane, I couldn't get it out of my mind. They should've canceled my flight before I ever left Houston knowing they didn't have a plane, pilot, or crew for the flight to Williston, North Dakota.

Just because you plan a trip and buy a ticket, don't expect to get there. Fortunately, in this situation, they offered a full refund immediately since I had absolutely no forewarning.

Had I known I couldn't run North Dakota, I would have found another run. Now that puts pressure on me to juggle races because smaller, northern states like North Dakota don't run as many races as bigger or more southern states. A quick search showed only three runs remaining for 2021 in the state. Unfortunately, I have a run already scheduled for each of those days. I'll need to figure that one out.

Turning my attention to next week, I travel to Michigan. Let's hope the airlines don't mess that one up. to meet legends out there. As long as I can run with his quads, all is good.

You might wonder if a week off would help. The answer is, not really. The rest is good, but I need the intensity and rhythm of running every week.

My plan is to travel to Laramie, Wyoming the next week to run on the 14th and then to Snoqualmie, Washington on the 15th. Since Washington is a more protective state, I will need to get a negative test to run there. I also know they will have a staggered start and test to get a permit.

For training this week I will do two, one-hour cross training workouts, one on Monday, another on Wednesday. I have swelling in my lower right leg and wear a protective stocking. In one of those workouts, I got to see just how my muscles are misfiring. My nephew, who is also training me, asked me to hold my right hand, and I responded, raising my left. "What? Why did that happen?" It was the wrong muscles getting the message. Then I did a squat and it burned. Then I tried getting up and out to find that wasn't easy.

My nephew, Nwankwo-Ikechi Nwankwo graduated from Texas Lutheran University with a Bachelor degree in Applied Physics . Once an athlete, he left that for education. I'm proud of him because he is a role model, being the first black graduate in that major. He is very smart and wants to start his own company. In addition, he is taking a couple of other courses to specialize in it.

A new development occurred this week when the race director for a Hawaii race gifted me an entry. That means I will travel to the islands for a trail run in western Oahu. I'm looking forward to running in their forests. Unfortunately, there won't be much time for tourist activities.

Meanwhile at home, I'm changing my training to run trails with friends. I need to build my trail endurance and know that an hour in the trails translates to two hours on the road.

I keep revisiting the challenge in my head and recognize that it has given me hope, purpose, and direction. I am pleased to have seen God working and know that when I move, God does. He likes a moving target.

Week 26: Riley Trails Marathon & Relay Marathon, Michigan, Aug. 7

Do I dare trust the airlines?

After the cancellations, I was hesitant to step on an airplane. But I can't let that fear freeze me in my tracks and crash my quest.

I was excited to be running yet another trail run on an old railroad track. The Riley Trails Marathon promised a sweet run that made five and a half trips around a loop slightly less than five miles. I expected this to be fairly easy. But as I was finding, the ones that look easy often have a problem. Sure enough, that held true.

As I exited the cab at 6:15, I immediately noticed familiar and unwelcomed sounds. It was the sound that sent chills up my spine. "Oh no!" Flashes of Pine Line went through my head but were quickly trampled by memories of that fateful night in Houston. "That's not the way I wanted to start."

I crossed the electronic timer and tried to focus. "Hope that doesn't last all day." Unfortunately, it did. By the time I ran three miles, I was on the backside of the loop for the first time. That is when I not only heard the gunshots, but I also felt the vibration of each blast.

Boom. Boom. Boom.

I have tried to condition myself, but nothing prevents my physical and emotional reaction to gunfire. The only thing I could hope for was that PTSD wouldn't become too debilitating.

This was especially unnerving because the shooting range was particularly close to the course. Looking around, I could see that others were also unnerved.

233

"Aren't they too close?"

"What if they hit us?"

Many of the runners felt like I did. This range was so close that they too could feel the vibration from the volleys.

Even those without PTSD were unnerved by it. They wondered if they were going to get shot. Some wondered whether they should turn around. I pushed on, fighting my fears. On my second loop, I felt like I was losing my control. I was spacing out, my heart was racing, my stress level increased drastically. As I got back to the trailhead, I looked at the race director and said, "I can't do anymore." He apologized, stating, "They weren't supposed to be back there shooting like that. Those were big farms." After a moment, he looked at me and said, "I'm worried about Aaron." He knew my story. Unfortunately, this was simply a private group of people who decided to go shooting on their land that morning, hunting and killing animals destroying their crops.

I fought to get to the half marathon mark. While I was running well, I turned in a time of 16-minute miles that included bathroom breaks, photos, etc. I was running a 5/2 split for a 10:47 pace. I felt very good about that progress. If only they wouldn't have been shooting those guns.

I was pleased that the race director presented me with a wooden finisher's medal, since I didn't finish and didn't earn a medal. The Race Director stated that they had decided to hand out finisher's medals to all participants whether they finished or not because of the pandemic.

I embody the saying that "Success isn't measured by what you can do, but what you can't do that you tried to accomplish." I don't run to collect medals. As one man told me, "Sir, get going, you are inspiring people you don't even know yet. Success is in thinking bigger and reaching higher.

That brings back memories of Mr. Dallas, that college science teacher that I had in high school. "If you only learn what you already know, that isn't success. That shows no effort spent. I was grading to see what you learned." Like a preacher who preaches my favorite sermons, we need to ask, "did we grow?"

That's my mantra during this challenge. Many finish a race injured and don't want to do another one. But I say, "People are my medal Mondays." Finishing the half isn't pushing me for my mental, emotional, spiritual growth. No sir, it doesn't challenge me at all. If you can do what you always do comfortably, even if you run 50 states, that wasn't a challenge. You must push the envelope. When I was running 30 or 40 miles, I was pushing my time and also working to get to 50 miles. I could easily have done 50 half marathons but that wasn't challenging.

Photo: People are my Medal Mondays.

But I need to be honest. When I started the 50/50/50 challenge, I sincerely thought I would finish all of them. Only one had a 5-hour limit and I was determined to finish that one in time. My original goal was 5:05 but even after I started and realized how my body reacted, I still wanted to finish in 6.5 hours. I wasn't deceiving myself because I knew Chicago, Berlin, New York I turned in a 6.5-hour run. But I didn't recognize the transition my body needed. I didn't realize that I needed to hit bottom to come back up.

I think I hit that bottom recently when I was doing sub core exercises working with a trainer. Marcus understood I hadn't hit bottom and kept me progressing until I did.

Returning to Houston, I met a guy who worked for United but saw him in Indianapolis, remembered him, stopped him. He beamed as he saw me, "I can't forget you."

That was very refreshing because I don't know what seeds have been planted or watered. I know what he has to do to hear the Lord say, "well done good and faithful slave." I do everything for the glory of God and am grateful for the journey. I have a thousand reasons why I shouldn't be doing this challenge. But I know I'm doing this for the glory of God. That keeps me going.

Next week

I fly home and then head north to Alaska for the Anchorage RunFest. Fortunately, it is a direct flight from Houston to Anchorage on Delta. That will be nice. I leave Thursday and run on Saturday so I should have plenty of time to recover. I'm looking forward to a movie night on Friday and relaxing on Saturday.

Unfortunately, we want everything planned out, parceled out, before we move out. I shared with a guy at the hotel and found myself complaining about my pain. I quickly apologized as I don't want to burden anyone. He kindly replied, "don't apologize, because if you hadn't tried, you wouldn't be here."

Now it is time to go north, north to Alaska.

Canceled Alaska Flight

I never made it to Alaska. Once again, the airlines let me down when, at the last minute, Delta canceled the flight. With no chance to make it in time for the race and the end of the Alaskan running season in sight, Alaska was scrubbed from my schedule for 2021. That meant it was the first state I won't be able to run. I still have five others that are questionable. The quest is becoming a challenge not only for my physical and mental conditioning but for navigating the covid logistics.

These flight cancellations have a ripple effect. They not only cause trouble for me but for those I planned to run with. For example, one running friend shared that one of her friends is a double agent, meaning she is a member of both the Half Fanatics and the Marathon Maniacs. To be a member of either club, you must run 3 races in 90 days or 2 within 16 days. That means a double agent must run at least two, or three of each race in ninety days. These are serious runners. Anyway, she was going to Alaska to run with Ronita Blend who once finished her 50 States Half and will complete the 50 States full marathons all under five hours. Unfortunately, she was stuck in Atlanta for 2 hours and that threw everything back. She arrived late but still finished. I wanted to cheer her on but also to run. She is officially a double agent, done half in all 50 states, and now has done a full marathon in all 50 states.

Next on the schedule is the Tunnel Vision Marathon in Snoqualmie, Washington. Set in on the edge of Snoqualmie Pass in the Cascade Mountains.

I don't see how anything could go wrong.

Week 27: Tunnel Light Marathon, Washington, Aug. 15

I knew better. After running for seven months in this challenge, I should have known that the race wouldn't be that easy. It became apparent as my flight approached Seattle.

Somewhere over smoked filled Seattle Washington. Smoke came from forest fires in Northern California.

That's when I noticed the smoke. Wildfires in northern California blanketed western Washington to such an extent, I could hardly talk. That meant I couldn't cheer on my fellow runners, who needed the help, given breathing was an issue. A day or two earlier, the winds shifted and there were clear skies. But when the race approached, the winds shifted back and brought the perpetual haze. I would be hoarse from the smoke for several days.

The Race

This was a point-to-point race where they bus us to the start line and we run back. We started near the tiny town of Hyak, just on the west side of the Snoqualmie Pass, which is 2600 feet in elevation. As was becoming an unwanted tradition, I was in last place shortly after the start. Fortunately, there was a Chinese guy just ahead of me. In our running conversation, he didn't think he would catch up with anyone as the course was known to be one of the fastest for Boston Marathon Qualifying.

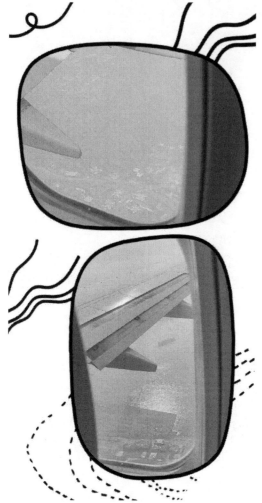

Photos: Flying into Seattle.

The course is so beautiful that I don't know how anyone can cross one of those bridges and not stop and admire the panorama view of the mountains, trees, and lakes. It was spectacular. I knew this from running it in both 2017 and 2018, when I paced it for the 5.5. hour group. So, I knew what it took to meet my goal of running it in six hours.

This course is easy and fast for two reasons. First, it is downhill the entire way. Second, unlike most trail runs, there are no ruts, roots, or boulders. The trail has grass in the middle and trails on each side. We do run through an old railroad tunnel where it is pitch black. That's why they require us to wear headlamps. The tunnel does have concrete, but you must watch for the potholes. The rest of the course is a towpath. Given there were only 400-500 runners and included only marathoners, this was a piece of heaven. No wonder so many qualify for Boston in the race.

I felt great because my glutes were working well. But because they haven't been firing at that level, it was pulling on all the other muscles. Marcus warned me this would happen, and that I would be limited in my production, in part because of the pain. Running downhill helped because I was using my quads and taking the pressure off the glutes. My glutes now felt as good as my quads. It had been a long time since

I felt that. But now, those other muscles reminded me that they hadn't been engaged in a while, and they started complaining.

My strategy, since it was all downhill, was to run intervals. I settled in to run 5 minutes and then walk 2 minutes until I caught up to the other runners and then settled into their pace. My pace brought me to a 13:50 pace, which I was very happy with.

But by mile 10, the pain said, "That's about enough." Every time my foot hit the ground, I felt like I had stepped on a live powerline. My whole body became a nasty sensation. By mile 12, the pain screamed at me, "That's it. No farther." I relented and walked to mile 13 in tears. The tears aren't because I was disappointed, but because the pain was so intense. The pain was so debilitating that I couldn't move enough to shower for several hours. I felt like one big, irritated nerve.

Usually when I run, as I decide to push it, my body responds. But not today. The more I pushed, the more pain I felt. It was like pressing on the car accelerator and nothing happening except getting an electrical shock that travels up your leg, through your hip and straight to your cheek and finally to the top of your head. The pain required that I slow down to a 21-minute pace. I tried  speed walking but that still hurt. I had used speed walking through the tunnel early in the race and determined that I could have done that the entire race. But not at mile 12.

I put my hand up for the guy on the bike behind me to signal my surrender. Unfortunately, I had to wait until I was in an area with phone reception to let the sweeper guy know to pick me up. Finally, seeing the "Sag Wagon " was a relief but getting into the car was a challenge. I gently lifted my foot and gingerly bent over to ease myself into the car. From there, it was a frustrating drive to the finish. That's not the way I expected it to happen.

Again, the run was bittersweet. The pain is a sign that I'm getting better, exactly what my trainer said would happen. It is the crucible I must endure to reach my goal. While that is important, it is also intensely incapacitating. I didn't imagine the pain would be so extreme.

Photos: Scenery along this flat, downhill course. Bottom Photo: Start line.

Yet, this race encourages me greatly. The first 9 miles went very well. I knew ahead of time I was going to slow down at mile 10 and shift to a one-minute run and one minute walk. I knew I could do that. Unfortunately, as I tried to slow down, I couldn't. I didn't think the 5/2 pace was too much. I think what happened was that the process my trainer had explained simply needed to take its course.

I don't like to admit it but when I get upset, the memories of the shooting engulf me. I experience the same emotions, images flash through my mind and my body responds as if it once again threatened. It is hell.

The smoke in Seattle messed with my mind. I don't know how long it took for the skies to clear, but that smoke wouldn't clear from my upper respiratory system. Fortunately, it didn't go into my lungs.

Looking Ahead

Meanwhile, life goes on outside of racing, but it isn't that great. Yesterday I learned my aunt was given hours to live. At the same time, my cousin from Florida was supposed to come to Houston for cancer treatment. He was doing well but then took a turn for the worse. The doctor put him back in the hospital with cancer that is now terminal.

Through the smoke and haze of recent happenings, I look ahead to Clarksburg, West Virginia in two weeks. The flight is supposed to be about an hour and a half with a connection in Chicago. I'm not confident flying United Airlines with smaller planes on the connecting flight. I've been burned too many times in that situation. It seems like United is taking money but not taking passengers to where they need to go. I do have another option to get to West Virginia. I could fly into Washington, D.C. and then drive three hours. That reminds me too much of the Oklahoma run where I drove and the memory is so vivid, my leg still hurts.

This will be a trail run, which is fine because I won't be able to run very fast anyway. I just don't want to get stuck in an airport.

I learned this week that the Air Force marathon was canceled. That means there is only one more run in Delaware this year, and sure enough, it is the same week as the Marine Corp Marathon.

This is where things got confusing. When the Marine Corp Marathon postponed the race in 2021, they offered the option to defer the race to 2022 with no cost or go virtual for 2021. Ok, no problem, I'll defer it to 2021. But then, when the pandemic wave subsided and the races opened up, they changed the rules. If you deferred to 2021, you couldn't change your mind. But if you chose the virtual, you were good. Ok, so I'll go back and change my choice, retroactively switching to virtual. Nope, that wasn't going to happen. Then, in another twist, once they decided to run a live race in 2021, they put everyone in the live race. That's not what I wanted. If I want to run live in 2022, I have to pay an $80 deferral fee to get what I originally wanted. They seem to be a typical big race that doesn't care for the runners that help build the race.

For the quest, I don't need another Virginia race, so I'll pay my deferment fee and run Delaware on that weekend in October. I may still need to juggle some other things.

I'm still afraid I'm going to miss Hawaii as I'm not confident in the restrictions. I fear they will still shut down the race I have planned for December. The stress of scheduling and rescheduling races, airlines, and hotels does take its toll. The rest of missing a race has been good for my body but my emotions take a hit. At the same time, I didn't realize how much just attempting a race is helping my mental well-being.

I did receive good news. I can leave earlier for London, following the next attempt to run North Dakota, the Fargo Marathon. I can catch a return flight to Houston, and then nonstop to London. That is good because I need 5-8 days to process the covid protocol. Two tests are required with a quarantine until cleared. Fortunately, they lowered the price of the covid test. At this point, I appreciate any money I can save. It will be nice staying at the Moxi, but I'm still concerned whether or not they will straighten out the debacle of 2019. Because they messed up so bad, they were supposed to extend us to 2020. But then 2020 was canceled and the Delta strain may require deferment for 2021, I'm not sure how they will work that out.

I will be running for Scope, Team for Kids, or possibly another charity. Three quarters of those that run London are running for charity. I like how they emphasize the charities but that means I need to raise 1250 Euros, less than $2000. A lot of banking institutions block those payments, so donors have to make more efforts. Boston uses giving gains which is in Finland, so they have to do the same thing. That adds additional stress and effort to raising funds.

I know of another Six Star marathoner, Felicia White, who raised $5500 in two days for Boston. Naturally, when I heard that, I reached out and asked her what she did. "Social media posts and appealing to family and friends. In the end I had 85 people donate, providing the funds I needed."

I like that but haven't found that to be my case. I appealed to people who knew me personally and professionally. Most promise but don't deliver. Only thirteen people in two years have followed through. I don't understand, but very few of my family donate. Strangely, most of those who have donated are complete strangers. Despite having fifteen living siblings, only four have donated. Despite Felica's success, I need to find a different strategy.

But enough about that. It's on to West Virginia.

Week 28: Moonlight on the Falls, West Virginia, Aug. 28

As I prepare for West Virginia, I'm realizing how my workouts are so crucial. I'm in my eighth month of this running challenge and appreciating how my work with my trainer and cross trainer have continued to strengthen me. Then, my own diligence with running and cycling adds a different dimension. Now if I could only figure out a way to get some, good, quality sleep.

As I fly east, my mind flashes to Boston where I will run in just 6 weeks. I really want to get that star for the Abbott World Majors. London is right there as well but, with the difficulty of traveling across the pond during covid, I would prefer to defer London.

Unfortunately, as I learned this week, they won't let me. I either must run it this year or forfeit my deferment. I don't think there is any way I can run London this year, so I'll forfeit my opportunity. There is nothing easy about the logistics in this quest. Too bad I didn't decide to do the challenge in 2018 or 2019.

I chose to fly into Clarksville, a small airport in West Virginia where I met a couple headed to the race. I learned later, everyone else came into D.C. and drove. Recognizing the remoteness of the race, I was preemptively trying to arrange a ride back to the airport. The driver taking me to the race informed me that there was no return service, but after hearing that I was raising funds for St. Jude's, he gladly volunteered to come and get me.

As the name implies, Moonlight on the Falls Marathon is run at night. I can see why, because no one should be forced to look at the hills they were about to run. The rolling "hills" were relentless, nothing but big mountains and valleys, stereotypical of West Virginia. The views, however, were stunning with cabins, forests, mountains, and streams.

Photo: Moonlight rising on Blackwater Falls State Park.

One advantage to running at night is that I didn't need a hotel room.

The Race

The race started at 10:00 p.m. and ended at 8:00 a.m. but required that we make the last cutoff by 6:00 a.m. They allowed us an early, optional start, and some did, starting at 5:00 for the sole purpose of reaching a certain vantage point to see the glorious sunrise.

This was the inaugural race for this run on a quarter marathon loop. Beast Pacing was there to literally set the pace. Every loop had 647 feet in elevation with the 2400 feet in elevation near the Black Water River. One portion went off road to the trail by river, that was very rough, and that is understating it. It was sloped, uneven, and difficult. I ran down conservatively, careful not to slip, or take a tumble. Then I walked up the steep hills. By the time I got to the top, I had to take a break because my old nemesis Pain was making a return visit.

These hills were straight up and straight down, no curves and no plateau. As you can imagine, I was relieved to find a flat spot at the top featuring a bathroom. Going down was nice, but once again, I had to be careful.

At the conclusion of the first loop, my nemesis made a second loop impossible. While it was a nice run, I just couldn't do any more.

The pain started by mile 4 and was greater than the Tunnel run in Washington. Going up I could feel the glute working and the foreign object buried inside. I sensed this pain was more dangerous because I felt a cone injury from the inside of the left knee. I could tell my right adductor was off because my leg drifted to the right. Pain traveled down to the Achilles and into the foot. All those symptoms combined sent a clear message, "That is it for today." Like a NASCAR driver with a blown engine, I spent the rest of the race on the sideline.

Photo: Exposure Therapy: 4 Pistol Shots to begin each race.

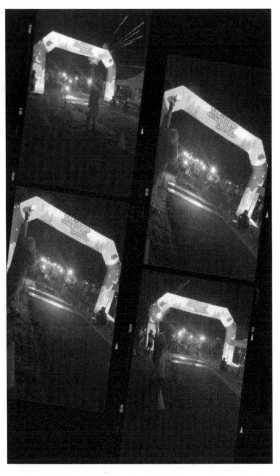

But I couldn't let it end there. I found my place and cheered everyone on until the last one was finished.

My pre-bullet racing would've loved running all night, but not so much in these hills. They were very disrespectful. Those mountains loved me going down but hated me running up.

You know how I at least push to finish a half, but not this time or I would have injured myself. As it was, my massage therapist worked hard on my right knee and foot to get me back in operation for next week. Meanwhile, I'm comforted knowing my glutes have been firing, working, and fully functional.

Recap

The rolling hills made it the hardest marathon many have run. The Blue Ridge Marathon is more difficult but doesn't compare with rolling hills. This course didn't have one big hill, it has multiple rolling hills. Nothing was flat and therefore, there was no relief. There wasn't even a parking lot or grass. The main reason I signed up was because it was a night run.

I don't mean to say it wasn't enjoyable. It was, especially with the bands playing along the course, the weather was cooler than anticipated, and the views stunning. I also met friends from the 50 States who were running the half.

Then, of course, there was the opportunity to cheer others on. That #RunningServant with his loud voice, filled the valleys. One woman was struggling, so I asked her to look up and told her how to run up the hills. She needed to use the front part of her foot, not the back. Later she told me she followed my advice for the rest of the race and loved it. "Thank you so much. That made the difference."

Another lady was struggling with her breathing. I suggested that she should walk but not push it. "You are burning yourself out." Walking with her, I showed her a few tips. After she finished well ahead of my pace, she thanked me, "I run with a group, but nobody tells me anything like this. You have information that no one else seems to know about."

Returning Home

With West Virginia checked off my quest challenge, the next logical step was to go home. That would serve to be as difficult as running the race. I remember thinking, "hopefully I can finish that part of the quest, or I'll need a new lifestyle."

Remember, I flew into Clarksburg, West Virginia. The driver on that trip to the race warned me that there was no cab, Uber, or Lyft drivers that served that area. Never-the-less, he volunteered to return on his day off and drive me back to the airport. But when I called him, I learned that there was some sort of emergency where he couldn't keep his promise. Now it was up to me to find a ride to the airport.

I asked everyone, I mean every last individual for a ride but I came up empty. Quickly running out of options, I spotted the last runner crossing the finish line. As I cheered him on and we started talking, I posed the question. "Could I get a ride to the airport?"

"Sorry, I'm going to D.C."

"I can make that work" I said aloud, knowing that wasn't in the right direction but offered the best option.

"The only problem is that I need to take a nap."

He once was a drummer in a popular band that traveled the country, however, he wasn't happy, so he quit and found a job working for Appalachian Trail. He bought a van, fixed it up, and lives in it.

Today he is an avid ultra-marathon runner who came to crew for another runner. The last race he had run was a 250-mile race in May, so he wasn't intending to run this one. But when he learned of the eight-hour competition time, he couldn't resist. His goal was to run farther than any other runner in the eight hours allowed. By the end, one runner logged 51 miles, but he logged 53. Now, completely exhausted and needing to sleep, he wanted to help but knew his limits.

"Can you drive?"

"I've driven all over this country" I said, both confident and needing to get to an airport.

"Great, let's go."

We chatted while he drove the first 51 miles. Having a common connection in the music business, we discussed how difficult it is to make money making music.

I took the wheel, and he settled in for some much-needed sleep. I said I had driven this country, but that drive was one of the most treacherous ones I've ever made. The mountains were steep and the road winding. We drove to such heights that we literally were engulfed in the clouds. I talked my way through it, "Don't panic or you will drive off the edge. Stay focused and you will be fine."

As we approached the airport, after having changed drivers, I called United. Fortunately, they understood and changed my departure flight from West Virginia to Dulles. Without any further delay, he was off to the Appalachian trail where he checks on hikers, picks up trash, and maintains what is broken. I really enjoyed his company as much as I did the ride to the airport.

Looking Ahead

Remember I said in the last chapter that I was worried about Hawaii canceling? Well, they did. Once again, it's time to reschedule.

Meanwhile, the Mad Marathon in Burlington, Vermont asked me to pace on September 12. That is such a beautiful area with the picturesque lake with the Green Mountains nearby.

I learned that the Air Force Marathon on September 18 was canceled in Dayton, Oh. I didn't find another run to replace it but will keep working.

My schedule for now looks like

Sept. 12 - Vermont,

Sept. 14 - Chadron, NE,

Sept. 16 - South Dakota.

Sept 19 – North Dakota

We will see how long that schedule lasts.

That leaves several states that I still need to schedule, including Delaware, Maine, New Mexico, Alaska, and Ohio. If I can't find a race in those states, I will run them as soon as I can in 2022.

After I returned home to Houston, I was laying in bed trying to sleep. Suddenly I heard sirens on the beltway. I flashed back to the shooting, remembering how I was laying on the pavement. I could hear police sirens as they mistakenly flew past the store to another location five miles away. Then my mind shifted to the previous night, when I was standing next to the man with the starter pistol at the Moonlight run.

The next morning, I talked to my psychiatrist, who helps me to control my thinking. Unfortunately, at one point I had slept only about 4 hours and been up for 30 hours. Last night I was angry and irritated. That doesn't make relationships easy as most people don't understand it. Unfortunately, I don't really know that I'm being difficult until someone like my friend says something. I sleep on the floor because it is more comfortable. That's not a product of the shooting, I was doing that before. Last night, after sleeping only four hours out of eighty, I knew I had to sleep, so I prayed and finally God answered, providing some well needed sleep. I woke up but knew I needed to rest so I canceled my cross training with my nephew.

Having crossed the sleep challenge, I turned my attention to Vermont.

Festival Fun before, during and after the race.

Week 29: Mad Marathon – Vermont, Sept. 12

The Mad Marathon had a reputation for being bad. Not that it was run poorly but that with trails on the side of a mountain near Burlington Vermont, it promised to be an intense challenge. It might not surpass the Blue Ridge marathon, but it ranks right up there. Like so many other races, this race is usually run in July but was rescheduled due to covid.

I first learned of the Mad Marathon from Dorey, who I met online while trying to book my Hawaii race. She lives half the year in Hawaii and the other half in Vermont.

"If you are running all 50 states, you need to run the Mad Marathon."

"The what?"

"The Mad Marathon in Vermont. I'm the race director."

From there we hit it off immediately, she filled me in, and I was hooked.

My intent was to connect with Paul and Carey Miller for the OnPace Team in Hawaii. Through a number of connections, including a different Paul who is the race director for the Chicago Marathon, I was trying to volunteer to pace the race in Hawaii. I sent the email as requested but didn't hear back. At the same time, OnPace was trying to get into the Mad Marathon and asked me to pace it if they did. Finally, everything came together. I was given the responsibility of pacing the sweepers. Some might feel slighted by that, but I love the back of the back runners, especially those struggling to finish. After all, that's where I've been running lately.

Before the shooting, I set a goal to pace a race in all 50 states. Unfortunately, that didn't happen. The guy who accomplished that feat is Ken Fattmann, a humble guy who usually paces the 5-hour group. Although I was disappointed that I wasn't the one to set that record, I still enjoy pacing because it fits within my servant's calling.

The course was, as promised, difficult. In the following image, you can see the elevation increase and decrease. Notice how it begins at 800 feet and immediately drops approximately 100 feet before increasing over 300 and then dropping about 450 feet. That's quite a roller coaster in the first four miles. After four miles of smaller increases and decreases, look what happens about mile eight or nine. I needed to become a mountain sheep. That reputation was spot on, you must be crazy mad to run this marathon.

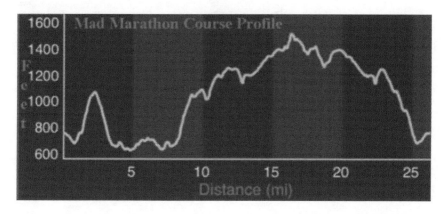

Remember, I'm supposed to be the pacer. That first uphill stretch proved troubling. The second incline at mile 8 or 9 provided a worse blow but I continued. Unfortunately, I fell behind but, determined to succeed, pushed to catch up to the 7-hour group. I'm learning that is usually when bad things happen. My glutes are like a spoiled, stubborn child. The more I push, the less they respond.

Notice on the map to the right, the half and full courses split at mile nine. The half marathon runners veer to the right to finish their last four miles. The full marathoners continue straight.

Despite my intentions, the incline in the middle of mile twelve proved too much. My back locked up and left me immobilized. Fortunately, I was near an aid station and a kind lady volunteer ran to her house nearby, grabbed a bag of ice, and delivered it to me. My back and glutes were so inflamed and in pain, that I was laying on the ground while everyone was running by. Other pacers, Jerry and Paul, saw me and stopped to ask how I was doing. They know that when a runner is lying on the ground reeling in pain, they have done all they could. There is no shame or judgment, simply empathy and encouragement. "Take your time.

OFFICIAL COURSE MAP

We'll call you when we get to finish" they called as they passed.

As soon as the ice delivered its therapy, the pain subsided enough that I could move. Slowly rising to my feet, I pointed myself in the right direction. It wasn't the direction I had originally planned but rather a shortcut to the finish. Yes, I surrendered. The course had defeated my quest to run the entirety.

Photo: "Ice, I need Ice Baby"

Those last 3.5 miles were bliss. You might not expect that given being previously paralyzed in pain. Return to the elevation map and you can see why. I was mostly running downhill where my glutes weren't needed. My quads took over and I felt great. I even took a video of myself running so I could appreciate the perfect form I was displaying. "This is what I used to feel like." Meanwhile, Carey came back to pace my sweeper corral.

Photo: On Pace is on point.

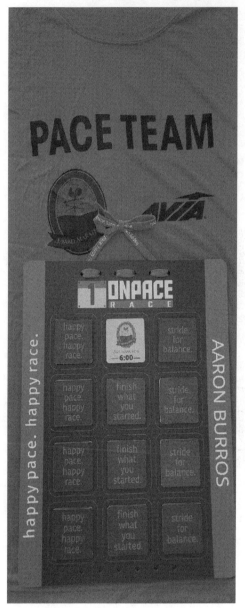

As much pain as I was in, I thought about finishing since the race allowed eight hours to finish. However, I knew no one would be out there for the full. Dorie even told me to finish, but I knew that the intense inclines and pushing too hard early in the race had taken their toll.

This race was very encouraging, despite the pain. This quest is about progress, and despite not finishing the Mad Marathon, I made progress. I only made it to mile 11 in the Blue Ridge race but finished the half on this difficult course. That's progress.

There is some consolation in knowing that you are not alone in the struggle. I met several people from Texas that were not used to the hills and struggled with the Mad Marathon. Then I also remembered what others had told me about the race. It lived up to its name and reputation. You must be mad to run those mountains.

Running the Mad Marathon reminds me that it was easier to drop 171 pounds, from 390 to 219 pounds and run ultramarathons than it has been running after being shot and carrying a bullet in my glute. Previously, when I got tired, I kept running. That's the way I'm wired. I need to push myself. But the difference is that I used to be able to work through my discomfort. Unfortunately, my physical and mental ability to run has diminished. Mentally, I used to be dialed in and could keep going. But now, when the immense pain strikes, my body says, "I'm done. I'm stopping." Like I mentioned earlier, it's like a spoiled child who throws a fit by sitting down on the floor and refuses to move.

Last two miles are literally downhill.

Looking Ahead

This is how my schedule looks at this point.
Sept. 18. Bismarck, North Dakota Marathon
Sept. 25. Akron, Ohio Marathon.
Oct. 3. Run Crazy Horse Marathon, South Dakota.

Oct. 9. Baltimore Running Festival, Maryland.

Oct. 11. Boston Marathon, Massachusetts.

Oct. 17. Des Moines, Iowa.

Oct. 24. Colorado Marathon

Oct. 28. New Mexico Running Day of the Dead in Las Cruces.

Meanwhile I'm considering running the Marine Corp Marathon in Virginia even though I have already done Virginia. It is a deferral form 2020.

I still need Hawaii and Alaska, as well as Rhode Island, Maine, Connecticut, Delaware, and Nebraska. Then there are the complications from rescheduling. Coastal Delaware Running Festival is the same time as Tunnel Hill in Illinois, and Rehoboth Beach, Delaware is the same day as Tennessee St. Jude's. I may need to switch Illinois to Nov 24 to knock out Delaware. I've already resolved that I will need to delay Rhode Island, Maine, and Connecticut to 2022 as part of the New England Challenge. I have Hawaii scheduled for December but am leery that they will cancel. If they do, I will run in June with Petra Montgomery who is finishing her 50-state challenge. At least, that's my plan.

Next week is my second try to run in North Dakota. Hopefully the airlines will cooperate this time.

Week 30: Bismarck Marathon, North Dakota, Sept. 18

I get nervous whenever I think of flying into a smaller, less populated state. It's not that I fear the people or being out of place. But struggling with the airlines traveling to Havre, Montana and having other flights canceled, I am not confident in the airlines. United canceled the previous flight forcing me to miss a scheduled North Dakota race. I'm also uneasy that, with the fall setting in and the weather getting colder, any cancellations push that state into 2022. This is a quest to run 50 marathons in 50 states in 50 weeks, not two years. I know I haven't finished all the races but I'm not going down without giving it my best shot. I just wish the airlines were more reliable during 2021.

As has become my habit, I drove to the Houston airport, parked, caught the shuttle, and made my way through security and waited to board. I was pleased to see my flight listed and even more pleased to see the plane and then be allowed to board. "Yes, this is actually going to happen." I was relieved when I landed in Bismarck.

But don't expect me to give United a lot of credit. I would have been running another race and checking off another state had they not canceled the previous race. Just because they finally did their job doesn't mean they deserve a lot of credit.

But the Bismarck Marathon does deserve a lot of credit. They have been running this race for thirty years and it shows in their professionalism. They start at 7:00 a.m. and allow six and a half hours to finish, closing the course at 1:30 p.m. As many races had done, the course was altered for Covid. The race wove through parks and towpaths with the last 2 miles on a paved bike path. It was a beautiful course lined with people in parks cheering enthusiastically. There wasn't much of a need to close streets since most of the course didn't include neighborhoods.

The course is the polar opposite of the Mad Marathon, flat except for a few small hills. It begins by following the Missouri River, crossing a bridge, looping around, and then back, returning to the start.

I met gentlemen Ken Lempka running his 24th marathon, we connected, and planned to run Pittsburgh together. Unfortunately, he fell shortly after the race and needed rotator cup surgery, so our plans are delayed. Ken Lempka thanked me saying "I wouldn't have finished Bismarck if it weren't for you. I'm proud to have been part of your 50-50 quest."

I started at the very end and was enjoying the run. I definitely enjoyed the plains and lack of mountains. That told my glutes to relax and enjoy the race.

At about mile eight or nice, I met a young lady from OnPace who also paced the half at the Mad Marathon. It is always fun when we can connect with people who have shared experiences. This young lady, Mattie Biertempfel, pictured below wearing a white shirt, was a teenager and intended to run the half marathon in Bismarck, but took a wrong turn, and ended up on the full marathon course. We met at mile eight or nine when she asked, "how do I get back to the half marathon course?"

"How do you feel?" I inquired.

"I feel good."

"Then keep going. If you have trained to run a half, you can run a full marathon." I encouraged her with a message many don't realize.

"Really?" She wondered.

"Congratulations, you are about to run your first full marathon." In the end, she prevailed and did what she didn't intend.

By the time I reached the halfway point, I was feeling good. You might find it hard to believe after reading the challenges in previous races. But I felt even better in the second half, even though it was a bit tougher with the rolling hills. The familiar push and pull of incline and decline, as long as it isn't too extreme, works well in alternating between my glutes and quads. It also felt great knowing that I was going to finish in six hours. That hadn't happened in a while, and I was excited.

But as you have come to expect, something was about to happen. And it did.

As I was enjoying my stride, I came alongside an older man and was about to pass him when he said, "Sure, pass me so I'll be the last one." I was just trying to catch up, not meaning to embarrass him. As we talked, I learned that he really didn't want to finish last. I mean, there was something more than just a little disappointment.

Ken was 78 and was frustrated that as he aged, he

was getting slower. While that might seem natural and predictable for most, that didn't set well with him. He was an experienced runner who wasn't accepting life's fate. As we talked, he expressed his determination to connect with his trainer and get stronger.

Maybe his frustration was a misdirected grief. Maybe the deeper reason was that his wife was suffering from dementia, and he was her caregiver. The one privilege he allows himself is to run marathons. As his sanctuary, he was determined to get stronger. It is all he has left of his former life.

Ken lives in Vancouver, Washington but has run the Bismarck Marathon before. For some reason, I got his name wrong in the beginning and kept calling him Ben. He was discouraged that he was not going to finish under six hours, in part because as a younger man he always finished under five. In his frustration, he had determined that if he couldn't finish under six hours, he was done running forever.

Thinly veiled in his aging frustration, Ken felt selfish by taking the time to run. He hated being away from his wife and wondered if he was breaking his wedding vows to stay with her in sickness and in health. I reassured him it wasn't and encouraged him to take care of himself. "You need time for yourself." Yet, I could see, he was unconvinced. His love and commitment to her was unwavering and the guilt of separation in her time of need was haunting. Then to finish last pushed the guilt and embarrassment over the top. How could he possibly continue running?

Instinctively, I determined that #RunningServant would help him. But that doesn't mean it was entirely selfless. After all, he had run the race before and knew the course. I didn't want to make the same mistake the young lady did in making a wrong turn.

I would've finished in 6:15 but because I stayed with my new friend Ben, I mean Ken, I finished in 7:13. But my time didn't matter. There was a higher purpose.

Yet I was conflicted. I was extremely pleased I ran well, was in very little pain, and finished. I appreciate that. I am also extremely pleased to help Ken. But I would have loved to have finished in 6:15. That would have shown my progress.

At one point, Ken had to stop. Determined to prove to myself I could have finished in the time allowed, I took a photo of when I would've finished. At 3 hours, I was at 12.4 miles. At 13.1, I was at 3:11.09. At 6 hours, I was at 22.62 miles. That left me 30 minutes to run the last 3.6 miles. I know I would have done that, but I just couldn't leave Ken out on the course. At 7 hours, I was at 25.74 miles. Unfortunately, Ken was in such tough shape that it took thirteen minutes to finish that last half mile.

How can anyone walk away from someone like Ken? He was so determined that he had spurts where he speeded up, and then panted. I took the role of trainer and coach, imploring him to slow down and pace himself. I kept talking to him and, as we approached the finish line, he confessed again that he hated finishing last. That was a clear signal for my role that day.

"Take it in" I said as I purposely backed off. This was his moment as I let him cross the finish ahead of me. I watched with satisfaction and concern as he crossed the finish line barely able to stand up and then promptly and violently throwing up. He was totally spent.

After composing himself, he thanked me, "I'm so glad you were with me."

I could only respond, "Wow, what a pleasure and honor." Ken's determination was inspirational.

Photo: Ken Lempka finishing strong.

Nearly 250 finished the marathon before us while another 450 ran the half and several hundred ran the 5k. In addition, several hundred joined together to show support for mental health concerns by walking one mile the day before.

Unlike many runs, this race needed only four full marathon pacers since this was a fast field, most runners finished under five hours. Ken and I were the only ones slower than that.

I feel great about my performance and especially good about what I could have done in the last half. I feel even better about helping Ken.

Inspirational People

After the race, I connected quickly with a couple that noticed and appreciated how I stayed with Ken. We traded numbers and they quickly offered to take me to the airport. I appreciated that kind gesture.

One guy was part of a running group and said something surprising. "We need more of you here." I hadn't really thought about it but had noticed that there were only two other black people. There was a black woman, and a Jamaican man. He used to drive trucks and when running a race in Bismarck met a man who offered him a job. He loves everything about Bismarck, except the cold. With over a thousand people running in the races over the weekend, it was odd to have only two blacks. I encouraged him to reach out and invite groups like the Black Runners.

I understand what that Jamaican man said. This weekend was filled with beautiful scenery, trails, and neighborhoods. I loved running the trails, across the bridges, and alongside the Missouri River.

This weekend rebuilt some trust in the airlines and in my running. It was what I needed.

Now it was time to go home. Not just to Houston, but to the land where I was born.

Week 31: Akron Ohio Marathon, Sept. 27

Going home. That's what I sense every time I return to Akron, Ohio. But sometimes going home isn't the return to the pristine, picket fenced neighborhood of the 1950s sitcom. Sometimes, maybe too often, it is the return to the grimy ghosts of greed and laziness.

There is an ugly underbelly to the running world that is driven by the quest for money. Instead of doing things the right and honorable way, they cut corners, choosing to do what is easy rather than what is right for the runner. Too many races, as we saw during the pandemic, promise but don't deliver. How many races were promised to run live and charged the in-person fee but then went virtual? How many offered deferments that were not in the runner's best interest?

I apologize if the tone of this chapter is not the upbeat one you expected for going to run in the town of my birth. Maybe that is appropriate for a man who has sixteen siblings and has longed for family support but found little. Maybe that is the angst from being promised a loaf and receiving a stone. Maybe it is magnified by the PTSD.

It really is a simple thing and an easy solution. But the problem occurs more than you would expect. After all, it's just a shirt. But when it happens time after time, there becomes a tipping point.

You have read earlier that I need at least a 2XL if not a 3XL shirt. So, I pay extra at registration for the bigger sizes. I was really looking forward to the half zip offered by the Akron Marathon. So, you can imagine my frustration when I arrived to find they had given it away to someone else who wanted a bigger size but didn't pay for it.

This hit me hard. Like I said before, maybe it was the PTSD kicking in. That distrust was amplified during the shooting. While I won't go into details, the very organization I was trying to protect turned against me. Family members who are supposed to love and support me, cast doubt on my story. Some even claimed I was involved in the crime. Then to have them doubt my pain and dismiss my injuries magnifies my distrust. You see, the PTSD isn't remedied by simply thinking positive thoughts. No, PTSD is a serious and complicated brain and body reaction to a horrible trauma. I can't simply "get over it" or "let it go." I've tried many times and will continue to work through the process. If I had my choice, I would be healed of this illness. I don't like what it does to me.

As I stood at the packet pickup, all of that history came crashing down. Simply stated, I had an emotional breakdown. It is similar to what happens when the PTSD hits me when running. I lose control of my emotions, much like using an ax to shatter the glass of a large aquarium. That dam breaks and there is no way to retain the water.

All I could do was to walk over and sit down. With my head in my hands, I couldn't see beyond the moment. I no longer wanted to run or serve. It was so bad that I decided to forfeit running and catch the first plane back to Houston. I no longer cared about the race.

To make matters worse, I had supported Akron Children's hospital, the benefactor of the race. In my PTSD state, all I could think was that these companies don't care about me or doing what is right. All they care about is doing what is convenient and easy. When the volunteer said she would take my name and see what she could do, I didn't doubt her sincerity but knew that's where it would end. Being from Texas, this isn't my first rodeo.

I flashed back to the 2019 London Marathon in 2019. I never did get that shirt. Then the other races, where the same thing happened, flashed through my mind. I couldn't get the distrust out of my mind. "They promised to order one for me, but I never received it. I never even received an apology." It was like a rapidly repeating loop of Groundhog Day over and over and over. All I could do was sit there with my head in my hands.

Fortunately, there was a kind soul who understood. Her husband had run the Burning River 100, from Cleveland to Akron in July. Hearing the situation unfold, she offered me her husband's 2XL shirt that he had received at registration. He already had a half zip and was glad to offer it. While I was pleased to get what is rightfully due me, I don't want to create an unnecessary conflict. I want them to do what was right the first time and avoid this disappointing situation.

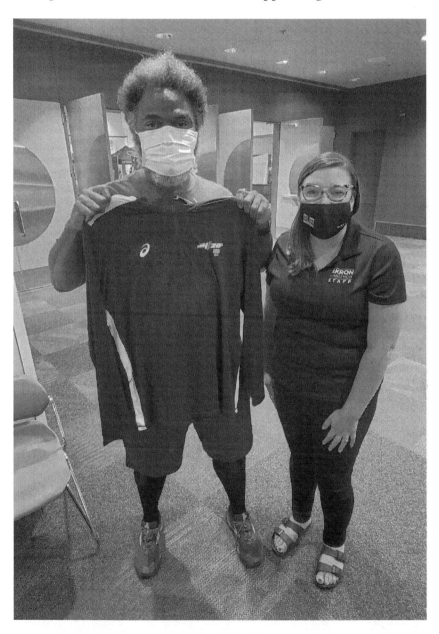

"Thank you. That is very generous" I said, extremely humbled that another runner gave up their half zip for me. They shouldn't have to do that.

I recognize that many companies are using clothing vendors from overseas and that sizes can run smaller. That creates requests for exchanges. I get that but that doesn't excuse giving away shirts specially ordered by runners who are charged extra.

It comes back to greed. The Rock n Roll run is owned by Iron Man. They were advertising the San Francisco Rock n Roll run in 2020 or 2021 and then declared it would be a virtual race. It turns out they hadn't even pulled the permits for the race. In other words, they had no intention of running an in-person race when they advertised and accepted registrations. They deceived the runners. That is not simply wrong, that is criminal. No wonder they are being sued.

Darin, who gave his quarter zip, along with his wife, brought it to me while I was still sitting with my head in my hands. Up to that point, I was irritated and maybe even angry. But when he offered it, I started crying uncontrollably. Remember, the PTSD drives this truck. I can't even steer it or put the brakes on. That's when I realized how much I was still suffering physically and emotionally. It may just be just a cheap race shirt, but this is a part of everything I have gone through and how I have been treated. In that PTSD state, I felt like my life didn't matter. It was as if I was fighting that thug while he was telling his buddy to kill me. I didn't matter to them. I didn't matter to the corporation I worked for. It didn't matter to my family. It didn't matter enough for a race to deliver a shirt that I had paid for.

Up until this moment, I hadn't realized the entire impact of the shooting and this quest. Although I had recently learned what my physical body needed, I didn't realize how emotionally fragile I was. I get it. This is just a cheap running shirt. It is nothing that should ruin my life. But emotions are not logical. Almost dying from being shot five times takes a heavy toll on the emotions. It creates a deep seeded terror that makes trusting anyone for anything very tenuous. There is some evidence that PTSD becomes a muscle memory that responds unconsciously.

When I pulled himself back together, the #RunningServant reappeared, a smile came to my face, and a laugh from my lungs. I quickly pulled out my phone.

"Let's get a photo." Together, the three of us posed for a selfie. I treasure that photo.

The Run

The run itself went extremely well. Over 10,000 runners ran the half and full. As with many bigger races, we started in waves, and as was becoming my new practice, I was in one of the last corrals, #11. Given that they release a new wave every five minutes, it was close to an hour before I crossed the start line. To my surprise, there were still quite a few people that started behind me.

Start Corral 11 and back

The marathon was run downtown Akron, with an altered course due to covid and a huge bike ride. To complicate matters, there was also a biking event at the same time, although we never crossed paths.

We ran out and back for the first 4-mile loop before crossing a nice bridge and enjoying a beautiful sunrise. The timing for me turned out to be perfect as the sun rose while I was on the bridge. That is one of the beautiful results from being slow. The elite runners didn't see that sunrise from the bridge.

Then we ran back into downtown where the terrain shifted from flat to hilly. We ran to the west side for another out and back, separating from the half marathoners who ran along a canal towpath.

Akron, Ohio Canal Towpath

I had fully intended to do the full marathon, but a family commitment required I cut the race short. My daughter was a student at Prairie View A&M and had recently joined the cheerleading squad. While any proud papa would want to be there, this was important for another reason. My relationship with her has been strained since the shooting. I recognized recently that I needed to prioritize time with her and show my support. When I learned that she was named to the cheer squad and had a game near Houston, I knew what I had to do. Prior to picking up my race packet, I went to the help desk and asked if I could drop down to the half before check in. They told me to get the full marathon registration, and if I wanted to drop to half, just run with half at the split. They promised to make note of it. "Ok, cool." That meant I didn't have to decide until I approached the full and half split on the course. But I didn't need to wait to decide. I knew with the time crunch; I would only run the half marathon. This proud papa couldn't resist an opportunity to see her cheer in her first game. So, I cut my run short to fly back to Houston.

Akron is known for their hills, so I was looking forward to running down them. I had hoped the finish would be downhill or slightly flat. That was another disappointment. They put the finish line at the top of a hill after an incline of 5% over the last half a mile. No one was running that beast. Everyone was walking and I had to wonder, "Who does this?" Evidently the same person who gave away my shirt planned the course.

Despite the pre-race meltdown, I ran great. While I usually do some version of a run/walk, this time I ran the first twelve miles at a 13:00 pace without walking. Even during the last stretch with the hills, my time only slowed to 14.38 per mile. That is progress!

Enjoying time with My Daughter, Calah at the Texas State Fair.

I used this race as a test for Boston, which is coming up fast. I was seeing how I could keep my glutes strong enough to finish in the time allowed. I believe I will be able to finish in under six hours. If my glutes decide to support me, I expect to finish in about five and a half hours. I used the Akron Marathon to figure out the best combination of running and walking. Bismarck didn't have hills and, without helping Ken, would've finished in 6:15. Boston has a hard 6-hour cutoff and is projected to be 70 degrees on October 11. The charity runners don't

start until 11 so I'll be running in the middle of the day. If it gets too hot, I'll run without a shirt. I hope that doesn't cause too many women to faint.

Take Away

Going home seems like it is always a mix of emotions for many people. We have the highs and then something happens to take us to new lows. Mine started with the lows and ended on a high note, not just by finishing at the top of a hill. (Who designs a course that way?)

I do love coming back to Akron. The city is so beautiful. One surprise was that I got to see Captain America on the bridge. To make it even better, Captain American gave me a shout out for my birthday. Isn't that cool?

Photo: Captain America on crowd control.

But I am disappointed that I didn't have the Running Servant in this race. The PTSD put me in a funk at registration over that stupid half zip and I couldn't break free. That's not like me. I love to be the "Mouth from the South" and raise the energy everywhere I go. I don't like being down in the dumps. I was pleasant and spoke to people but didn't live up to the calling of the running servant.

Looking Ahead

I'm looking forward to running the Crazy Horse Marathon in South Dakota. One of the things I'm anticipating is seeing Mt.

Rushmore for the first time. This quest is great for meeting great people and seeing the country. As I have worked on the logistics, I plan on flying into Rapid City and looking for a ride. That's 47 miles and takes over an hour. I learned from friends who just ran a race out there and rental cars were $400 a day. That's too rich for me. As with many of these more remote locations, Uber will take you out, but it is tough to find one to get back to the airport.

My plan is to continue on to the Run Colorado Marathon in Denver before working my way south to the Running of the Dead in New Mexico. I'm reconsidering New Mexico. The race is a 1.1 mile out and back then loop that is a pretty boring track. The upside is that I'll be able to rest and then continue running. Like a trail run, they allow 24 hours to run it. My strategy is to run quarters or 5Ks, rest, and then run another. That will take the stress off my glutes, making it an easy trail run.

After I returned home, the Akron Marathon sent out a survey. One of the questions asks, "Is there anything else you would like to share?" I simply wrote, "Keep the 3XL shirts under lock and key. Assign someone to watch them."

With Akron behind me, I looked to the west. Like the carving of Crazy Horse, this quest was a work in progress. It's time for the next step.

Week 32: Run Crazy Horse, South Dakota, Oct. 4

What a difference a week can make. Last week I was returning home and this week I was traveling to a place I had never been before. On the top of my list was seeing Mt. Rushmore for the first time.

"Can you take me by Mt. Rushmore?" I asked my Uber driver as soon as I met him.

"Of course. We will drive right by it on the way to your hotel."

Driving southwest on the edge of Rapid City, we entered the Black Hills and saw signs for Keystone and Mt. Rushmore. I was enjoying the hills, which are really mountains. I don't know who named them, but they have the tallest peak east of the Rocky Mountains. We entered Keystone, an old mining town that now caters to tourists. Now quiet with the tourist season ending at Labor Day, I started to notice how Mt. Rushmore was the theme. Then, as we left town, we faced a steep incline that soon took us above the trees to provide a grand vista.

Then I saw it. Like a little kid anxious to see the surprise, I saw a glimpse of the four presidents carved in granite. But they disappeared

as the road followed the contour of the mountain. Not to be disappointed, the road turned again with an even better view. With my eyes wide open, and probably my mouth as well, the driver slowed and pulled to the shoulder of the road, directly in front of the  monument. I was immediately impressed since I hadn't seen it except for history books. We didn't drive into the parking lot because we could see it from the road. I got out for a better view, and of course, a photo.

It was surreal. You see something like this so many times on tv, in the movies, or in advertising, but when you see it in person, it comes to life. Somehow, I felt like I became a part of history that day standing alongside the road.

My hotel was a few miles away, at the Palmer Gulch KOA campground and lodge. It sits about halfway between Mt. Rushmore and Hill City, where the race would be finishing. Palmer Gulch KOA looks like a little city with cabins, campgrounds, and an RV section. Normally packed with tourists during the summer, this was a popular place for runners this weekend. Many enjoyed horseback riding and hiking in the surrounding mountains.

Hill City is a town with only about 900 residents but swells during the Memorial Day to Labor Day tourist season. The feature attraction of the town is an 1880 train that runs from Hill City through a historic ten-mile route in the central Black Hills to Keystone, on the other side of Mt. Rushmore. With restored period locomotives and cars, the ride turned back the clock while appreciating the beautiful and peaceful views. I can imagine this ride would be crowded at the height of the tourist season. I was exhausted but still didn't sleep at night. Oddly enough, I can sleep on an airplane, in part because the air pressure, cabin, buzzing, and everything else relaxes me. Maybe I need to turn my apartment into an airplane. Now that's a thought.

One of the reasons I stayed at the Palmer Gulch Resort is that the race provided school buses to transport us to and from the race. Since Crazy Horse is not in town, located between Custer on the south to Hill City on the north, everyone needed transportation to the start of the race. Return transportation left Hill City beginning at 10 and ending at 2:00.

The Crazy Horse Marathon was started by Jerry Dunn, an ultra-marathoner and begins at the Crazy Horse Memorial near Custer in the southern Black Hills of South Dakota.

The weather during the first week of October is definitely turning past summer and deep into fall at this elevation exceeding 5,000 feet. The air was brisk that first night, dipping to 32 degrees but warmed to a perfect 50 degrees to start the race and finish at 72. But standing in the shadow of another giant monument in the making, Crazy Horse, it was cold yet impressive. The native American, Lakota Sioux venture refused any government funds and is slowly carving away the rock to reveal the head and outline of their great leader, Crazy Horse sitting atop his horse. It warms my heart to see such honor being bestowed but I was wondering if I should've brought gloves. But then I came to my senses and realized that I would need them after about two and a half miles.

Arriving early, I had a few minutes to look around the Crazy Horse Memorial. I was intrigued that if I donated, I could take home a rock from the carving. I liked that idea, both donating and getting a rock. I was seriously considering which one to take from the bin sitting on the ground. Again, coming to my senses, I started to wonder. "Can I get this through security? Or would they think I was stealing Crazy Horse?" I decided my carry-on didn't need any more weight.

Photo: Model of the Crazy Horse Monument

I've noticed since the beginning of this quest that races attract some very nice people that I want to stay connected with long after the race. In this race, just prior to the start, I met Maria and Dan Kasher, a wonderful couple from Chicago.

Finisher **Certificate**

Congratulations

Maria Kasher

on completing the

2021 Run Crazy Horse Marathon
Marathon

84		
Overall Place		
30	6:28:17	Timing Serv
Gender Place	Time	
6		P

The Course

I chose this race because it is a point-to-point course, beginning at the Visitor's Center at Crazy Horse Memorial. For the first 3 miles, we run within their Memorial Grounds on both paved and gravel roads. We actually run to the base of the carving and then turn around, spending most of the race on a trail named for a former governor, George Mickelson. By mile 3 we head south to Custer in a steady uphill climb to the town of Custer, yes, named after the former general who died at Little Bighorn in southeastern Montana. Turning around, we get to the fast part of the race. By mile 15, the entire last half is a steady downhill run to main street Hill City.

As you can tell from the description, most of this is downhill, therefore it should be fast. It was. The lead marathoner was at mile 14 at 1 hour 35 minutes on his way to a sub-3-hour run. It didn't look like we would need the seven-hour limit.

I was having a great time, in part because I had a good couple of days seeing the sights. I was taking photos and laughing it up, allowing the #RunningServant to do his thing. That's when I met George, a big guy that kind of looks like me. He said, "Your taking pictures and everything is turning this into a fun run. Everyone else is simply running, turning around, and going back up. Not you." I couldn't resist and asked George to pose for a photo together. He was a volunteer that helped make the race fun.

Photo: With George

Since we were running mostly on the trail, they didn't close many roads. The only cops they had were at the Crazy Horse Memorial, in Custer, and then at Hill City. All other street crossings had volunteers.

The Run

I knew that if I could do those first five miles to the turnaround in Custer, the rest would be pure fun running downhill. But that first section was tough. Actually, it was a relentless, demanding run with mostly a long incline. You know I love to run hills, but I really needed them to be more rolling. 'Sorry if that sounds picky.

By mile five the incline was reminding me that I still had a bullet in my butt as my glutes were on fire. After the turnaround in Custer, the pain eased, and I ran a sub 7-minute mile returning toward the Crazy Horse memorial. But then I had another tough incline. I liked running the trail because it went down for 6 miles, to mile 10, but had to turn around and do 6 miles coming back. I decided quickly to simply walk back up. I tried trotting for a quarter mile but couldn't do that. By mile 11, I could only walk for the next 4 miles.

While I loved the people, scenery, and running, I was becoming irritated that they didn't shut the trail down for the marathon. That meant we encountered a ton of bikers riding from Crazy Horse to Hill City. Later I learned that there were several close calls between bikers not wanting to share the trail with the runners. There were several near accidents and the bikers complained to the authorities about the marathon runners. That reminded me of the truckers in the Utah run.

With the early inclines in the race, I knew prior to the race that I would need to see how I felt when I returned from the turnaround and approached the Crazy Horse memorial. At mile 15, my leg buckled. Unfortunately, that is about the point where the eleven-mile downhill run begins. Had I not had Baltimore and Boston in the next week, I might have pushed through to finish. But also realizing my stabilizer muscles were fading, I called it a day.

That disappointed me because I was on pace to finish in six hours. Since they didn't have an official sag wagon, I asked one of the volunteers who graciously drove me to the finish line.

You only needed to look at this guy and you knew he was something else. He was dressed in a running outfit that looked like a tux. We bonded immediately, exchanged contact information, and had a number of laughs. I learned he ran marathons and, in one year, he ran 189 races. He even has a page on Wikipedia. Now retired, he travels the world looking for runs and people to run with. At one point he spent five months in El Salvador. I was envious, especially as he prepared to run the 100th Boston Marathon. He ran the course every day for 25 days and officially for the 26th day. Had I not been shot, I could have imagined running with him. He now splits his time between the Black Hills and Florida. It turns out that between 1995 and 2000, he set up several runs in the area.

Photo: Jerry Dunn, America's Marathon Man
(Photo by Mark Warren)

Instead of a sag wagon, they had sweeper bikers. I met one lady who said that she loved being at the back because the lead bikers are just riding to keep a pace, running with their ability. But those at the back are running with their hearts. I thanked her, sensing a kindred spirit, and then shared some of my story as I ran. "That's amazing that you are out here" she replied. While she definitely wanted me to finish, she understood when I weakened. That's when she got off her bike and walked with me. What a kind gesture. Her husband, who had paced the half, joined us, and helped me when I couldn't go any farther.

I enjoyed meeting Maria Kasher who is running #31 on her 50-state marathon challenge. Her friend, Renetta Blend has already completed her 50-state half marathon challenge and another 50-state marathon challenge. She is also a Double Agent for the Marathon Maniacs which means she has run three marathons and three half marathons in ninety days.

The people were phenomenal at this run. That includes the volunteers, runners, town, and everyone involved. I met a gentleman and his wife who asked what I was doing. I told Him I was running to raise funds for St. Jude's. They responded, "We support St. Jude's." He quickly gave me a $100 donation, telling me, "God brought me to you."

Two anonymous donors each gave $1250. A third one gave $50. For that race, I will exceed the donation requirement.

It was nice to have people recognize me from the Pine Line marathon in Wisconsin. (Remember, the race with the gun range.) I always enjoy taking photos with the ladies who treat me like I was famous.

Then there was Jake, who used to do some dangerous job but retired to move to Hill City and become a barber. After the race, I paid him a visit at Jake's Barbershop where he cleaned up my hairline and beard freehand. That is a rarity and very cool.

I was pleased to find that they had the chocolate milk on ice, like it should be.

I enjoyed this run. On the return to the airport, I took a last look at Mt. Rushmore and then headed home.

Photo: My new friend that served as a bike sweeper.

Returning Home

Arriving home, I always look forward to a good massage. Actually, I usually get two to keep my muscles happy. Fortunately, I have a massage therapist I can trust.

Or at least, I used to. But suddenly she didn't seem to hold up her end of the agreement. Earlier I had worked with her to establish a game plan for Boston. Since she was so important to my running, I was going to pay for her time to fly her to Boston. I was paying for her hotel, tickets to the race, and food. Critical to this agreement was that we have regular sessions every Monday. But then, without notice, she decided she was taking Mondays off.

"What's up with that?"

I sought answers but it was apparent that my plans and needs didn't matter to her. For the first couple of weeks, I found a replacement. As time progressed and Boston was getting closer, I realized I wasn't her priority. So, I sent her a text terminating our agreement, canceling the flight and hotel reservations. She is great at what she does but if she isn't doing it when I need it, it doesn't benefit me.

With South Dakota done, It's on to the big weekend.

Week 33: Baltimore Marathon, Maryland, Oct. 9

This is the weekend I've been training for. That may sound strange reading a book about a quest to run 50 marathons in 50 states in 50 weeks. You might think that running every state is more than a warmup to running Boston and earning my fifth star for the world majors. But they all work together. My quest is to return to my former running performance, or at least as close as I can get. To me, finishing Boston means I have made incredible progress. That's why this is so important.

My plan is to run Baltimore on Saturday and fly to Boston to be there to run on Monday. That was the plan.

My mother and two of my brothers were accompanying me to the airport, on their way to Akron for the funeral of a cousin. Meanwhile, I was headed to Baltimore when my brother received a call that his son's vehicle was found in Galveston with keys, wallet, and other personal belongings. No one has heard from him. During the initial investigation, police found his phone thanks to a friend using technology to locate it. I had sick feeling in pit of my stomach because I-45 from Dallas to Galveston is known as "Murderer's Row." Whenever someone goes missing, the chances of surviving are very slim. I was numb with fear.

Baltimore

Arriving in Baltimore was the medicine I needed. They showered me with love. Corrigan Sports adopted me as a runner and showered me with love. They loved my story and shared it with so many different people and media contacts in Pittsburgh and at CNN. I enjoyed an interview with Baltimore WBAL TV.

Then, as if it were manna from heaven, I found a fantastic massage therapist before the run. I had a couple to choose from and went with a yoga lady. Wow, what a great massage. I felt 500% better.

I was lounging at my hotel, basking in the glow of the massage, when I wandered over to an Under Armour store. Being a runner, I am always looking for new clothing. I was taking a photo of something that caught my eye when I heard a commotion. I looked and saw a standoff between two black guys. Since I already had my phone up and taking photos, I instinctively switched to video and started recording it.

Suddenly, I realized I was in the midst of a possible shooting situation. One guy wearing a hoodie, rode his bike recklessly between a man and a woman, with hand in his pocket, and threatening to shoot people. The other guy turned out to be an off-duty cop who pulled his service weapon and his badge. Recognizing the error of his ways, the hoodie bike rider relents and retracts his hand, out of his hoodie and puts his hands up.

Not wanting to escalate the situation, the cop tells the bike rider to go on his way. "Watch what you are doing."

The bike rider recognizes the forgiving nature of the cop and attempts to give the cop a fist bump. The cop shrugs him off by declining the offer. That doesn't sit well with the bike rider, who got mad, and started making threats. The cop showed some amazing restraint, in part because his wife is with him. Seeing this, I thought I could help. Being a big guy and black, I thought the guy might listen to me. Besides, this is in the popular inner harbor with many families around.

I looked at the bike rider and said, "You need to apologize and leave."

That didn't sit well with the bike rider who started threatening me. "You snitch," he shouted as he rode away. I don't like being called names but if it defused the situation, I'm happy to serve.

With the matter appearing to be settled, I went to Under Armour to see if I could buy a t-shirt. As I'm walking up the steps to enter the store, this same bicycle riding gun toting guy reappears and threatens me.

"You better leave, or I'll call the cops."

"You are a snitch. You are going to die" the guy counters.

"I've been shot several times," I said, sharing my secret.

The guy reaches in his hoodie to retrieve his gun.

"Do what you have to do" I said as I took a step towards him.

The guy took his hand out of his hoodie pouch, stepped back, got on his bike, and rode away.

Suddenly an officer exits the Under Armor store, identifying himself as a federal police officer, approaches me. "Are you ok?"

I provided the details to him.

It turned out that the second cop had a previous encounter with the guy. Explaining the situation, the bicycle riding guy claimed to have a gun with seven extra clips, intending to shoot people that day.

"You didn't think he was serious?" I wondered aloud. "It is people like you that caused me to be shot several times in a workplace shooting."

"I didn't know he was serious." The cop tried to explain, but his words were lost on me. "It might have been a BB gun."

"I don't care. If someone makes that claim in a city with a big concert, marathon, tattoo convention, and an NFL game all in one weekend, you need to take it seriously. After all, why are you here?"

That's when I took out my phone and showed the video of the guy threatening a police officer shortly before.

Photo: The Suspect with backpack, the officer and wife outside Under Armor's corporate store, Inner Harbor.

Then a woman working security near the harbor returned from lunch and approached us. The federal cop informs her of what has just happened.

"I've had complaints about this guy," she reveals.

"And you didn't take him seriously?" I ask.

Earlier, while I was talking to the security officer and a tactical officer, people continued to come up telling of a guy riding a bike threatening to shoot them in the head. But the federal office kept bragging how he was a federal cop like that was supposed to make his inaction right. He insisted that they needed to talk to the local police force. I figured he must have been close to retirement and didn't want to jeopardize his pension by getting involved in a dangerous situation.

By now, this is attracting attention from a tactical officer who contacts Baltimore Police. Having told my story, I went back to the hotel.

Shortly after, a Baltimore Police Officer calls and asks me to send him the video I had of the guy. A few minutes later, sitting in my hotel room watching television, I saw a report with the police chief asking the public for help with any information of a suspect going around randomly shooting innocent victims, and that the four people had already been shot and transported to local area hospitals. I text the Baltimore cop. "This could've been prevented."

They didn't even detain him when they encountered him. They just thought he was high. Never mind he told the federal officer he had a gun with extra clips and was threatening to shoot people. You don't take that stuff lightly.

As we were lining up for the marathon and I was doing the interview, there were several officers, tactical teams, swat personnel, canine squads, as well as bicycle cops looking for the gun toting bicycle riding guy.

As the race was about to start, I was standing alone with a guy and his wife when they asked, "Are you the guy we saw on the news?" It is nice to be noticed for something good. Can we get a photo with you?" Obliging, he continued, "I'm glad to have met you.

The Race

With all the commotion, I had to remind myself that I had a race to run.

When I run, I like to keep my shoes loose until it is time to run. So, when it is time to get into my corral, I sit down and tie my shoes. I saw a chair and a lady standing beside it.

"Can I sit down and tie my shoes?"

"Sure" she replies hesitantly. "Are you the guy I saw interviewed on the program?"

"What program" I said, playing dumb.

"I read your story" she counters, quickly displaying the paper.

Photo: with Ester Weir of Elkridge, MD.

"You got me. Yes, I'm the guy."

She was a teacher from Baltimore who was there to run her first marathon. To say she was nervous was an understatement. "I can't run like I used to." Trying to calm her, I offered a few tips and congratulated her on her courage to run.

Fortunately, she had a friend there to cheer her on. I shared my story and a lady sitting nearby who was listening in, quickly chimed in, "It's true." As I shared, my story struck a nerve with the runner to the point she was in tears. Another asked for my autograph.

You know that is my first marathon autograph. In return, I asked them to look up #RunningServant on social media.

I also met a man with a 10-year-old daughter who was running the 5K. It is always cool to see young people getting into the sport and being supported by their parents. It is a great way to build a great relationship.

The media coverage from the tv interview and Corrigan Sports created a buzz as I ran through ghettos going to the zoo. People kept shouting, "I saw you on the news." I stopped to take photos several times before realizing, "I can't continue this, or I won't ever finish."

I met one guy whose friends told him he didn't need to train that hard. So, he only ran an Army 10 miler and ran no farther than thirteen miles. He didn't bother with hill training. To make matters worse, he ate all the wrong things just before the marathon started, including beef

jerky, and heavy foods. This guy was writing a book for failing in a race.

Photo: These sweet ladies are trying to marry me off.

It turns out his name is Marques Ken, a politician seeking office in Baltimore's District 44. Together, we laughed and had a good time, exchanged information, and I offered to train him for next year. One of the things I promised him is that I would teach him how to run up hills. In his ignorant state, he was trying to sprint up the hills, leaning in, and pushing off his heels. That's not the way to do it. You run on your toes and use your calves to go uphill. That is needed to drive the knee up and use the glutes.

Along the way I was coaching whoever wanted help. One woman said, "I didn't know the Baltimore 10K offered coaching on the course." I laughed, knowing this wasn't an official offering.

I really enjoyed that last incline before the split. We had so much fun and even had people dancing. Maybe I should have been a DJ.

Then there was this young guy in his shorts standing alongside the course. He was built and displayed his cut physique. I stopped and told him to come dance with me. Together we were Chip and Dale cutting the rug right there on that pavement. A lady up the hill joined in, going low and I followed. Then she shouts, "Get back on the course. This was a lot of fun." I tell you that there were a lot of people jamming with me.

One elderly lady screamed from the porch that she saw me on the news. I stopped and took a photo with her, and said, "My auntie has been looking for a wife for me. Maybe you are the one." She was happy and posed quickly for a selfie with me. I forwarded that photo later to the lady with the news.

Maybe that is why, by the time I came to the split with the 5K course, I was already at the back of the pack and five minutes behind the slowest marathon runners. I had to forget my run/walk sequence and just ran just to catch up. But as I crossed a street at a traffic light, my legs cramped up. I made my way to the curb where a spectator tried to help me. Both calf muscles needed what I call an "eagle beat" where someone pushes their finger into it. I was able to persuade a guy to help me and then talk him through the process, ensuring he wasn't hurting me. That got him up on my feet but by that time, the sag wagon was right behind me.

"What do you want to do?"

"I want to at least finish the half."

I felt I was having a good race, setting a great pace, feeling the rhythm of the rolling hills. The guy helping me promised to help me get to half. I even ran ahead to see if I could find salt tablets but was unsuccessful, however, I did find some chicken broth at an aid station. They added, "Drink Gatorade too." Not being an underachiever, he drank a bottle and a half. By the time we reached mile 13, I was too late to finish in the seven hours allowed.

Photo: Marques Dent of Baltimore, MD, and I completed the first half and walked back to the finish chute.

The finish line coordinator appreciated my contribution and offered me a full marathon medal.

"I can't do that. I didn't finish."

"I'll make you a deal. I will give you a full marathon medal, but you will owe me half next year since you did half this year."

He definitely wants me to come back.

Progress

I am so grateful for all of these people. The race weekend started off looking like another PTSD disaster but ended up being a big celebration. How did that happen?

I handled the shooter situation well. One of the questions my doctor asks is, "How would you respond in another shooting?" I didn't

291

know until that day in the Under Armour store. I got involved so nobody would be shot. Even then the people in authority wouldn't listen to me. him. Had I not had the video, they wouldn't have taken him seriously. That still bothers me.

I look back and recognize I'm healing because I processed the situation in a healthy manner. It does bother me that I never did learn if anyone died or if he was ever caught. However, the important part for me was that the PTSD didn't appear. That is progress.

On a sour note, I learned that my nephew was indeed murdered. They found his body near Tipi Island in Galveston. However, the investigation is still ongoing.

There have been too many deaths in my family this year.

With Maryland checked off my quest, I turned to the biggest target of the year, the Boston Marathon.

With Barry Bieler of Annville, PA

Week 34: Boston Marathon, Massachusetts, Oct. 13

The very mention of the Boston Marathon strikes a chord in every runner. It is the world's oldest and, therefore, the granddaddy of all annual marathons. I was about to participate in the 124th running of this legendary race.

The Boston Marathon is the pinnacle for the elite runner, seeking to compete with the world's best, and be named, "Boston Marathon Winner." It is also the ultimate goal of recreational runners as they train diligently to become a "Boston Qualifier." The standards are high, competition intense, and the satisfaction immense. Then there are those who cannot dream of qualifying but want to run. I'm in that group now. Boston provides an opportunity to run by raising funds for charities. Everyone in this last group is seeking to be a "Boston Marathon Finisher."

Running to support charities is a wonderful way to run in the world majors. You still must finish in the time allotted, but the joy of running and raising funds for a worthwhile cause is doubly fun. I've run for several charities including Hale Education in Boston, St. Jude's for my 50-50-50 challenge, and Team For Kids for Berlin, Chicago and New York Marathons.

While Boston has been my focus in earning my fifth star for the six world major marathons, I approached this race with some misgiving. You see, the Boston Athletic Association made a very questionable decision during the pandemic. I was ready to run in 2020 having raised the required $8,000 for Hale Education. Unfortunately, the BAA changed the race from an in-person run to a virtual race due to covid. I understand that.

But when the BAA canceled the 2020 race, qualifying runners were given refunds without an additional charge. I understand that. However, that wasn't the case with those of us running for charity. We were required to raise another $8,000. I not only don't understand that decision, but I also don't think that was right. But I went to work and raised the funds again.

I wanted to look forward to Boston like the other runners do. To do that, I had to put that out of my mind and focus on the good things that were about to happen.

A Short Flight?

Unfortunately, just making the short trip from Baltimore to Boston would prove to be a monumental task. As you read earlier, air travel in 2021 was problematic with airlines struggling with staffing shortages. I was scheduled to leave at 6:20 a.m. Sunday morning to run the Monday race, flying on Southwest Airlines for less than an hour. I was preparing to board the flight when I received notification that the flight was canceled. Southwest claimed it was due to the inclement weather near Atlanta that caused a ripple effect throughout the system. In a follow-up notification, they blamed the FAA for air traffic problems. A few days later, we learned that there was a shortage of pilots and flight attendants that caused Southwest to cancel more than 2,200 flights.

The reason didn't matter as much as the fact that I needed to find a flight quickly to make the race.

By this point in the challenge, I was pretty savvy in rebooking flights. Working my phone, I avoided the long lines in the airport waiting to talk to a representative. Knowing I only had to go from Baltimore to Boston, I was hoping there was an easy fix. Unfortunately, with the massive cancellations almost everyone that was going anywhere was affected, as indicated by a two hour wait in line just to speak to a representative at the airport. Meanwhile, I was on the phone and finally heard back, but the news wasn't good. They couldn't get me to Boston until Tuesday. That wouldn't work. I persisted in my pursuit, asking them to continue looking. They finally found a flight that left Sunday night at 9 pm scheduled to arrive at 11 on American Airlines. That wasn't ideal but it would work.

Meanwhile, I'm hearing about people who had boarded but then had to deplane because pilots were not available. I was hoping and saying my prayers when I finally got a seat on Southwest going from Baltimore to Long Island. From there I took a taxi to a train station, the train into New York, and hopped on a bus that took me to LaGuardia Airport. Danny DeVito had nothing on me in the movie, "Planes, Trains, and Automobiles." The final leg would take an American flight to Boston.

But then I had another of my Holy Spirit unctions. "Find another flight." I've learned over the years that I need to listen to those urgings. I returned to the process and found a Delta flight that would get me to Boston in time. I pressed the "purchase" button."

"Insufficient funds."

"How can that be?" I wondered aloud at the instantaneous message, continuing the sequence of frustrating dominoes to fall. Then I realized, in the frantic attempt to find a flight, I made so many purchases and was waiting for so many refunds, I didn't have the money I needed. Feeling like I was on "Who wants to be a millionaire" I used my last lifeline and called a friend, Darrell Jones from Innocents' Convicts. He was the one wrongfully convicted for a murder in Boston and spent 32 years behind bars. Because we connected at such a deep level, he told me to reach out if I needed anything. Well, this was the time to use that lifeline. He quickly and generously agreed to send $110 to secure the ticket on Delta.

Again, I clicked "purchase" and this time the purchase was confirmed.

It was a good thing it did because that urging by the Holy Spirit once again proved true. The American Airlines flight was delayed and was later canceled. Thank you, Jesus.

You might be thinking, why not just rent a car and drive the four hundred miles from Baltimore to Boston? After all, it only takes about eight hours. But remember Tulsa? It totally messed me up. I just can't sit on that glute for several hours and still race the next day. I did drive to Louisiana but had a day to recover before running the race.

I boarded the flight and was relieved when I felt the plane take off. Even more, I appreciated arriving in Boston in time to take a covid test, pick up my bib, check into the nearby hotel, shower, change, and catch the bus, walk to the corrals, and wait to start. There was no packet pickup so all I had was my bib and wristband required to enter the race. Hurrying through each step. I felt as if I was running a sprint just to get to the marathon. I made it just in time with only 1 or 2 minutes to spare.

If only I would have had time to sleep the night before. That's not what a runner needs before running a marathon with tight time limits, but it is what I had to do.

Joining the throng of 23,000 runners, we boarded shuttles to the start line. Using smaller waves for covid precautions, we began with rolling waves.

Meanwhile, I was one of the fortunate ones. Many couldn't get to the race in time due to Southwest Airlines meltdown. Even crazier was the fact the Boston Marathon deferred the entries for runners who couldn't make it in time but wouldn't defer charity runner's entries because of the pandemic.

Although I didn't have a lot of time to think about it, the weather was in the 60s and beautiful running weather.

The Race

Despite everything that happened, the #RunningServant was in rare form. I had everybody, runners, and volunteers alike, laughing in the brief time I was waiting to start. I love having fun but love lifting the spirits of everyone around me. My antics motivate people as well as help them to relax. You might say I lead the party on the pavement. I played out one scene acting like I was the sprinter racing the hare. One of the guys filming the event told me I helped make the start the best one he has seen.

There was also a somber note. I couldn't help but think about my nephew who I knew was not just missing, but knew he was dead. I suspected murdered due to the circumstances, but that wouldn't be confirmed for a few days. The race had the potential to be overshadowed by all the other struggles.

But when my body is responding, running helps me escape the cruel world. Today was one of those days and I felt great. I worked my strategy of walking up the hills and running down. My glutes showed up to play and I was loving it.

I called to tell Paula of Hale Education to tell her I was still running, and everything was going well.

"Everyone likes you," she responded. "Everyone is talking about you on the course."

As I approached the last water station before mile 18, I put my phone on speaker so she could hear what I was about to do.

"On the count of 3, everyone shouted, "1. 2. 3. 4. What the Hale are you running for." They responded perfectly and Miss Paula busted out laughing. We had all run for several hours, and covered eighteen miles, so we needed a little levity. No wonder so many thanked me. The police officers and volunteers surprised me with comments like, "You were the only fun thing being on the course with the runners" and "you make this fun."

I particularly enjoyed pumping up the energy at every aid station. We definitely had fun, especially mile twelve, where everyone enjoyed my shouting and singing. We had so much fun that afterward, I had 30-40 videos from people. I love cheering people on to make noise. But then I encourage them to get louder and louder. At mile 12, I got them to chant. At Mile 16 I received a pair of white wristbands from one of the cops who told me Paula from Hale sent them in honor of my slain nephew who wore a pair during his dancing performances. Paula had the wrist bands because she saw my Facebook post asking people to help me locate a pair and left them with her husband, a Boston Police detective, who passed them to an officer to hand to me.

Photo: Holding the wristband Paula sent for me to wear in honor of my nephew.

Mile 13-16 is a steady incline that, like the Crazy Horse Marathon just a week ago, hit my glutes. Fortunately, the armbands reminded me that I dedicated the race to my nephew. That gave me strength and determination to continue.

There was one problem, or should I say two. Twice I needed port-a-potty. That rarely happens to me, and I hadn't factored the extra 25-30 minutes into my strategy.

Prior to mile eighteen, I was running through a neighborhood when a lady came out with her drink. She was something else, running with me and flirting with me. She was trying to get something going by asking me how long I would be in town. While I had my bootie slapped in the London Marathon, I hadn't had a spectator propositioning me before. I tried to deter her by telling her about my Hale Reservation fundraiser, but she was persistent. You know she ran a quarter mile with me. She didn't quit until I invited her to come to Hale with me. Evidently that was enough, and she left me alone. She never did show at Hale. Evidently, she couldn't fit it in her schedule, or she found another runner.

Then the unthinkable happened. By mile 18, the BAA crashed our party on the pavement. I know I was toward the back of the pack but I had been running well, outside of the emergency bathroom break. I started to notice the trucks and workers tearing down the course. Beginning at the start line and working forward, they came from behind me, and it wasn't long before they passed several of us, collapsing the aid stations, and trucking away the port-a-potties, even the medical tents were being broken down.

"What's happening?" I wondered aloud. This was reminiscent of 2019 London, and I hated that.

I was genuinely confused and felt deceived. I was told we would get six hours to run the race. I was on track to finish in six hours so what was going on? I have eight miles left to go, another 105 minutes, and I have been running for four hours. That meant I could easily finish in six hours. But now, with everything broken down, I didn't know where the course was. At first, I ran with a guy but then he told me to keep running as he went in a different direction, saying he knew a shortcut. Getting his medal was his main concern. I wanted the time and the integrity of knowing I ran the course. I wasn't about to take a shortcut, so once again, I was alone on the course.

Looking forward, to the side, and even backward, I noticed a couple of ladies running two hundred yards behind me. I stopped and waited for them to catch up to see if they knew the course. Fortunately, one of the ladies had run the race seven times so she knew the way. She was running with her mom who was much slower. And that meant that I either had to run with them or try to find the route myself. I ran with them for a while, and then, anxious to finish, tried to find my own way. At one point, my confusion must have been evident because spectators told me which way to go.

Now realize, at this point, there were no
- mile markers,
- course directions,
- aid stations,
- hydration stations, or
- port-a-potties.
- volunteers
- police

That meant I had nothing to drink beyond mile seventeen. By mile nineteen, I was thirsty, so thirsty that a spectator offered the half a bottle of water he had been drinking. I gladly accepted it and I drank it. How desperate is that for desperate? That is all the hydration I had for the last eight miles and two hours of the race.

To make it even more frustrating, there was no sag wagon to pick up those who were not making the time restrictions. I would have understood if I were so slow that the sweepers took me off the course and then they closed the course. But that never happened. There were no sweepers and no sag wagon.

By the time we entered Boston proper, the traffic on the streets and sidewalks was crazy. Running past famed Fenway ballpark, the streets were open to traffic and people flooded the sidewalks going to the Red Sox's game. They were cheering enthusiastically, and I appreciated that, especially with the confusion on the course.

One cop yelled at me to move to the sidewalk because there was a car behind me. That's when my frustration boiled over.

"I paid to run this race, so you guys need to run this race like you do for the elites."

Another cop, trying to be helpful, gave better advice. "Take the street to the other side and go under the bridge."

He knew what he was talking about. I did and it helped me avoid an incline and run that last mile at a good pace. Meanwhile, they were trying to erase the blue line.

An amazing thing happened from there to the finish. The Spirit of God empowered me to run as if I were on the wings of angels. I ran my best segment of the day, cheered on by a number of lingering spectators. I was encouraged and exhilarated as they cheered for me to run harder and faster.

With the finish line ahead of me, the Holy Spirit came over me. I suddenly stopped, and bowed, thanking God for getting me this far in my quest and recovery. I was humbled by his grace, love, and forgiveness. In that moment, I was alone with my Lord, worshiping heaven from this tiny piece of earth.

Suddenly I heard an overwhelming chorus, "Cross the finish line!"

I knew what they meant, but could only respond, "You don't know what I've been through to get here." I knew that, beginning with my shooting, this had been a long, winding road that led me to do what God had laid on my heart. That's why I stopped and had to glorify God, thanking the one who made it possible.

With my worship complete, I stepped across the finish line. With that final step, I had just earned my fifth star of the Abbot world majors. There was now only one star left and that is Tokyo.

Unfortunately, I had no idea of my time. My Garmin died sometime after Baltimore. Not having a chance to charge my watch or my phone, I couldn't use an alternative app. Garmin was supposed to last 21 hours but obviously didn't. But I wasn't worried because races, especially the granddaddy of them all, used the timing matts.

Knowing I didn't have a finish time irritated, disappointed, and then demoralized me. By shutting off the timing mats, they ruined everything. Without announcing their policy change that was publicly stated on their website and in their emails, we wouldn't get six hours to run the race. Instead, the clock started with the elite runners. That meant I only had about five hours to finish the race, given I started toward the back and didn't cross the start line for about an hour after the elite runners.

That infuriated me. I am an honest man that lives with integrity. I expect others to do the same, especially well-established organizations that run signature events. If we can't trust them to do what they say, how can we do business with them?

My Reflection on the Race

I wish I could've experienced the Boston Marathon without all the hassles.

I will be honest with you. After all is said and done, I believe I finished in under 6 hours. My glutes caused me a little pain and then I had the bathroom issue. Yes, I did a song and a little dancing but that was insignificant. Even had I not done that, I still would have finished in time. What hurt the most was shutting down the course, waiting for directions, and lacking any hydration. Without those barriers I would have easily run the course in five and a half hours. But had the BAA not torn down the course, I could have finished in the allotted six hours.

But that doesn't let the BAA off the hook. They failed to live up to what they promised. I understand their main focus is on the elite runners but that doesn't mean you can't make it a landmark event for the charity runners. London does. In fact, London prioritizes charity runners by providing them approximately three quarters of the registrations. But London race organizers also tore down the course before they were supposed to in 2019.

I don't look forward to running Boston again, but I have to. Without a recorded time for the Boston Marathon, the Abbott World Majors won't award my fifth star. That means I must run it again and receive an official time. I raised $8,000 twice, fought through airlines, weather, and a lack of sleep to take two planes, one taxi, and two busses to run a race that I didn't get credit for running.

I may be the only one who feels this way about the Boston Marathon, but I don't believe I got what I paid for. Twice I had to raise $8,000 and then they crashed the party early.

To make matters even worse, I didn't even receive my packet and shirt. I hope that doesn't sound petty. But to only receive my bib when I paid for the shirt, I'm personally offended. They didn't even offer an apology or offer to mail it. I had to email them afterwards and demand it. Even after I told them that I would be in town for two additional days they refused to provide a time for me to stop by and grab my packet after being told I could when I got my bib. How does an elite organization operate that way?

While the BAA didn't control the weather or Southwest Airlines labor shortage, they did accommodate runners trying to get to the race in time. I appreciated that.

On the opposite end of the emotional roller coaster, the highlight of the Boston Marathon was running with Hale Education. I love running with a purpose, especially for such a good group of people. I also loved the volunteers and the other runners. The people are always the highlight of every race. For example, I met a woman on the course that was running Boston for the 27th time. That's impressive. But I can imagine her pain as she came in after me and didn't get an official time either. That just doesn't seem right.

In some ways, the Boston Marathon is over-rated. Specifically, Heartbreak Hill wasn't that bad. Actually, the hill before that was the difficult one. It was definitely far less challenging than the Blue Mountain Marathon.

I'm also disappointed in many of the runners. I suspect a few got rides farther up the course or cut across since there is no timing mat. Sure, they get their medal but that shows no integrity.

At the same time, I'm grateful to have the experience. I'm most happy to be there when some of my running friends received their sixth running star, completing the Abbott World Majors. That is quite an accomplishment and one that I'm looking forward to earning.

Another Hotel Issue

But there is one more bitter disappointment. Despite paying months in advance to stay at the Moxi, which is a beautiful building, the customer service is terrible. The people and management were condescending, refused to listen, and one claimed, "I'm the manager on duty." No logic or proof of payment swayed them because he claimed, "we don't have a record of payment."

I paid extra for the river view but was given a room without a view. So, there are three reasons I want the view. First, I paid for it. Second, I don't want a street directly below me. Remember, I still have people targeting my life. Given they are part of a nationwide gang, I never know where they are or what they look like. Third, my PTSD is easily triggered by sights, smells, and sounds.

In the end, I finally convinced him to call the owner of the company who sponsored my room. Even then, he couldn't see the problem. I paid for the river view but got a city view. They were two different rooms with the river view being more expensive. Marriott tried to do that to me in Baltimore as well. Then to hear the manager claim, "You are not my customer. You are acting like you want something from me. I am the customer." Wow, what an attitude.

It was only after I persisted nicely but took out my phone, pressed the record button, and informed him that he was being recorded that his demeanor changed, and he put me in the right room. Along the way, I had to pay for the room three times. Then, finally getting to the right executive, they remedied the problem.

Making it worse, I had reserved the weekend in the hotel prior to the Boston Marathon choosing the postponed date. At that point, I was only paying approximately $175 per night. By playing their games, the sponsor had to pay $400 a night. The hotel was grubbing for money, demanding more money for the room. To make matters worse, when I ran Boston the next April, the Moxi manager offered to comp three nights and would talk to his manager to comp the entire five days. At that point, the cost of the room was over $700 a night. I called a couple of days before the race, double checking logistics, to find they would only comp one day. I chose to find a different hotel and won't stay at the Moxi again.

Making my way to the room, hot, sweaty, tired, and frustrated, just like my first run at Daufuskie, I was ready to relax. But no, there was still another insult. There were no washcloths. I called housekeeping, and they brought washcloths fresh out of the dryer. They were still hot.

Looking Ahead

I stayed an extra couple of days and was finally able to receive my shirt. Again, that is a small item but part of the package.

Returning home, I learned that my nephew's funeral would be held in ten days, on the 23ʳᵈ, the same day as I was supposed to run the Colorado Marathon.

I leave on Saturday for Des Moines, Iowa.

Looking farther ahead, my doctor said I need to have 2 veins burned in my inner thighs to improve blood flow. That will require that I rest for 3 weeks. I plan to do that on Tuesday following the January 16 Chevron Marathon and the

Martin Luther King holiday. That procedure uses a laser to reroute the veins inside the muscle, forcing the blood to flow outside the muscle.

Once completed, I won't have swelling in my lower right leg. That will help my leg from buckling as it did at the 30K mark.

While I did have some issues, like my leg buckling twice at the 18-mile mark, I am pleased that I didn't have as much trouble as I have at other races. Most of the problem for the Boston Marathon was not due to my physical or mental challenges.

Most of the problems with my performance had to do with the BAA. I really thought the race organization was much humbler than they are. But then, as I looked into their history, I learned how they didn't allow black elites from other countries, and even when they did, and they won, they refused to give them the prize money. I understand that was a long time ago, but you would think the 2015 bombing would have humbled them. I'm not sure it did. Maybe they need to experience the #RunningServant. Maybe I am their covid vaccination for humility.

I know there was a purpose in what happened. I look forward to seeing what it is. I know ego gets in the way when a celebrity sets in. "If you don't want to do it, we have plenty of people who will take it." I need to remember that I am serving the Lord and therefore, God will put me in situations not just for my enjoyment, but to help others.

A Decision

I've been contemplating running New Mexico's Day of the Dead Marathon for some time. I like to honor those who have gone before me. After all, we do stand on their shoulders. However, as a follower of Jesus and one who is committed to his teachings, I can't worship the dead. When I thought about running this race, something didn't feel right in my spirit, so I never did register. I know that leaves me without a race in New Mexico. With the end of the year approaching quickly, New Mexico becomes the second state to officially be pushed to 2021.

Week 35: Des Moines Iowa, Oct. 17

Since I had raised funds for Hale Education, my plan was to stay a couple of extra days in Boston to connect and develop relationships. That strategy played well in the aftermath of a very hectic week. I was emotionally spent after missing a night of sleep simply trying to travel the four hundred miles between races. Then I had a hard time working through the frustration of the race. Worst of all, I knew returning home meant coming to terms with the murder of my nephew.

That hit me hard.

It wasn't just the death of a young person who should have had his long life ahead of him. No, it was more than just losing a family member, if that wasn't horrible enough. But he was murdered. That complicated things for me. The death of anyone close is difficult, but I will say it again, he was murdered. I could feel the terror he must have felt. I felt the emotions. I felt the pain as the bullet entered his body. I felt the pain of life slipping away. I was there but I was spared.

After an uneventful flight home on Wednesday, I made a hurried turnaround, leaving Friday afternoon for Des Moines. In between I got in as many appointments for training, massage, and doctors as I could. In the midst of it all, tucked in the not quite unconscious part of my mind, was the aftermath of my nephew's death.

Des Moines

In many ways Des Moines, population 215,000, offered an escape for me from the drama of the previous week. While the large, elite races in cities like Boston are thrilling, I thrive on the personal connections at these smaller races. They are down to earth, honest people who live beyond politics and elitism. I like that.

I arrived in time to hang out, relax, enjoy the expo, visit with people, and eat a great spaghetti dinner. I even had time to hear Jeff Galloway speak. Both he and his wife were there to address Jeff's recent heart attack and share his signature run-walk method. As a Transformational Coach, I'm always interested in learning new techniques.

Photo:
Jeff Galloway poses with his friend.

The dinner was nice but rather steep at $35. I'm used to pretty thin and weak sauce for these pre-race meals but this one was at a banquet hotel that knew how to do it right. They offered grilled chicken breasts, Andouille sausage, with plenty of veggies, coffee, and desserts. The Tiramisu was a nice touch. It was worth the extra dollars.

The hotel was just a third of a mile from the start and across the street from several bars and restaurants. I was a bit leery of the situation, but given the relaxing time I'd had, I decided to make a brief appearance. Retiring to my room, I had been relaxing for three or four hours when my peace was shattered.

Bang. Bang. Bang.

Hearing the too familiar sound of gunshots, I knew something bad was happening to someone. That unsettled me and I tried to just relax and watch tv. The next morning, I watched as the news reporter detailed how three people were shot at Third and Court, directly across the street from my hotel where I had been just a few hours before. To say that it really bothered me was an understatement, especially on the heels of the Baltimore Inner Harbor incident.

Forget sleeping well that night.

The frustrating part was, once again, the hotel didn't listen and assigned a room on the wrong side of the hotel. I specifically asked for a room with a river view, not a city view. Had they given me what I asked for, I wouldn't have heard the gunshots. I really wish these hotels and other organizations would do what they say they are going to do. While I hate to claim race has something to do with it, I have to wonder.

One of the downsides of a race in a smaller city is that it can be hard to find the services I need, like a good massage. I'm not looking for a relaxation massage but rather a deep tissue session to relive the pain in my glutes and other areas. Unfortunately, I couldn't find a therapist in Des Moines. Maybe I should have flown back to Baltimore. But that was out of the question and meant I would start the race behind the eight ball.

The Race

I was pleased that the marathon didn't start until 8:00 a.m. and that the weather was beautiful. Starting in the 40s made for perfect running and warming to 68 degrees made for a comfortable day.

The first 10k went well, completing it in 1:22. That was because it was mostly downhill, and easy on the glutes. But the next 5k was a totally different story, taxing my already exhausted glutes.

As I was approaching mile 8, I met a lady, Erin, attending a birthday party. She was friendly and enjoying the festivities, so I stopped, snapped a few photos, had a few laughs, and kept going.

As I passed the nine-mile mark, my glutes were telling me, "That's it Mister. This is where I check out." But I was not going to give up just yet. You just never know what miracle is about to happen.

The first angel came in the form of a lady working the water stop at mile 9. She walked and talked with me to distract me from the pain. Erin, one of the many Erin's on the course, helped get me to the next angle.

Between mile 12 and 13, the course took us through the campus of Drake University where we ran around track and the announcer called out your name. One of the advantages of being at the back of the pack is that there aren't as many runners as possible so they can talk about each one. As they were talking about me, I felt like I was running in an Olympic stadium. Coincidentally, they hold Olympic tryouts in this venue.

Drake Stadium, which has a capacity of 14,557, is home to the football and men's and women's soccer teams as well as the annual Drake Relays.

At mile 9, the course travels under the I-235 bridge for a 5k out and back loop. As I rounded the corner, I couldn't believe what I saw. There was a tent and it appeared to be something medical. As I trudged on and drew closer, I was elated to see it was a chiropractor providing, guess what? Massages. I'm not a shy guy so I picked up my pace and quickly asked if I could get some relief. This guy was an angel sent from heaven who knew how to exorcize my pain with a massage gun. That angel ushered me into a few minutes of heavenly relief.

Refreshed and recharged, I ran on, completing the 5k loop. But as I approached the I-235 bridge again, I thought, "Another treatment would help me finish." But as I rounded the corner nearing mile 15, I was disappointed to see they had packed up and left. I assume that since I was at the back of the pack, they didn't think anyone else needed their services. I should have made an appointment.

As I approached mile 15 marker and the Bill Riley Trail, my body said, "No you don't. I said before that I was done. I mean it this time." It wasn't just my glutes but also my back, I.T. band and hip flexor felt like they were so tight they were ready to snap. I had to wave the white flag and call it quits.

They were generous and gave me a half marathon medal, which I appreciated. That is the difference in smaller races. They see the people, not the rules.

Photo: Bike Marshall gives me a hug and a half marathon finisher's medal prior to me being carted off to the finish line by the Sag Wagon.

I was disappointed that after two good races in Baltimore and Boston, I couldn't finish Des Moines. If I could have had another massage at mile 15, that would've helped me make it to mile 21 or 22. Then, if I had yet another treatment, I could have finished. That's how weak my right side was at that point.

Along the way I met several 50 state marathoners working toward their goal. As usual, there were some working on running the half in every state while others ran the marathon and even some the ultra. As usual I also met some of the Marathon Maniacs and the Double Agents.

After the race, I got a ride from the Supervan back to my hotel, the Hampton Inn. You know they accommodate you well when you are in intense pain, and you don't snap at them. Because I'm a Marriott platinum member, I asked for one of the perks, a late checkout. They obliged, giving me until 3:30 to shower, change, and rest. I packed up and the massage lady picked me up. She normally didn't work Sunday but decided to and it turned out well for her with several appointments. That had to be a $500-1000 day for her.

Looking Ahead

Going home meant re-entering the aftermath of a family murder. Although I wanted to try and run the Colorado Marathon then return to Houston in time for the funeral, I can't get a flight early enough for the funeral.

I know it will be a closed casket funeral, so it's not like I will see him for the last time. I also know there will be lots of family, so I don't want to miss it. But I also want to run in Colorado. My challenge is important to me.

Some might think that is a little selfish on my part. After all, shouldn't family come first? But they need to understand that I have sixteen siblings and each of them have a family. If I attended all of my family events, I wouldn't do anything else.

Then there is another concern. How will the funeral affect me? I have a hard time with my memories and giving an interview about the incident is difficult. Notice I have a hard time even saying the word, "shooting." In interviewing for this book, we didn't spend only a few minutes with the details of the incident. It hurts too much and sends me into a bad place. The very thought of attending the funeral and repass worries me. I don't think it will be good.

Yet I'm committed to my family. I was considering canceling Boston and Baltimore to help look for my nephew's body. At first, we only knew he was missing. We didn't know what had happened to him. Then, just before I ran, I learned he had been murdered. Now, we still don't know much more beyond that it happened near Galveston. Oddly enough, I met a district attorney from Galveston on a flight back from Des Moines. As we introduced ourselves, I shared about my nephew, who was supposed to be at work. He didn't offer much hope, knowing that area but did encourage me that the Galveston PD is great at solving murders.

My family doesn't fit the traditional, tv sitcom image. My dad was a rolling stone before the Lord saved him, having seventeen kids with five women. Dad was never married to my mother but had two children together. Mom had another two. I'm close to my full brother and lost one of mom's other sons in 1994. As strange as that sounds, Dad married and stayed married following his conversion to Christ. His wife likes to say, "Jesus makes all the difference." Together they have five children. Between the kids my stepmother had and the ones my father had; it all adds up to seventeen.

In the end, I decided to stay in Houston for the funeral. Colorado will need to wait for next year.

Then there is the rest of the schedule. It is mid-October and rescheduling any race is highly unlikely without going into 2022.

Meanwhile, the Marine Corps Marathon was canceled, freeing up a little time, due to the political atmosphere with President Trump and the democrats trying the whole insurrection insanity. That still leaves three races in the Northeast Challenge, Rhode Island, Maine, and Connecticut as well as New Mexico, Nebraska, and Alaska. I have no choice but to push those to May of 2021.

The concern for Hawaii canceling continues. I want to do this trail run and know I could do the Honolulu Marathon, but that course runs mostly in the city. I'm not a fan of that.

But I don't want to obsess over those details. The next race for me is another big one, the New York City Marathon.

Week 36: New York City Marathon, Nov. 7

New York, New York, yes start spreading the news. The city that never sleeps hosts a great marathon weekend that I never want to miss. There is something about the massive number of runners and the crazy support from spectators that makes returning to New York easy as eating pie. Besides, this was the 50th anniversary of running this iconic marathon. Mix that with my 50th birthday challenge of running 50 marathons in 50 states in 50 weeks, you don't have to invite me twice. Actually, you don't need to even invite me once because I'm just going to show up for that party.

Photo: We both turned 50.

In returning this time, I already had my fourth star of the six world majors, having earned it in 2019 which boasted a world breaking non-non-elite 53,627 finishers from 141 countries in the non-elite race, a 98.9 percent completion rate with 578 dropping out making it the largest race in history. That meant this run was just going to be fun, but also part of the 50-50-50 challenge.

Not everyone gets to run New York. Despite a cutoff of over 50,000 in a typical year, they hold a lottery for acceptance. It is totally random beyond the very elite runners, but unlike Boston, there is no qualifying time.

The other option is to run for charity. There are several charities, as with Boston, but require far less fundraising. You are required to raise only about $1400 to 2600. I have enjoyed running with Team for Kids because of how they help kids in so many ways, educating them for life while getting them running.

Of course, the cost of running any race goes well beyond the entry fee with airfare and hotel factoring in. I stayed in the Jane hotel in 2021 to cut my expenses. It is where the ships come in and the crew and captain often stay. Instead of a nice suite, there are single and double bunks with common areas, except for the captain's area, which is much nicer.

Meanwhile other runners chose their hotels depending on whether they were a charity or lottery runner. It's not that the marathon discriminates, but to get to your start line, you can either take a bus or ferry. That dictates which hotels are closer to your departing point. Some, like Teen for Kids, are so large that they have their own dedicated ferry. It left from the Ferry Beth N.N.1 West 34th pier. As you can imagine, moving even 30,000 runners, much less the usual 50,000 runners, takes great planning.

Photo: Team For Kids Runner Tanya Graham of Glendale, California.

The Preliminary 5k

I can't say enough good things about the New York Marathon. The weekend is filled with fun races, beginning with the Abbot 5K Dash on Saturday, so I arrive on Friday.

Waking on Saturday morning, I sensed something was wrong. For some reason, I was in pain. Despite doing everything I knew to ease the pain, like warmups and stretching, I couldn't get rid of it. The pain was affecting my back and mentally causing doubts about running. I ever left the hotel. I started to wonder, "Can I even run a 5k? If I can't run a 5K today, how can I run a marathon tomorrow?"

When I say I was in pain, I mean that it was excruciating, as great as when I shot. I couldn't explain it. I had not heard shots the night before. I wasn't wrestling with my air mattress or sleeping on the vanity. I couldn't explain it.

But I wasn't going to give up. I remembered the words my doctor said following the shooting. "I can run, it just depends on how much pain I was willing to endure." This was a test of my will to run. I determined I wasn't going to fail.

Standing in that start line, the pain felt like a shattered window from a single point. The pain radiating from my back throughout my body. If not for my pride, I would have been crying if not in front of all those folks. I was grateful that I was able to control my emotions, unlike Akron.

You know that when you are in pain, it is hard to focus, much less run. But you also know that when you are determined to do something, you push through the pain. That's what I did. I pushed myself through the pain to finish.

As soon as I could, I found a therapist and asked for both a massage and a stretch session. My muscles were so tight that they felt like a banjo string. The song they were playing could have been an old country song about how much I hurt. I needed more than just the usual one-hour appointment to loosen those strings. From there, I went back to the hotel and stayed off my feet for the rest of the day.

The doubts continued to flood my mind. "That 5k run took everything out of me. How can I possibly run a marathon tomorrow?" The pain wasn't just physical but also emotional. I started this quest to help me get back to where I was in my running career before the shooting. As misguided as you might think that was, that was a legitimate goal. I legitimately thought I could do it. Maybe I was foolish or simply misguided, but with the exception of Boston and Baltimore, I wasn't anywhere close to that level. Now, as I look New York in the eyes, I'm doubting my future as a runner and that takes a toll on my identity and ego. I am a proud man, proud of who I have become but also proud of what I have been able to do. This pain chips away at that confidence, weakens my mindset, and challenges my future. Maybe that is why the PTSD brings me to tears. It's not just the physical pain but how it pierces my identity.

Photo: Team for Kids Runner Janice Character about to grab her 4th Abbott World Major Marathon Star.

In those moments, I dedicate myself to rest, physically and mentally. Dozing on and off before finally retiring in hopes of a good night sleep, I calmed my mind with prayer and worship.

I woke up but was a bit afraid to move but curious how I felt. Gently opening my eyes, I wondered if this would be another bitter disappointment, maybe the worst of the year, or if this was yet another one of God's miracles. As I opened my eyes, I discovered that it was the latter. It was as if yesterday never happened. I felt much, much better, the pain erased, and my energy restored. I quickly changed into my singlet and shorts, before walking out the door and heading to the Teen for Kids ferry.

"Are you cold?" one person asked as they were bundled up, guarded against the 42-degree temps. "I thought you were from Texas. You should be freezing." Looking around, I noticed that everyone else was wearing jackets, hoodies, gloves, and anything else they had. I know I'm a big guy, and the cold doesn't bother me that much. Maybe it is because my body has grown so used to enduring pain that the cold isn't that big of a deal.

The Race

Our Teen for Kids section filled an entire ferry and then had our own wave in our corral, as we waited on Staten Island. Our scheduled start was 11:20. One of the perks of running for a big charity is that they had tents for us that were closed and heated, protecting runners from the elements. Unfortunately, with covid, the tents were open. As an alumni runner with Team for Kids, I didn't have to go through the interview process again, all I had to do was raise the money. After taking the ferry, which was dedicated entirely to Teen for Kids, we set sail for Staten Island. Teens for kids had their own ferry and a tent in the runner's village. Many runners were layered up with old clothing that they usually discarded along the course. However, that is a practice that will get you disqualified in New York. You must discard the extra layers while in the coral.

The start is marked with a cannon. In the past that has bothered me, but since I expected it, it didn't. That was a small piece of progress that I greatly appreciated. It was also a sign as I sensed this was going to be even more fun than 2019. Maybe it was because it was the 50th anniversary that told runners "This is special." Even though they reduced the numbers by 20,000, the streets were packed with spectators. New York showed up for this party.

Photo: The Queens welcome committee.

Crossing over the bridge into Queens, a lady held a sign, "Welcome to Queens, now get out." Everyone laughed. I don't think she meant it, but hey, this is New York and stranger things happen.

Beyond her, Queens was off the chain. As they do every year, they pushed past the police barricades to cheer us on. I'm not talking about any quiet applause. They rivaled the most zealous soccer and football fans. Crowding close to leave only the blue line, every spectator was giving high fives, screaming, reading the names on our bibs, and shouting our names. It was bedlam but it was runner's heaven. I wished I could have looped back to run that again.

Start to finish this race was great. That doesn't mean I didn't have problems. My knee buckled at mile 7 and pain kicked in at 10. Despite that, I was on track to turn in a 2:45 half but my old friend pain greeted me at mile twelve. This pain felt like needles in my butt. It wasn't debilitating so I used periods of walking and running to push myself through the pain.

Entering the second half of the race, we had to run a two-mile bridge between mile 14 and 16. Shortly after that we came to my second favorite part of the run. Mastercard sponsors a DJ where I always stop and dance. My favorite is to perform the "prep dance" and other throwback dances. That fits with my "preppy run crew" shirt, one tied around my waist for after the finish.

Photo: Silence 🔇 🦉 isn't golden on this bridge. And no one, no not one runner, was talking.

The next 5k is the longest stretch in Queens before crossing the bridge. At this point, my glutes and hip flexors were hurting. But other

318

than that, I was doing fine. I was tremendously pleased that pain in my neck and shoulders was gone.

The "last damn bridge" as I like to call it, is the fifth bridge that they don't tell you about. Going over the Queensboro bridge the spectators suddenly disappear. The silence is eerie, only hearing the pounding of runner's feet on the deck. As I mentioned in my 2019 run, to break the monotony, I start singing and creating noise for the other runners. That's what the #RunningServant does. I vowed in 2019 that when I ran it again, there wasn't going to be silence. I was shouting out cadences, praises, and singing songs. I'd come up on people and I could see them lifting their heads and smiling, getting life back. Without some noise, that bridge as a capital B, boring. I truly believe you could actually fall asleep running in that silence. Later, people reached out to me thanking me for what I did in that situation. "You woke everyone up with your chants and comments."

If you run the marathon, you'll appreciate this guy and his sign, if you run it twice, you'll long for them and if you run it thrice, you'll love them unconditionally.

Coming off the bridge is like walking out the door to the sound of a jet engine. The spectators were anxiously awaiting, greeting us with a wall of noise.

As we neared the finish, we had one last incline before going into Central Park and finishing. Boston brags about Heartbreak Hill but that is all hype. That is nothing compared to the NYC incline. Actually, the first of Boston's hills are worse than Heartbreak Hill and that incline in New York tops anything Boston offers.

From there it was a sweet run through the park and across the finish line. Yes, it was almost that anticlimactic, but immensely satisfying. As you have witnessed by being along for this ride, there have been many marathons where I couldn't finish. Finishing, especially New York's 50th anniversary marathon, was special.

Photo: My victory pose.

The People

Part of the fun was all the people I knew running this race. Over the last ten months I have met so many runners from all over the country, that to see so many at one race was exhilarating. As much as this is a running challenge, the joy has been meeting and building relationships with so many runners doing amazing things of their own. Not only are they part of my journey, but I'm blessed to become part of their journey.

Photo: Marriage, in many ways, is like a marathon. A couple hold hands during the home stretch when the course gets the toughest.

Just before the finish, I noticed a man and wife. She was struggling and he was showing patience and support, holding her hand, and encouraging her. I was so intrigued that after I finished, I stopped to watch and film them as they finished. Standing in the glow of their joint accomplishment, I noticed her rubbing her stomach. I couldn't tell it when she was running, but now it was apparent. They were pregnant. What a special moment for them. This new family just ran the 50th anniversary New York marathon together

I was so pleased to reconnect with so many from this last year. One very special connection was the woman I met and who told me about Aiden. Aiden had been in my heart and at the center of my fundraising ever since. Naturally I asked for a photo together. I was disappointed, however, because Aiden was supposed to be there and couldn't make it.

Photo: Running in honor of Aiden, posing with Melinda Howard.

It is these stories where I grieve how ESPN and other media only seem to focus on the elite athletes. I realize why but there are so many uplifting stories that they ignore simply because they weren't one of the leaders.

I was immensely pleased to have my body respond so well. Despite some pain, I felt like I was in the same running condition that I was before I was shot. For most of the race, running was effortless. Now that is the progress I was hoping for.

One of the aspects I appreciate most about the New York City Marathon is that they keep the finish line open until the last runner is done. There are no time limits, and no man or woman is left behind. After reading my struggles, you know how much that means to me. Not only could I have used more time in some races, but I have also seen the humbling stories of others doing what others never imagined finishing this race. They are running with physical limitations, sometimes even a broken foot or with a disabling disease, yet they pushed through. They cannot begin to dream of winning, but they are pushing through their pain, pounding the pavement, putting one foot in front of the other to finish a marathon. That is impressive. That's why I love to go back and watch the last finisher. Every one of them has a great story to tell. That year, the marathon workers stayed until the last finisher crossed at 2:00 a.m.

Looking Forward

Having run Boston and New York, I'm looking forward to running another iconic race, Disney World's Marathon weekend, before wrapping up the challenge at Houston's Chevron. Doing the Dopey challenge.

But next on the list is Illinois' Tunnel Hill Marathon in Vienna. The Race Director is letting me run on Saturday with the ultra-runners but has assured me he will have my medal at the 26-mile mark. This will be good as it is a trail run.

Then my plan is to board a plane and fly to Philly to run the Delaware Coastal Marathon on Sunday. This will be a similar schedule as running Boston and Baltimore.

I'm scheduled to fly back to Houston on Monday before a quick turnaround flying to Little Rock and then Space Coast.

Week 37: Tunnel Hill Marathon 100, Illinois, Nov. 14

Even after running almost every week since I started in January, predicting results is still a mystery. I never know whether or not my glutes are going to show up for the race. When they do, I can run well, as I ran 7 miles in the first hour and a half in NYC. When they don't, it is frustrating.

I'm convinced that massage made a difference. I have found the best results when a therapist uses a massage gun with a vibrating head and different attachments. Stretching is good, but for me, that massage made the difference. To a lesser degree, the foam roller helps to work out the facia, the white part of the muscles.

But when my glutes aren't happy with me, the pain gets to be too much. Instead of finishing a marathon, I struggle to finish a half.

The Tunnel run is a Boston Qualifying race and promises to be fast with the last nine miles a gradual downhill. If I can make it to mile 17, that should be a good finish.

Prepping for the Run

One of the fun parts with any race is the spaghetti meal the night before the race. Many races do this and then bring in a motivational speaker. Traci Falbo was our speaker. She ran the fastest known time for 100-mile race by a woman, setting that record on this course in 2014. I arrived early, went through the line to get my food, and by then, the house had filled up. I found a place to sit in the overflow room and it was filled. At times it was hard to even hear the speaker.

323

But that didn't matter. I was intrigued and inspired by what she had done. As she finished, I made my way to meet her, knowing I needed a photo with her. We hit it off so well that I surprised her by literally scooping her off her feet to create a fun moment where we all laughed. She insisted on autographing not only my bib but a picture for the TROT Tribe, Trail Running Over Texas.

Photo: I sweep Traci Falbo off her feet.

The Race

Running on a crushed rock trail, we followed the first mile to turn and go through the famed 800-foot railroad tunnel. From there it was an out and back, running to a wetlands center before returning to the timing mat. My plan was to run out and back, cutting the race short before flying to Philadelphia and run Delaware.

One of the most inspirational people I met was Lisa Gunnoe from Little Rock, Arkansas. She had a brain injury, yet still runs ultras. You know I'm going to like her because I can definitely relate to those runners overcoming a physical trauma. She used a run-walk pace of 1/30, 1 minute run, 30 second walk, to run a 50 miler that day. Lisa has short term memory difficulties but functions better when running. We ran together for 10 miles and enjoyed a beautiful conversation. With her beautiful spirit, she encouraged me when all I could muster was a walk, "You can do it." Like healing salves on a wound, her words soothed my spirit. She is such a beautiful person.

Photo: Lisa and I take a moment to get captured during this captivating course by a citizen who each year looks forward to people asking him to take their photo.

She had a friend running with her that also had an injury. Although she was once an elite runner, she now runs to serve. Part of that involves speaking to groups.

Both women are believers and that reassured me that I am on the right track. I was in excruciating pain, once again not able to minister. That brought moments of doubt about my quest, purpose, and direction. Her friend encouraged me, "You can't help everyone on the course." She realized as she was always stopping to help people. That encouraged me, helping me to shift my perspective and that led to walking faster. As she completed the turnaround before me, she caught my eye, she saw my pain, and once again said, "You can do it." Those words were therapeutic oil, even though I knew finishing wasn't a matter of my will. My muscles told me that finishing the race today wasn't possible. Even two angels couldn't lift me on their wings to the finish line.

In this run, the first 10 miles went well but then the continual flat course took its toll. My glutes need the play of hills, up and down, pushing and then relaxing, to perform at their best.

In the middle of my pain, I took out my phone and recorded a video that showed how the pain had taken me captive. I was 2.5 miles away from turnaround and was walking at that point. Already, I was no longer planning but simply hoping that walking would get to the half marathon point. Mentally I am good if I can finish the half. I know I'm challenging myself to run a full marathon each week but, by now, I know that my body isn't going to respond each week. When it fails me, the new challenge is to get to the halfway mark. I was now at the point where every step felt like stepping on pins and needles that shot electric shocks throughout my body. It is as if my friendly glutes became my moral enemies and were playing dirty.

But by the time I reached the turnaround, I could barely walk. I appreciated my angel's kind encouragement. But my body failed me. I had no choice but to take my marbles and go home.

Unfortunately, I was two miles from an aid station. That created another problem. Like most trail runs, there was no ride available. Here I am, unable to even walk, and needing to get back to the aid station. My initial thought was to call an Uber. But was there an Uber available? Of course not. Fortunately, I met a kind soul crewing for a lady running the ultramarathon. He was waiting on her and volunteered to give me a ride to the aid station. I quickly learned that he had a podcast and that he emailed the race director to have someone pick me up. I definitely needed that angel.

I rented a Ford Explorer to get back to the airport. My original plan was to continue on to Philadelphia and then drive the short distance to Delaware and run the race the next day. But on the way to the airport, enjoying heated seats that felt fantastic even though it made me sweat, I knew there was no way I could run the next day. I knew ahead of time it would be a race day decision and now I knew. Just getting into the car was bad enough. I couldn't imagine driving, flying, and driving again to get to the hotel and then run a marathon. I learned that painful lesson in Tulsa many months ago.

I only considered it because I was hoping rest would make the difference. But there wasn't enough time for rest. I would have needed another day before the Delaware race.

Arriving in St. Louis, I changed my flight and returned home.

Looking Forward

By the time I arrived home, I hurt so much I couldn't even get out of my chair and stand up. Since I slept on the floor, I couldn't even just lay down without a whole new process. First, I had to sit in my chair, then get down on my knees, and then lay on the floor. You can imagine what it took to get back up.

That wasn't the worst I felt, but definitely in the top 3 of all the races I've run.

I didn't even need to think about my first priority that week. I needed an extensive stretching and massage therapy session. But this would be no routine appointment with Ratif of Reach Stretch Studios Memorial in Houston. To say I was tight was an understatement. He worked on me for two and a half hours, stretching and massaging my body.

"You weren't lying" he said as he worked through the knots and tightness. "You are so tight you can't even move."

To tell you how bad it was, it was worse than after driving to and from Tulsa. Even driving 8 hours each way and only finishing a half didn't compare to how tight my body was. Ratif reminded me that scar tissue causes pain. At this point, I've scheduled a surgery next January that should help with numbness by increasing blood flow. In the process, I might call Kim Kardashian to see about butt lift or tuck. As long as I'm doing some work, I might as well do it all.

You know I'm kidding about the last part.

As the pain eased, I was able to appreciate the Tunnel Hill Marathon more. It was a fast course where two guys were trying to set a new record. Not only is it fast, but it is also a beautiful and easy course. There are no crowds but lots of nature. I had some friends finish 50 miles in 12-14 hours, which is a decent time, even for some that did the run-walk.

If not for the glutes, I would have hung out with my new angel Lisa the entire race. If only I could have continued my past. I was on track for running the first 10k in one hour. But knowing I'm doing a full marathon, that pace is too aggressive.

Looking at the calendar, one date jumps out at me. November 28 marks 6 years since I was shot. Oddly enough, I am running the Space Coast Half Marathon in Cocoa Beach, Florida that day.

But before I get to that, next week I am running the Little Rock Marathon.

Week 38: Little Rock, Arkansas, Nov. 21

If I were labeling each marathon with a title of a song, the Little Rock Marathon would be titled, "It hit me like a wrecking ball."

I didn't want to focus on it, but this race fell on that fateful anniversary of the shooting, November 28th. Those things have a habit of lurking in the dark regions of our subconscious, then rear their ugly head at the least opportune time.

It started with the nightmares on Thursday night and waking up in the throes of PTSD. I could hardly breathe and spent the entire day trying to relax and calm down. Unfortunately, my efforts were ultimately defeated, and the PTSD prevailed. After a long struggle, I finally fell asleep, and to my surprise, awoke feeling grateful. Somewhere in the darkness of the night, my PTSD dissipated. I didn't know why or how, but I was glad it was gone.

Before leaving for Little Rock, I drove to watch my daughter cheer for Prairie View A&M. The Aggies of Texas A&M were highly favored in this early preconference game designed more as a scrimmage for the major conferences that padded the finances with another home game. Meanwhile, teams like Prairie View enjoyed a nice payout and a chance for players to compete with the nation's best, even though the chances of winning were slim. But I wasn't there to enjoy the game. I came to experience my daughter cheering in her first college game against a major division one nationally highly ranked school. I was filled with pride as I watched my intelligent, smart, and beautiful baby girl Calah.

Photo: Calah, my youngest daughter, cheering for her Panthers at Texas A&M.

But it seems that every time something good happens, there is an equal and opposite force. Every time A&M scored, they fired off a cannon. I didn't know that was going to happen. To make matters worse, Texas A&M scored seven touchdowns and they fired that cannon each time. Boom. Boom. Boom. Boom. Boom. Boom. Boom. Then at the end of the game, they shot the cannon off consecutively for each of the seven scores. Boom. Boom. Boom. Boom. Boom. Boom. Boom.

Each blast sent shock waves through my body and triggered another round of anxiety. It was like being shocked with a cattle prod over and over and over without being able to move. I cringed after each one.

My old nemesis PTSD, who had just left the night before, came rushing back like an unwelcomed, hungry family member hurrying back for yet another free meal.

I drove back to Houston unnerved, discombobulated, and disoriented. A massage would have been great, but there wasn't room in my schedule. I had no choice but to jump on a plane to Little Rock.

I arrived and went to my hotel, tired, and emotionally spent. Although I fully intended to get up at 6:00, like Montana, I couldn't. All I could demand of my body and mind was to get up in time for the 8:00 a.m. start.

That extra hour allowed me to relax, recover, and breathe comfortably.

The Run

As I started running, I felt it was going pretty well until my Garmin watch started vibrating. Quickly looking, I saw my heart rate was in the danger zone. I'd never experienced that before.

I tried relaxing, refocusing my thinking, and walking. Nothing helped. My heart rate refused to drop into the safe zone. Wanting to make the right decision for my short- and long-term health, I decided to call it quits at the half.

That was a good decision. By the time I finished, I was lightheaded, dizzy, and had a pounding headache. My heart rate dropped to 158 but needed to be much lower, about 48-52 beats per minute at rest. This was troubling, in part, because I haven't had trouble like that before. Even when working with my trainer running on a treadmill for 15 minutes, my heart rate peaks at about 90 bpm. Running marathons usually peaks at 138. Normally I'm running at about 120.

I waited on the course for 10 minutes, but it stubbornly refused to drop below 122. Not wanting to mess with God's timing, I sought out the medical tent. "You made a wise decision" the doctor looked me in the eye, confirming my choice to end the race prematurely.

"Your blood pressure is 133/89."

"That's not bad for me."

In the process of taking my blood pressure, my heart rate calmed down to 84-89, and then went back up to 122-129. It wasn't until I was back in my hotel, showered, and changed that my heart rate settled under 100 bpm. I went to bed with it beating between 64-69 bpm.

Before slipping off to sleep, I checked the readout on watch from previous races. That is one thing I truly like about my Garmin watch. It records and saves all that data, even though I didn't think it would be necessary at the time. That's when I noticed the data from the Medford, Wisconsin marathon where they had an unexpected shooting range alongside the course. My heart rate spiked then, but not like today. That was the last time I felt this bad. Looking again at my current rates, I noticed my oxygen dropped 3% when it was usually 99. It spiked on occasion but didn't stay there. A couple days later, my heart rate remained about 55. That is in my normal range. At rest I'm usually at 48, and while moving around, in the 50s and 60s.

Battling PTSD

That is how powerful and suddenly PTSD can take over my life. Even though I'm a committed believer in Jesus Christ, I can't go to church because the snare drum in the worship band triggers my PTSD. I tried sitting in the church until the band started and then exited the lobby. That helps. Unfortunately, I cannot even worship like everyone else.

Then to attend a game to support my daughter and be triggered is extremely frustrating. Instead of focusing on her, I was guarding against an all-out PTSD assault. It was important for me to be there for my daughter. It was also important for me. Despite trying to prepare myself for the crowds, noise, and band, I didn't anticipate the cannons. I sure didn't expect blast after blast.

I didn't need to see another doctor to know the prognosis. I need to stay out of those PTSD inducing situations.

There is no treatment available for my PTSD. I know because I've seen some of the best medical professionals in the country. I was checked out by a doctor in Boston, who was head of Boston University (or was it Boston College). He is the world's leading PTSD expert, the former head over Veteran's Department under Clinton, and an independent researcher actively working on a revolutionary treatment. If he doesn't know of a treatment, there is none. Along with the others I've consulted with, they all agree that after three and a half years, there is no cure for me at this time. The only thing I can do is to adapt, learn to live with PTSD, and not let it rule my life. I must learn my triggers, manage the environment, and avoid situations where it can be triggered.

One of the lessons I'm learning came from a guy I met recently. He was diagnosed with cancer and his therapist told him "Learn to live with cancer, not for it." In passing this nugget on to me, he has helped me pivot my perspective and find an advantage in fighting PTSD.

"Learn to live with it, not for it. In other words, don't live for it, PTSD, live with it. Don't ask PTSD what you can do, tell it what you are going to do."

Before I was shot, my mom claimed I had a Superman complex. She believed that I thought I was invincible. Maybe she was right. Maybe I still have some of that. All I know is that weeks after the shooting, I was still in shock because my whole life came tumbling down like a house of cards.

I was driving west on I-10 when my vehicle broke down, forcing me to pull over. My mom, seeing the teaching moment, said, "I was wondering when you would break down." Not talking about my vehicle, in her mother's wisdom, she noted, ``You need to realize you are a human, not superman."

It took a while, but that reality finally set in. Several doctors examined me and diagnosed an extreme form of PTSD because of the constant bullet and pain. But there was more to their diagnosis. I suffered from how my employer treated me, as if I shot myself instead of how I was trying to save coworkers' lives. Then add to that how I had to wait in pain for a surgery. It wasn't that my doctors couldn't get it scheduled. It was waiting for the company to give approval to pay for it. There I was, in a fragile state and this battle raged. The prolonged agony persisted, and the PTSD prevailed.

The Ultra-Marathoner's Mindset

To run an ultramarathon requires a superman complex. To run anything beyond a marathon, especially a 50 or 100 miler, you must think beyond the expectations of others. Most are not runners and quit when something gets uncomfortable. But the ultra-runner exceeds the mindset of even the marathon runner. The 5k or 10k might be fun and require far less training. The half marathoner is bolder and accepts the challenge to run 13.1 miles. That separates them from the sprinters or fun runners. Endurance runners learn to persevere through the pain and drudgery of pounding the pavement mile after mile. The marathoner learns to push through the proverbial wall at mile 20 to finish as only 1% of the population does. In the process, the endurance runner learns to train, listen to their bodies, and ignore their ego. They find their purpose and peace, resolving their practices and priorities. The ultra-marathoner thinks beyond merely finishing to pushing themselves through to better themselves. Theirs isn't just a challenge, it is a quest to be and do. It isn't so much a competition with others, but rather a personal journey to connect with their ultimate source of strength and do what others never thought possible. For me, it is a spiritual quest to serve and be my ultimate self.

When we adopt that mindset, we have the identity of Superman. We are not ordinary and want nothing to do with the ordinary. We are on a quest, living beyond mere competition to surpass the expectations of others. But it's not in simply doing, but rather being our best. Some days, that best isn't what we intended or what others expected. But it is the best we can do on that day. That's when we ignore the internal and external critics. The mindset of an ultramarathoner is pushing ourselves higher and higher and then faster and faster. It is the ultimate challenge.

That ultra-mindset is what sparked my running a decade ago. That is also what drew me to lose 180 pounds and what carries me through this 50-50-50 quest. It is what powers me through PTSD attacks. It isn't about what others think I should be doing or being. It's not about getting attention or being the life of the party. It's definitely not about just getting a medal. It's about living an abundant life even though it might be difficult to get through the moment. It's making the world better by encouraging, assisting, and connecting. The ultra-mindset is serving what others need and accepting help in my times of trial.

Little did I know that mindset and body transformation would save my life, moving just enough to redirect a fatal bullet.

The People

Each race provides so many wonderful moments of reconnecting with old friends and meeting new, fascinating ones. I first met a couple at the Mississippi River Marathon. It was her first marathon in February or March. Although excited, she was struggling and praying for someone to help her finish when God put her in my path. I turned out to be her angel that day.

It is always good to reconnect with pacer friends. At Little Rock, I met the friend who had beat me to the title of pacing a race in fifty states.

I especially enjoy connecting and reconnecting with race directors as they are good collaborators for what I'm seeking to do. In this race, I reconnected with the Crazy Race Director for the New England challenge as well as meeting the race director for the Little Rock Marathon. She was really kind and let me get the double medal for doing the 10K and the marathon. Another lady I met worked for a newspaper in Little Rock. Kelly, hearing my story, said, "If I had known you were coming, we could have done a story." That makes me want to go back next year and run the entire marathon. Although

March is cold and rainy, like an ice bath when running, I will be prepared and ready to go.

Then there was George, a man with Down Syndrome who wants to be first to run 50 state half marathons with Down Syndrome. As is my practice, we took a photo together, and, after learning about it, tuned into his YouTube channel.

Photo: posing with George, celebrating our accomplishment and his audacious spirit.

That wasn't the end of the connections. There were others that I met at east coast marathons I had run. In the end, Little Rock was like a big reunion. Next year is their 20th anniversary run so I really want to run it again.

Looking back, I realize that I have re-evaluated my definition of hills. Before I ran West Virginia or the Blue Ridge Marathon, I would have thought those hills in Little Rock were pretty big. But not now. Although it was not nearly as flat as those flat railroad bed races, they were nothing compared to what I have run.

In the end, I was pleased with how my body performed. My glutes were activated, and I am convinced I would've finished the marathon without the PTSD induced heart problems. Every race I seem to learn more.

One important lesson I learned surrounded the Garmin watch alert. I didn't know what it was doing when it started vibrating, alerting me that my heart rate was dangerously high. I will from here on.

I also learned that I really enjoy the landscape of the Little Rock Marathon. The rolling hills mixed with flat stretches make this a perfect place to return. Besides, it is a short plane ride from Houston.

Looking Ahead

Next week I travel to the ocean side of Florida to run the Space Coast Marathon in the shadow of Cape Kennedy. I plan to arrive Friday and leave Monday. With a generous seven-hour finish time, I fully expect to finish. The following week I'll check off Tennessee when I run the St. Jude's Memphis Marathon.

With only a month left before the end of the year, I'm doubtful that I'll get to run a handful of states. I still need Nebraska, New Mexico, Wyoming, Alaska, and Delaware. Unfortunately, with winter approaching, those will either have to wait until next year or I'll simply consider that part of the quest unmet.

Anniversary of the Shooting

Six years ago, today.

I laid on my back in a parking lot looking up into the barrel of a weapon, warding off death.

As I answered a frantic page for all male assistance, I noticed several guys outside the store; and after hearing one guy tell another guy to get the tool and put in work, instantly, I knew they were trouble. Unfortunately, my coworkers didn't recognize what the two were intending to do — I, however, fully understood. If I didn't intervene, many would have been shot and more likely than not even die.

I'm a spirit-filled man of God and know that my eternal fate is secure by faith in Jesus Christ alone. However, my coworkers were not, and that concerned me, especially in this situation. Someone must interrupt their actions, or they would spend the rest of their lives in torment.

That someone was me.

Why?

Because not only am I'm the #RunningServant, most importantly, I'm a slave to Jesus Christ.

"Get inside" I shouted as I grabbed the first guy from behind, wrestling with him, dragging him down and holding him from behind. He was desperately trying to retrieve what I perceived to be a gun in his pocket, I frantically grabbed his hands, preventing him from removing it.

Sensing he was outmatched, the thug showed his nature, "Get the tool and put in the work" he shouted to his accomplice. Moments later, he returned blasting shots.

After getting the last coworker loose, I look up to see the second thug with a gun aimed directly at my heart. Instinctively I rolled to the left, jumped to my feet, and fled.

Bang. Bang. Bang. Bang. Bang.

The hot metal pierced my body four more times as I rolled to protect my heart from receiving the kill shot.

Week 39: Space Coast Marathon, Florida, Nov. 28

Arriving Friday for a Sunday race allowed me time to relax and connect. While in Starbucks, I noticed a lady wearing one of the medals. It was huge! I quickly connected and she let me hold it, when I learned that it was also heavy! Portraying the image of the nearby space launch facilities, it featured a Space Shuttle celebrating the 50th anniversary of the oldest marathon in Florida.

I often fly out late in the afternoon, which doesn't give me much time to pick up my packet on Friday. I like to take care of that as soon as I can, but I can always do it Saturday morning. We would have cut it close but made it in time except the Uber driver needed to stop for gas. We arrived a few minutes too late for packet pickup.

Staying at the Hampton, I ran into an old acquaintance that I've seen at several races. Woody is a man who was fully functional until he turned 21. Then, for whatever reason, his body quit processing copper. As the metal built to a dangerous threshold in his brain, it immobilized him, and made his speech indecipherable. His motor skills diminished, he smiles broadly from the seat of his racer's stroller while mom or dad push. His brain is sharp, spirit unquenched, and love of running overflowing. He understands what others say and loves to give "pounds" otherwise called high fives. Woody and I connected at a previous race, and every reunion brings smiles and laughter. It was good seeing him in the lobby.

The Race

This race was the polar opposite of Little Rock, West Virginia, and the Blue Ridge Marathon. It was more like the Pine Line except we were running along the street. With absolutely no hills, I think the curb was the highest point in the race. While I prefer the rolling hills, my mind and body were relaxed and ready to run.

This race offers two loops, one running north, the other south. Similar to the Hatfield and McCoy race, half marathoners chose their course. Marathoners ran both. Numbering about 1400, we begin by running north and then continuing to the south loop. Meanwhile, about 5600 half marathoners shared the course. Two thousand chose the north loop while 3600 chose the south.

Shortly after the start we were greeted with a beautiful sunrise and a glimpse of the vehicle assembly building at the launch site. The out and back loop was very fast in part because it was so flat.

The first half felt good, but I didn't want to push it. My glute was hurting, and I knew what that meant from previous races. Yet, I was making good time. If I was just running the half marathon, I would have pushed and finished in 2:45. For me, in my current condition, that was excellent. That success propelled me farther.

But as I approached the end of the first loop, I realized I had a problem. But this was a problem I hadn't experienced in any other race. I was hungry. That doesn't even express it. I felt like I was starving. Never before in this quest have I been so hungry throughout the entire race. If there would have been an opportunity, I would have stopped and eaten an entire meal. As I approached the 13.1 mark and the split to the south course, I saw a woman offering donut holes. I goggled down five of them, hardly taking a breath, consuming this manna from heaven.

To this day, I still don't know why I was so hungry. I know I was in pain but didn't think that was enough to create an intense craving for food. It's not like I hadn't eaten enough the night before when I consumed a medium pizza. I intended to order a large one, but it came in two boxes, and I didn't think I needed all of that. But my stomach growled and saturated my brain with the constant demand, "I'm hungry. Get me something to eat."

As I thought about it later, I think it was from a recent change in diet. Having picked up a few pounds and wanting to lose them, I calculated that I was burning 4700 calories on an average day. Then by running a marathon each weekend, I was burning even more, to the point where my reserves were depleted.

Before I was shot, I ate 5000-7000 calories a day, 10,000 when doing long runs. But I burned it off by running and biking all over Houston. That's how I lost 100 pounds the first year I was running. I outworked my diet. I know it works because Michael Phelps, the Olympic swimming champion, ate 10,000 calories while training and he is fit. By adjusting my intake, evidently, I didn't leave enough fuel in the tank for running. No wonder I was hungry.

Continuing onto the south course, I passed mile 15 but didn't see the marker so I was expecting to see 15 when I saw the mile marker for 16. That is a happy surprise and turned out to be an indicator of how much fun that south loop was going to be.

The south loop impressed me with how more runners there were but also how many spectators lined the course. I connected with so many people and wanted to take photos with so many, that I switched from photo to video. I checked later to learn I had taken 407 photos just on the south loop. Imagine how many I would have had If I hadn't switched to video for 15-20 minutes. That was fun.

Notice for me to say it was fun means that I wasn't in much pain.

Angela

At mile 16, I noticed a gal in a gold blouse and black skirt sitting on the grass with her husband. I could tell she was a runner, but he was not. I teased her, even though I didn't know her, saying, "Are you all taking a break?"

That prompted her to get up and start running. She quickly passed me. When I reached mile 18, there she was again, taking a break. This time, she was complaining, "I can't do it. I'm done."

Photo: Angela, the Birthday Girl, getting it at mile 16.

I wasn't going to let her quit. I figured if she had made it this far, I'd help her finish.

"Come on. You can do it. Let me tell you my story." I recapped my story and convinced her to get back on her feet.

As we reached the south end of the south loop, marking 19.5 miles, we turned around and headed north. But she hit a mental wall, in part, because she had never run beyond 20 miles.

Recognizing the problem, I persisted, encouraging, joking, challenging her to keep going. Finally, I grabbed her hand and dragged her a bit.

She pushed back, "You are treating me like a little kid" but I didn't let go. We made it to mile 20 at the 5:28 in the race, we were on track to finish the 6.2 miles in 92 minutes.

Knowing this was her first marathon, her husband called, checking on her progress so he could meet her and walk with her the last few miles. He had run marathons before and knew what a special moment it is to finish your first one.

As we approached mile 23, her husband approached and wondered what was going on. "Who is that big black man holding my wife's hand?"

Sensing a problem, I quickly explained, "Angela wanted to quit but I wouldn't let her. I told her I would drag her across the finish if I had to." I'm glad he understood.

But I knew time was ticking away and we were not running fast enough to finish in time. "Keep up with me to keep her at the pace. We need to finish in time."

Shortly after, a lady volunteer came out onto the course with a cart to tell us they were shutting down the course. I quickly explained that it was Angela's 50th birthday and first marathon. Cheryl, the lady on the cart, was course manager and understood what that meant. "Tell you what. I will go ahead and hold the finish line open with the timing mat so she can finish. But keep going."

"Thank you!" we all said in unison, appreciative of Cheryl's kind decision.

At one point, her husband pleaded with me, saying, "She can't go any farther."

She adds, "I really need a bathroom."

I wasn't having any of that.

"No problem. Trail runners use the bushes all the time. Do what you have to do but let's keep moving."

She complied. I wasn't sure whether she didn't have the energy to say no or because she really did not want to finish.

Meanwhile, her husband kept saying, "She can't make it the next two miles."

I countered, "You can't quit now. This is too important."

She returned but wasn't anxious to finish. He played the trump card. "One of your best friends interrupted her vacation to see you at the finish line. You have to keep going."

That was the energy or guilt she needed to push on.

Photo: Angela and her husband, Shelton

Meanwhile, we didn't know that Cheryl had another surprise in store. As we made our way through several turns and finally emerged with the finish line in sight, we were blown away. Cheryl had returned to the finish, shared Angela's story with the race director and everyone else. Even though they had disconnected the timing mat, they reassembled everything and spread the news. Gathering every volunteer and spectator, they planned a party worthy of an elite finisher.

With about a mile left in the run, I told them to keep going because I was going to run ahead, allowing her to have her moment. I often drop behind my pacing groups to let them have their moment. In this case, knowing the timing was important, I decided to run ahead. I also had another surprise in store.

As Angela and her husband emerged from the last curve in the finish line maze of twists and turns, that small band of volunteers and spectators erupted with cheers and continued to crescendo until Angela crossed the finish line. Watching the crowd, you would have thought she just won the Olympic Marathon. Now, she wasn't just a runner, she was a marathoner. Her husband stood at her side, smiling with pride.

Photo: Angela with family and friends.

Then, on cue, her family, friends, workers, and volunteers broke out in a rendition of "Happy Birthday." I have to admit, that is one of the reasons I ran ahead. I wanted her to have the best birthday possible. After all, it was her 50ᵗʰ birthday. We were the same age.

Angela was consumed with joy. Her husband, appreciating my help, gave me a big, friendly hug. Her friend voiced their appreciation, "I'm glad you listened to Aaron and kept going."

Meanwhile, I'm starving. But, because we finished after the course was supposed to be shut down, the promised pancakes and other food available to the runners had disappeared. Now it was time to hunt down something to eat.

People

I appreciate a group that has become known as my old man crew. David runs with black top hat, white shirt, and shorts. Bob (Woody's dad) and a couple other guys, along with a group of ladies that run together, all cheered me on with shouts of "Big Sexy" as I approached the finish line. They are a few of the ladies that use the slogan, "Big Sexy's getting slim."

Looking Ahead

After arriving home on Monday, I prepared to leave Thursday for Memphis and run the St. Jude's Marathon. This one is important because it is for the charity I've sponsored this entire quest. However, I'm still waiting for final confirmation for my hotel and registration. I'm getting nervous about that. To protect myself, I secured a backup reservation. This needs to come together quickly as the run is on Saturday. Looking farther ahead, Hawaii is still scheduled, despite my worries. So is the Disney Marathon weekend on January 6-9 and Chevron on the 16ᵗʰ.

Week 40: St Jude's Marathon, Tennessee, Dec. 6

There was no question this was a St. Jude marathon. Everything was St. Jude's, and that means banners, aid stations, and clothing. If you weren't in Memphis to support St. Jude's, you were in the wrong place.

As I mentioned before, I enjoy arriving two days prior to the marathon so I can connect with old friends, meet new ones, and attend the runner's sessions. I'm glad I did that in Memphis because there was one question and answer session for St. Jude's heroes that attracted phenomenal runners that were also coaches. For example, one lady has run 128 marathons. Another person on the panel talked about listening to your body, yet another on prevention, and another noting that you want to be able to walk the day after.

At this point in my journey, I'm most interested in hearing how to run after an injury, because that is what I'm dealing with. I'm also interested in hearing how to push beyond your capabilities. For example, I greatly admire the woman who ran 128 marathons. There is no question that is impressive, but my question is, has she pushed herself beyond what she already knows she can do? Is she just doing the same thing as she has already done? She is very impressive to those who have never run a marathon or run only a few. But why do the same thing over and over without challenging yourself to do more? If you have conquered a goal, run a marathon, and are in marathon shape, wouldn't you want to challenge yourself to take the next step and run an ultra? Challenging yourself is more important than just proving you can do one more run. I'm most impressed with people who are pushing their boundaries, continually reaching higher for the next goal.

Logistical Problems

Remember, I was concerned about the logistics. I kept calling but wasn't able to secure my flight, hotel, and transportation until the day I left. That is cutting it way too close. I did get a hotel room, and that was fortunate because it was sold out. I didn't want to reprise the Tulsa experience and sleep at the start line.

The only challenge that they weren't able to work out was admittance to the race and hospitality area. Because I raised funds for St. Jude's during this entire quest, they were showing me their appreciation. But sometimes one hand doesn't know what the other is doing. They didn't have me registered for the race, and that meant I wasn't allowed to enter the hospitality area. That meant that when I arrived, the volunteer claimed, "You didn't RSVP." I don't like when an organization is supposed to do something, fail to do it, and then blame the customer. After trying to reason with them and getting no satisfaction, I had no choice but to ask who was in charge.

I called the woman, gave my name, and explained the problem registering for St. Jude's races. She still didn't get it, claiming I needed to recommit. I assured her I had done all that. I told her my name and that I had been fundraising all year. Finally, she got it. "I remember you. No problem. I'll register you.

"Thank you" I said knowing that now I could pick up my packet and find a place to relax.

Unfortunately, this all happened shortly before the race. It would have been much more relaxing had they worked this out at least a day before. At this point, I just wanted a place to relax without being around so many people. Unfortunately, my start window was approaching so I resolved to relax after the race.

The Purpose

Between all the races, the 5K, 10K, Half and marathon, 17,500 runners were involved. That's a nice size, smaller than the mega New York Marathon with 50,000 runners but far bigger than Havre, Montana or Morgan City, Utah. By this time, I've come to appreciate what each size of race offers.

One thing I noticed was how this race attracted the homeless population. They weren't there to run but to cheer on the runners, excited, and eagerly engaging the runners. I like the banter, so I asked them, "You want to run with me?" None of them took me up on my offer. But there was one guy, more excited than most runners, that I had to love. I offered him some of the energy drinks. That's when he revealed the motivation behind his enthusiasm. It was St. Jude's who was there to help his family when they were diagnosed with cancer. Instantly, my commitment to St. Jude's was restored. What they do is so important. Here was a family that needed help but couldn't afford the cost. They were the answers to his prayers. That is a great story.

The Unknown

I'm learning that I never know what to expect.

In the same way, as we begin December and I know I'm within a few races of ending my quest, one of the things I have learned is that I will definitely show up at the starting line, but I don't know what will show up with me. That makes every day and race interesting. I never know how my body will respond. I never know if or what will trigger my PTSD. I also don't know who I will meet or how I can help them.

The Race

Although the vaccinations had been out for 9 months, we were still socially distancing to guard against the second or third wave of covid. The race responded by creating rolling starts and assigning each runner a window for their arrival time and one for starting. It was a small window of six minutes. My window was 9:06-9:12. While I was waiting to start, the rain started falling.

This was something that hadn't happened so far in my quest. There was something about it that was unsettling. I double checked my surroundings.

I am standing at the starting line.

Security is tight.

Everyone had their wristbands with a chip.

No one is here that shouldn't be here.

This space is definitely secure.

So why is my body reacting so weird to the rain?

One of the reasons for this quest was to reintegrate myself back into society. I wanted to feel safe again. But the rain added an element that I couldn't explain. I wasn't feeling safe even with all the safety measures. I used my mental therapies to fight the anxiety, but my efforts were stymied, and I became as quiet as a church mouse. Those that knew me, wondered what was going on.

Photo: Posing with the 5:20 Pacers

I wanted to start with the six-hour pacer, but he was late. That meant I had to start on my own. Evidently the pacer showed up because their group caught up to me at the 10k mark.

That first 10k was great, walking up and running down the hills. Somewhere after the start I hooked up with John, who hurt his ankle, and decided to drop from the half to 10k.

The half-marathon course was awesome. It was a gorgeous scene with trees and homes. By mile nine, I encountered the party street that continued over two miles.

A block party that stretches for two miles. Now that is one big block party. There were plenty of kids enjoying the blowup games while adults were drinking and offering beer, wine, and fireballs. I don't drink alcohol so that didn't interest me, but everyone was having a great time.

Photo: The Party Street Host doing the most.

The best part for me was finding a doctor who was offering adjustments and stretching. I definitely wanted to partake in that revelry. She worked on my right leg which was already almost useless. When she lifted my leg at a 55% angle, I screamed. Then she stretched my hip flexors. They were tight because that was all I was using to run. My right glute never engaged, even after the treatment. I knew I was in trouble at the 5k mark when I tried squeezing glutes and couldn't. I had to wonder how much it had to do with the anniversary of the shooting.

To help you understand how much pain I was in, remember all the other runs where I've experienced pain. Now consider that the pain I was feeling in Little Rock ranked in the top two races. I was in so much pain that I couldn't cheer anyone on. Approaching the split between the half and the full marathon, the pain was so extreme I knew I had no choice but to bow out. Looking at my watch, I realized I was walking at a 22 minute per mile pace. At that pace, there was no way I could have finished in time.

If you have had a migraine, you will understand. If you have had some other excruciating pain, you will understand. Pain bursts the balloon, hides any hopes, and destroys any dreams. It shatters your spirit and turns you into another person. It tortured me just knowing that I couldn't cheer anyone on. My only focus was finding relief.

That's why, when a reporter approached me, instead of wanting to gladly engage, my only thought was relieving my pain. While I would never harm another, I would have punched his momma for some relief.

So why now? Why did the PTSD hide on the anniversary when I ran the Space Coast Marathon? Why did it hide that entire week and attack me today? Now it felt like my body was reliving every single moment of the shooting. Over and over, with every pulsation, I relived the scene.

I tried to ward it off. From the very beginning, I tried dancing and cheering, doing anything and everything I could to distract myself. But it didn't work. As the rain started while I was waiting to start, the DJ played "Purple Rain."

That is when the world caved in. I was suffocating under the weight of those memories of six years ago. If I would have sat down, I would have broken down.

Rain. Light rain. Persistent rain. That rain triggered my pain. Exactly like six years ago, it was a light rain, just enough to keep the wipers going but not a downpour. It had the same feel and smell.

Odors. Like the thug's odor of Newport cigarettes, specific smells, sounds, feelings, and situations trigger me. With the mental flashbacks my body reacts, and I literally felt the hot lead bullet pierce my body once again. That same fear of dying pierces my peace. I feel the bullet trapped in my right glute as I try to run. I feel the same sense of panic, wondering if this will be my last moment alive.

This experience at Little Rock was totally new for me because it wasn't a thought that triggered my PTSD. It was my body that reacted. Usually it starts in my mind, then moves to my emotions, then to my body. As the rain started to fall, I immediately looked to my left torso, the exact point where the first bullet pierced my body. It was as if I had just been shot again.

At this point I was following Pete, who I connected with after leaving the party street. I noticed Pete had an ankle brace. That caught my attention because my aunt wore an ankle brace. I learned that the broken ankle was healing nicely but had prevented him from training. Despite that, he wasn't about to quit. He definitely wanted to finish.

So here he was, exhausted but determined, with a metal brace for his foot, essentially a leg with a shoe. He was not going to be deterred from his goal. But that doesn't mean his body cooperated.

Beginning two miles from the finish, he started cramping but refused to stop. Instead, he slowed to a walk until his muscles relaxed, then he ran. He repeated the pattern by running until he cramped, then walking. Then repeat the pattern. I watched in amazement. That was one determined man who finished strong despite the pain.

Even though I was in pain, Pete (pictured below) needed help, so I started a conversation.

"How are you doing?"

"My feet are hurting."

"That is what is expected."

Pete grunted and kept going. I continued.

"Ever wonder why your head is on top and your feet on the bottom?"

"No."

"It's mind over matter. Your head is the leader of the body. It is above everything you are going through when running. From the waist below, you are good to go. Above, you need to reconsider."

I could tell he was listening. While I believed in what I was saying, the conversation alone helped Pete take his mind off the pain. Interestingly enough, it was also doing the same for me.

"Walk it out, Pete."

I was impressed with Pete because he kept his run/walk pace.

"Whatever you do, don't sit down once you cross that finish line." I knew if he did, his muscles would cramp even more, and it would be excruciating.

In that last 400 meters, he ran 200 meters and walked 200 meters. He only stopped running when the cramps started. Pete pushed through and I let him finish ahead of me.

Pete and I weren't the only ones running hurt. I think of Cabby and know she doesn't have a choice to quit. She has to keep going, but as runners, we have a choice. We can choose to quit.

The After Party

As we exited the expressway and ran onto the ramp and crossed over to the finish, it was another wild party. Spectators, well lubricated from their liquor, were gladly offering runners shots. One lady dearly wanted to hold hands with Pete and me. Unfortunately, she reeked of alcohol. We obliged and she kept pace. Meanwhile Pete's cramps were relentless, requiring him to drop her hand so he could massage his leg. One party of three, a guy and two gals, were toasting the runners. By the looks of them, they drank two shots for every toast they offered. Everyone was enjoying the festivities that reminded me of the Louisiana marathon in Baton Rouge. They even had bars on wheels and all kinds of junk food.

Reflecting on the Race

Despite the miserable pain, there was much to love about this race. For example, there were four or five ladies that stopped me and asked for a photo. They had read my story in Runner's World and showed their appreciation. Then there were other friends that I was pleased to see and renew our friendships. Memphis was one big party and I loved it.

I appreciate how God sends his angels to minister to me. In this race, it was Pete. By helping him, God helped me.

Looking Ahead

I've learned that the Abbot world major marathons want to do a story on me when I earn my last world major star in Tokyo. That's the good news. The bad news is that they won't make an exception for me concerning Boston because they must have a verified time to record. I cannot submit a time; the BAA must do that. I understand but that doesn't mean I'm not disappointed. In the end, that means I must run Boston again and finish in a time where it is official. Then it is on to Tokyo. By the way, they want to do the article but only if Tokyo is my last star. That means I have some work to do beyond the 50-50-50 quest.

In these waning weeks of the quest, I'm starting to branch out. I will be volunteering at the Dallas Marathon next week before traveling to Hawaii the following week. Yes, Hawaii is actually going to run. I will need to complete the covid testing before leaving and after arriving, but it is going to happen. From there, I run Disney and Chevron.

Week 41: Hawaii Running Project, Dec. 27

The paperwork to get into Hawaii during the pandemic is like paperwork needed to enter another country during wartime. It has to be double, and triple checked. It has to be checked when leaving Houston, and then entering Hawaii. I have to stand in line to get my required wrist band from United Airlines. If you don't have the band, you must sit in a room at the airport and wait. By the time all that is done, anyone is glad to leave the airport.

But that isn't the end of it. You still need to wear a mask and show your negative test or vaccination card to enter any restaurants or bar. Even though Hawaii is a beautiful paradise, traveling during the pandemic was a big pain.

David (Kiwah in Hawaiian) picked me up in his Mini Cooper. He is no small guy so together we looked, and I felt like the guy in Incredibles. Kiawah is the Race Director for Hawaii Running Project, where I would be running. On the drive to western side of Oahu, he explained how I fit into his goals. This was their eighth year of running the race, and each year they have sponsored someone with a good story outside of their running community. When he received my email, he knew I was the guy to feature this year. I was honored.

That was an answer to prayer because, as everyone knows, even a short trip to Hawaii is expensive. Kiwah budgeted funds to pay for my airfare and accommodations, which I greatly appreciated. This was all part of his plan to expand the awareness of the race and raise funds to help the community. Along with my expenses, David set a goal of raising $500 for St. Jude's.

The Hawaii Running Project has a very prestigious history with a famous ultramarathoner as a founder of the run. Over the years, they have made a significant impact on their community and have been successful in attracting runners completing 50 and 100 milers in 50 states.

Kiwah's story is equally impressive. He lives on the mainland and works a fulltime job. That requires him to leave work, fly to Hawaii, run an ultra, then return on Sunday to work on Monday.

The Hawaii Running Project

The Hawaii Running Project is quickly overshadowed by its older sibling, the Honolulu Marathon. Yet there is no animosity as they feed off each other, the Hawaii Running Project being scheduled for the week following the Honolulu marathon. Kiwah and other leaders of the Hawaii Running Project take the time to pace for the Hawaii Marathon.

The Hawaii Running Project is designed for runners to run at their pace as far as they please. It might be just a 5k or it could be 100 miles over two days. Last year, a couple that ran the Hawaii Marathon, flew back to the mainland, then returned to run the Hawaii Running Project because his boss wouldn't give him time off. This year, that couple is running a hundred miler together. Another guy, had only run 15 miles, but after reading David Grogen's book *Can't Hurt Me*, he committed to running his first 100 miler. The problem was that he didn't train properly. He was eating everything and burning some serious calories. He didn't carry much body fat, so he didn't have the energy to complete the race. While his feat was impressive, finishing 62.2 miles, his lack of training beyond two weeks limited his results. His body locked up on him, fatigue became his mortal enemy, and his limited training his undoing. Although he was fit, his muscles weren't used to running that far. His spirit was right, but he was misguided. Instead of trying to run 100 miles in 24 hours, he had the time to rest, replenish his body, before finishing the next day. But, for whatever reason, he set a goal of completing it in 24 hours. So, he stopped. Everyone has their goals. That's what I like about running ultras. Everyone is running a different goal.

Given this race included only 371 runners, I knew I would enjoy this race. Normally it isn't that small but the strict Hawaii covid restrictions limited the registrations. They run it twice a year, one during the winter and one in the summer, with the summer race bigger but more challenging. Meanwhile, the Hawaii Marathon's numbers also decreased, only drawing 6000 when they usually drew 20,000.

David dropped me off at my hotel, the Ohana East, in Waikiki. Beach just a quarter mile off the water. Due to the holidays and despite the restrictions, this area was packed. Many were Asian tourists, which is different from normal when it is filled with travelers from the mainland USA. Everything was sold out and all I could see for miles along the shore was beach umbrellas.

Every time I was on the beach, I looked at Diamond Head, knowing I was scheduled to hike it the day after the marathon.

The Race

I wished I would have known I could have started at 3:00 a.m. Instead, I started at 7:00 when the sun rose and revealed a beautiful blue sky. By noon, it was beaming like I expect in Houston.

The problem was with my medicine I take which forbids me from exposure to direct sunlight. But here I am, baking like I was sitting in an oven. My legs felt like someone gave me an I.V. of peppermint patties, emitting a strange sensation, weakening my knees, and creating a powerful urge to vomit. As odd as it sounds, I was also incredibly hungry, a reprisal of the Space Coast Marathon. Frantic for food, I looked everywhere for something, even a morsel. Unfortunately, there was only one aid station between the two loops. One loop went out .8 of a mile while the other extended for 1.8 miles, both through neighborhoods. The aid station was the only place to get something to eat unless I knocked on someone's door. I seriously considered that idea but dismissed it quickly.

The heat was about to overtake me when I stopped and sat down in the shade for a couple hours. That's the beauty of running a marathon in an ultra-race. At 3:00 pm, I got up and ran another lap, before sitting down again. A friend from Texas came by, and I greeted him with, "I'm done." David assured me the clear sky and sun was unusual for this time. By 3:30 the wind shifted, and the clouds appeared. Funny thing about the wind, it seemed to be blowing us no matter which way we went. Because of the valleys and surrounding mountains, the wind swirls creating that effect. This was a beautiful valley, once a hog farm that has since been transformed into a beautiful and expensive housing development.

Photo: Hiding my face from facing my disappointment.

Even though I proclaimed that I was finished, I rested while my body and spirit recovered. I got up and kept running. After enjoying the hill at the end of the short loop one more time, I finished the marathon. I was pleased that I was able to rest and allow my glutes to recover. In many of those races where I couldn't finish, had I been allowed to rest, the story would have been different.

With only 37 runners, all running their own distance in their own time, the finish was rather uneventful. I crossed the line but there weren't any crowds to cheer or fans that wanted an autograph. With a whimper, it was done. I quickly returned to Ohana East, found some food to fill my hungry belly, showered, and knew the day was a wrap.

I was looking forward to the next day, enjoying an island tour, hiking Diamond Head, and visiting beaches. That opportunity wasn't part of the run but rather extended from a guy I met on the beach. A lot of people have their own little tour company, and he was one of them. He was very welcoming, not just another pushy salesperson. Part of the package was a snorkeling adventure, but I knew I was only going to swim. But sensing I needed a down day after the marathon, I canceled the tour. I saved his number so next time I go; I'll contact him.

I didn't want to run the Honolulu run because I wanted to experience more of the island. Having run the Hawaii Running Project, I will definitely reconsider running the Honolulu Marathon now.

Hawaii is often considered a paradise but being tested every 48 hours took the edge off. I was glad to leave and get away from that. Before I left for the airport, however, I knew I had to take a certain souvenir home with me. I stopped at one of the three Leonard's locations to buy a box of donuts. I chose éclairs, both coconut and chocolate to bring to my Starbucks' crew.

I landed and went directly to share them at my "traveling office" as I like to call that location. We had fun, taking photos and videos, sitting outside, and enjoying being on cloud nine.

Photos: I brought Leonard's for my Starbucks barristers.

I knew I needed to be alone.

Out of Nowhere

Then, out of nowhere, a ton of emotional bricks dropped on me. I'm still not sure exactly what happened or why.

In an instant, I became depressed and went into a crying fit. I couldn't stop. My emotions overwhelmed me as I became upset, angry, and frustrated.

Yet, these are my friends, people who care about me. Having been through this before, I know that the best therapy is to sequester myself. My destination for that solitude, however, was a surprise.

Fast forward in what seemed like a moment later, and you find me sitting on the hood of my vehicle, staring at the place where I was shot. I sat there for several hours. The toxic stress overwhelmed me to the point of causing fever blisters.

Fast forward again. I'm sitting at home. I've taken my fever blister medicine and they are healing. Now it's time to sleep. It wouldn't be a restful sleep.

Fast forward to morning. My aunt, who has been staying with me, greets me. "You were yelling in your sleep."

Fast forward to days later. I'm still trying to process it. Even my psychologist was surprised to learn that I had returned to my old workplace. We decided that it is another quest, trying to take back my life.

Eventually I was able to process it mentally and return to my new normal. The hardest part was waiting for my body to work through it. A trauma, as I'm finding with my shooting, leaves a muscle memory that is difficult to handle.

I still am not sure why this all happened at that particular time. I suspect it was left over from the anniversary. Why it was triggered by returning home from Hawaii I am not sure.

Looking Forward

With a huge sigh of relief, Hawaii in the books. My original plan was to finish my quest by running the Dopey Challenge at the 50th Walt Disney World Marathon. I was going to arrive on January 5th and leave on the 11th. With how my body has been responding, or shall I say not responding lately, I have been thinking about running the 5k and 10k (scheduled on Thursday and Friday.) To save my strength for the marathon on Sunday, I would walk the half marathon on Saturday.

But I'm reconsidering. Since I ran the Space Coast, I've already checked off Florida. What is my purpose in running Disney, other than it will be fun? I need to think about that.

That leaves only Chevron postponed to my birthday weekend. I am looking forward to celebrating my birthday weekend by running at home with plenty of friends and family.

Week 42: Chevron Marathon, Texas, Jan. 17

I listened to my spirit and declined running the Dopey challenge at Walt Disney World. It's kind of hard to explain, but since I had already checked off Florida with the Space Coast run a month before, I was at peace in letting go of that part of the original plan.

I'm also reconsidering my revised goal of running the remaining states in 2022. As I listened to my spirit during my morning prayers, I'm learning to guard against my ego. Am I running to satisfy my ego? Am I going back to finish races I couldn't complete within the one-year period to say I did? If so, that's not the right reason. I'm here to serve, not glorify myself.

But maybe there is another reason to cancel Disney and the remaining states. I'm tired. Running so many races and working through so many obstacles has been hard. Maybe I'm tired and tired of having my PTSD triggered in so many ways. Maybe that last episode was the tipping point.

So, it is official. I am declaring Chevron as my race in this quest. I've been looking forward to ending my quest in my hometown and now it is going to happen.

One nice thing about this race is that I don't have to get on any plane, worry about them canceling the flight, or fighting with a hotel about my reservation. I'm staying in my apartment, driving to the race, and running on familiar territory. That's a relief. Besides, I'm hoping my family turns out to support me. That would be a great finale to the year. After all, they haven't been able to cheer me on the entire year.

I have my game plan. Starting in Corral C, means I have 5.5 hours to run the course. I should be able to do that as long as I don't go out too fast. I already know the last 10k of the marathon is the toughest part of the course with rolling hills due to underpasses. The hills are good but most of the course is flat. I figure if I give myself an hour and 20 minutes for the last 10k, I'll be fine. The challenge is to make the cutoff at mile 20. I must be there by the five-hour mark. From there they let you finish without giving you official finish time, you just don't get the finisher's photo or allow family to cheer you on at the finish line. They treat you like everyone else, allowing 6 hours before they break down the finish.

Chevron has always done a rolling start and allowed the half marathoners four hours to finish. Beginning together, we split at mile eight. From there, since there are always more half marathoners than full, there is plenty of space on the course for those of us at the back of the pack. My focus is on making the cutoff at five and a half hours. That's where we enter the park, have our bibs scanned, and reassured we will finish. If it was up to me, they would follow New York's model and leave no runner behind. But last I checked, I'm not the Race Director.

Say What?

Every year, since I turned 40, I go for a physical the week before my birthday. I have my blood work done, EKG, and any other test they require. Normally, there isn't a problem. But this year was different.

"There are abnormalities."

"That's not what I want to hear."

"Instead of spiking up, you are spiking down," the doctor said with more than a little concern on his face. "You need to see a cardiologist. You can't run Chevron."

I heard him but didn't comprehend what he said. "Did he just tell me not to run?"

"I'm telling you not to run this weekend." Seeing the puzzled look on my face, he repeated the message.

He knew I ran Boston and was attempting to run a marathon every weekend. He also knew this was the last run in my quest, and I was planning to push it with Chevron. Outside of hurting myself, I was going to leave nothing on the table.

"You can't run." He said it again.

"Can I walk it?" I said, attempting some sort of compromise.

"Yes, you can walk it but absolutely no running."

That wasn't what I wanted to hear.

Old Friends

The day before the marathon I ran the 5k. After thinking about the quest and that this was my last run, I decided to stay at the Marriott and enjoy the lazy river. It is the host hotel so all I had to do was walk out the door and join my coral. That was a good choice as I was able to connect with several old friends that I haven't seen since the covid shutdown. I also met some awesome people.

By now you can imagine I have a hard time putting names with faces or remembering where I met them. Fortunately, some people volunteered the information, refreshing my memory. Such was the case when I reconnected with a lady at the 5k. She recognized me and quickly approached, saying, "I ran with you for five miles in New York."

Photo: Nancy, another lady (below), saw me at Expo, unfortunately, I called her Marie. She was nice enough not to correct me, but I felt bad. The next day, when I saw her at the marathon, I specifically addressed her by her right name.

Unfortunately, I didn't sleep well that night. Sleep is a challenge for me most nights and this wasn't the exception. But that told me I made a great decision staying at the Marriott. Otherwise, I would have had to make an early drive downtown. As promised, I walked out the door and joined my corral.

The marathon this year was bigger than normal with 34,000 runners. That pent up desire to get out and run was evident.

With the quest ending and being in my hometown, I was excited to be there. I was even more excited about finishing the marathon, pushing beyond the frustrations in previous races across the country.

But then I heard my doctor's voice. "You can't run. You can only walk."

"But I know this course," I said in my head. "I knew when to run and when to rest."

Ask any runner what they would do in that situation. I'm guessing most would do what I was about to do and run their race while watching their heart monitor closely.

The Race

We started and I settled into my strategy. I was pleased that my body was responding well in my last race in my hometown.

That is until I saw Nikki Cannon ahead of me. I knew her from Facebook and knew she was celebrating her 40th birthday with her own quest. She was running 39 marathons in 39 days leading up to her 40th birthday. In other words, she was doing a 40-40 challenge. I can relate to that. But then I realized we shared birthdays; I knew I had to meet her.

She was a good distance ahead of me. Feeling good, I broke from my strategy and ran to catch up. When I caught up to her, I realized the error of my ways.

"I shouldn't have done that."

By the split at eight miles, I was doubting my stamina. I considered splitting and settling for a half marathon but decided to see how far I could get. I made it to 17.16 before the sweepers passed me. I knew what that meant.

The sweeper pacer was set at a rigorous 12-minute mile in attempts to catch up to the 13:44 marathon pace mileage from the gun time pace. They are easy to identify from other runners as they each carry two balloons. I've mentioned sweepers before, as well as the sag wagon. No runner wants an encounter with them because that means you won't finish the race and you won't meet your goals. For me, seeing them was especially humbling on this, my final run of the quest.

The only thing that went through my mind was, "maybe I shouldn't have run to catch up."

Photo: Angelina Wilson and Nikki Cannon.

Riding in the sag wagon, the medical lady dropped me and a couple of others off at the finish with a word of encouragement. "Go get your finisher shirts and your medal."

"But I didn't finish. I didn't think Chevron gave medals to those who didn't finish."

"You are going to take a medal." She sounded like my momma, so I wasn't about to argue. I learned later that this year Chevron changed their policy and gave every runner a medal. I was humbled.

The medals were small, the size of most 5k medals. But it was a great design. It looked great alongside my medal for the 5k. I don't run for medals, but this one marked the end of an incredible quest.

Photos: (Left) The "We are Houston" 55K (Below) George R. Brown Convention Center Medial Tent

What's Next?

My top priority is to find a cardiologist. They recommended someone but I can't get in until April. So, I'll keep looking. I need to check out my heart.

Meanwhile, there are several things happening with my family, none of them good. My main issue with them is that they haven't been supportive at any time during this entire quest. My immediate family, brothers, mom, dad, haven't been there for me. Only a couple have contributed financially or helped me in fundraising. They haven't supported me emotionally. Even though I was running in my hometown of Akron, Ohio, not one family member showed up. I even volunteered to pay for any one of them to run the 5k with me, but not one showed up. I was going to pay for dinner on September 25 and still no one showed up. Then I ran in my hometown of Houston, and no one came. I don't know why I expected anything different. While they don't specifically discourage me, they don't do anything to support me. It is as if I didn't

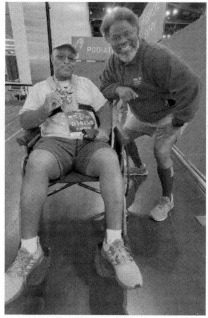

364

exist. Meanwhile, I'm there for them. I've learned that sometimes perfect strangers are the closest family. That leads me to make a difficult decision. For my own wellbeing, I will limit access to myself for everyone in the family, except for my kids.

But enough of that. To celebrate my son Brandon's birthday on the 13th and mine on the 15th, I went to Saltgrass with my son and his mom. After the 5K, a friend came and brought a card. That was nice.

Photo: My birthday celebration is carrying me away.

I took the weekend to contemplate my future and recenter myself. After a grueling year, I realize I need to focus on myself. I will still be the #RunningServant, but when it comes to my family, I can't let them drag me down.

Recapping My 50-50-50 Challenge

I realize that I didn't toe the line for all 50 races. Covid has prevented that. But I had hoped to make over 40. I missed two or three because airlines canceled flights. I almost missed Boston for the same reason. Then I missed Delaware because they canceled the race two days prior to the race because they didn't have the police officers to stop traffic. I wasn't able to work Nebraska and New Mexico into the schedule. Then I missed Rhode Island due to nephew's suicide and Nebraska due to nephew's murder. There have been plenty of obstacles in this quest.

One of the main obstacles has been my pain and discomfort. There is a difference in running with discomfort than running with a permanent injury. One is unpleasant and difficult while the other can be utterly debilitating. This quest has taught me to run in pain every week. I know each week there will be pain. I just don't know how much. I'm learning how to best fight through the pain. That means determining what I will do with the pain. Sometimes just sitting down aggravates it.

That creates many questions. What do I do? Sit or not? Do I dare drive? If so, will I have enough time to relax and recuperate?

I have learned that now, more than ever, I use cheering to distract me from my pain. The fact that I couldn't perform my rap at St. Jude Memphis showed how much pain I was in. I was alone in my misery until I came across Pete. Then, reaching out to help him, I distracted myself enough to finish the half marathon. Helping others helps ourselves.

367

Another lesson is that discipline is valuable, but it is, at times, not enough. I learned discipline in running ultras. But running through debilitating pain is taking me to a new level in discipline. Without my natural abilities to run, it would be easy to quit. This is much harder than when I was healthier. The mental discipline to continue when you would have previously given up. I have my critics, those who say I'm wasting money by registering for a full marathon when I don't know if I can finish or not. Those same critics wonder why I continue a quest that I know I'm not going to complete. Then there are the critics who doubt my ethics, falsely claim I'm scamming donors. There are critics who doubt my authenticity in pursuing the Abbot world majors. It takes discipline to counter the critics. It takes discipline to do your best, even when everyone knows you won't meet your lofty goals.

Some critics voice their caustic attitude in the form of a common question, "How can you afford to do this quest?" I also receive that question from those that are genuinely interested so they can do more.

First of all, I'm debt free. I live based on my needs, not my wants or desires and I don't use credit cards. Without debt obligations, I'm free to do much more.

Second, I lead a frugal lifestyle. I don't spend a lot of money on clothes, household furnishings, and other typical expenses — I've been labeled a minimalist. I don't drink alcohol and rarely go to a fancy restaurant.

Third, I prioritize my spending. This quest is my focus. At one point I contemplated subletting my apartment and couch surfing with friends and relatives in between races.

Fourth, I shop for good bargains on flights and hotels. The pandemic shut down travel and when it did open back up, I found many discounted tickets and hotel rooms. About the only ticket that wasn't dirt cheap was Hawaii. Even then, my initial ticket was under $400, but with the cancellations and rebooking, that changed. Originally, I was planning to stay at hostels in all races. However, because of covid, I would have needed to rent the entire room which would cost as much as a hotel. I found good deals on hotels. Then there were the points I earned. Because I'm in Houston, United is an easy choice to get me to most places, so I'm a platinum member with them. I will have flown 100,000 miles with them by the end of the quest. That often brings an unsolicited upgrade to first class, even if they are only providing bottled water and pretzels due to covid. My bullet ridden booty enjoys those nice, big, wide seats. Spirit is a good low-cost flight for certain markets, so I have points there

That discipline helps me contain the pain. When I began in January, the pain spread throughout my entire body. But with physical, emotional, and mental training and discipline, I can now keep it isolated to a certain set of muscles. Even though I cannot control the pain from the scar tissue or the PTSD, I can control other things, like my mind and spirit. That is progress.

Looking back, I don't think I would have had the drive to run this quest had I been healthy. I know a friend who ran 13 marathons in a row but had to stop. He told me he simply didn't have the energy to keep going. That's because ego rarely pushes you beyond your limits. The quest for attention or accolades isn't enough. Instead, it is the intrinsic things like hope and determination that push you through that wall at mile 20. Those aren't the things you work on in the gym. It might be the things that get you to the gym.

As I mentioned earlier, most people are content working within their abilities. It is the rare individual who becomes uncomfortable, overcoming obstacles and going beyond what they believe and understand.

I imagine some of you are wondering how I can talk about not quitting when I have not finished every race. Please understand, I didn't quit simply because I was tired or mentally exhausted. I quit because I didn't want to risk additional injury. There is no shame in quitting. As the one gentleman told me in a previous race, "It is ok to live to run another day." Angela wanted to quit because she wasn't mentally tough enough to finish on her own. I wouldn't have drug her on if she was risking injury. Sometimes we need someone to help us through that wall.

But the pain of injury is a different story. In this race, I could have taken out my phone and mapped the route so, if they closed the course, I still could have found my way to the finish. But I was worried about damaging other muscle groups that were overcompensating. Just finishing a race that I started is not worth additional injury.

Too many give up because they doubt, they can finish. In a similar way, too many cast doubt on anyone quitting due to an injury.

I've had people criticize me for not finishing more races. I've also had people criticize me for not giving up on the marathon quest and settling for running half marathons. They claim I'm wasting money.

But that is not my quest. My quest is to push myself further, running faster, and finishing more often. No, I haven't finished every race but, in the quest of finishing 50 marathons in 50 states, in 50 weeks, I have pushed myself farther than I ever imagined. The success isn't in whether or not I finish them all, it is in my progress. A quest is a venture into the unknown. It is, as dictionary.com defined it, "a search or pursuit made in order to find or obtain something." I was searching for my old life, but found I had to create a new one. I was in search of my old running form but found a new strength by pushing through obstacles I hadn't foreseen. I was searching for a reintegration to society, and I found it at the back, not the front, of the pack. This quest has been a search for a new life, and I have found it. Finishing would have been nice, but it would have prevented me from finding what I was really searching for.

Epilogue: Transformation

Throughout these pages, you have seen that I am a man of transformation. I am not content accepting the limitations others put on me. I am also not willing to live within the confines of physical or emotional restrictions. It is not that I'm being difficult, disobedient, or destructive but the opposite. I'm willing to be transformed into someone much better. God has worked wonders in me, stopping me on that road in Rockwall Texas, changing my direction, leaving the drug running behind. He pulled me up out of my chair and away from the food to start running. He transformed my body with the loss of just under 180 pounds. Then, when thugs tried to kill me with five hot pieces of lead, God put me back on my feet. He continues to work and brings me back. Yes, I still have work to do physically, emotionally, and spiritually, but I'm willing to be transformed.

Unfortunately, I'm finding that my family is like most people. They don't want correction, challenge, or change but are content in complacency and conformity of the culture. They definitely don't want transformation. Instead, they live critically and criticize you if you aren't willing to help them stay where they are. Like many, they refuse to learn how to fish but just demand you feed them fish.

I cannot do that. I will not do that. It is unhealthy. Instead, I will cheer loudly, encourage persistently, and push enthusiastically. I am not going to foster anyone's unwillingness. I am not going to enable anyone to settle for destructive lives. For those wanting to take advantage of me or anyone else simply because they are family or a longtime friend, I will not tolerate that. That is selfish greed.

Instead, I will Run and Serve those desperate for transformation. Why? Because I love them as God has commanded, "love and do as unto the Lord."

As you can tell, this is a sensitive subject. Only because transformation is what life is about. It is my passion and my purpose. The very idea of transformation is to become what you ultimately desire. It is to work through the difficult stages of growth, be willing to fail in order to become the best the LORD has purposed you to become. In the process of transformation, you learn and grow, develop, and emerge, discover and celebrate the life dreams are made of. Transformation is truly a glorious act of grace.

That's not to say it isn't hard work. My quest demanded more of me than I ever expected. Remember, I thought I was going to be able to run every marathon with a time of 5:05. That didn't happen and that is ok because it was part of my transformation.

Look back through the book to note all the challenges I faced. Take note of how I had to hit bottom in London to later work with a trainer to re-engineer my body. I literally had to learn to work different muscles. I've had to continually condition myself against emotional triggers. Yet there is so much more to do.

As you look back, observe a Superman was humbled into becoming the #RunningServant. But see how that has made me better. See how there are far more compelling stories at the back of the pack with those struggling simply to finish. Appreciate the elite runner's ability but consider how much more effort and drive it takes to run with debilitating injury. Notice also how easy it is to complain and blame, but how much more satisfying it is to encourage and serve. Relish the transformation.

Then celebrate the journey, not just the destination, because we won't be complete until that heavenly transformation. The journey is where we live each moment. Whether running uphill pushing in pain, enjoying the spectacular views from the mountain top, or flying downhill, dreaming of a glorious accomplishment, each step is a point in your transformational journey.

As I work to begin my fitness training practice, I am working under the label, Transformational Coach to transform, convert, change, and renovate lives. It is to leave your current lives in order to reach for something far better. It is to get off the couch and get out and run. Transformation is challenging yourself to run farther and faster than you thought possible. It is challenging yourself with a quest to do what you never imagined possible. It is becoming the best person you can be.

Transformation requires incredible energy and power to break through the concrete walls of comfort, compliance, and conformity. I found that strength in the Almighty God. Who else could have taken me through these trials? Who else could have literally saved my life from the fatal shot that should have struck me in the chest? What other source would have sustained me through the disappointments and depression of the last year? Why would anyone want to continue when they failed so miserably by the world's standards?

You probably picked up this book because it looked like a good story. I hope you have found that to be the case but hope it has been much more. I hope you are inspired to make your transformation. Be like Angela at the Space Coast who needed a little encouragement but was willing to be drug along to finish. Be like Pete in Memphis, who despite his cramping, kept going. Be like Gabby and Aiden, unwilling to quit.

From here, I will follow my habit and let you run ahead, enjoying your moment at the finish. I hope this book has helped you to challenge yourself, transform your spirit, and set your mind to finish strong.

Aaron Burros, The Running Servant
(Big Sexy to some, Nipples to few, but PAZ to all)
Transformational Run Coach
RRCA Certified Coach
Ordained Minister, Gospel of Jesus Christ
B. A. Bible / Leadership
Public Speaker: Sacred and Secular
Email: aaronburros@yahoo.com

Marathons

1. Daufuskie Island Half Marathon, Marathon & Ultra
2. Go Short, Go Long, Go Very Long   50K   Tulsa, OK
   Jan 23, 2021   4:20:00
3. Big Beach Marathon   Marathon   Gulf Shores, AL
   Jan 31, 2021   3:00:00 Big Beach Marathon   7K
   Gulf Shores, AL   Jan 30, 2021   57:32
4. Mississippi River Marathon and Half Marathon
   Marathon   Greenville, MS Feb 6, 2021   7:00:01
5. Run Oak Island (BAM! Race Series)   Marathon   Oak
   Island, NC   Feb 13, 2021   3:15:00
6. Louisiana Marathon   Marathon   Baton Rouge, LA
   Mar 7, 2021   Louisiana Marathon   Quarter
   Marathon   Baton Rouge, LA   Mar 6, 2021   1:40:39
7. Skidaway Island Marathon & Half Marathon   Marathon
   Savannah, GA Mar 13, 2021   5:15:00
8. Labor of Love Marathon   Las Vegas, NV Mar 20, 2021

9. Two Rivers Marathon Race Festival   Marathon
   Hawley, PA   Mar 28, 2021
10. NJ Ultra Festival   Marathon   Hardwick, NJ Mar 28,
    2021   Two Rivers Marathon Race Festival   Marathon
    Hawley, PA   Mar 27, 2021
11. Carmel Marathon Weekend   Marathon   Carmel, IN
    Apr 3, 2021

12. GO! St. Louis Marathon   Marathon   St Louis, MO
     Apr 11, 2021
13. Foot Levelers Blue Ridge Marathon   Marathon
     Roanoke, VA   Apr 17, 2021
14. Pine Line Marathon   Marathon   Medford, WI   Apr 24, 2021
15. Potomac River Run Marathon & Half (Spring)
     Marathon   Washington, DC   May 2, 2021

16. Tobacco Road Marathon and Half Marathon   Marathon
     Cary, NC   May 15, 2021
17. Zip Code 07662 Marathon   Marathon   Rochelle Park,
NJ   May 23, 2021   3:19:00
18. Coeur d'Alene Marathon (CDA Marathon)   Marathon
     Coeur d'Alene, ID   May 30, 2021   5:51:00
19. Bear Paw Marathon   Marathon   Havre, MT   Jun 5,
2021   5:14:07
20. Baltimore 10 Miler   10 Miler   Havre, MT   Jun 5,
2021   2:15:35
21. Delaware Marathon Running Festival   Marathon
     Wilmington, DE   Jun 12, 2021,   7:00:00
22. Hatfield McCoy Marathon   Marathon   South
Williamson, KY   Jun 12, 2021
23. Grandma's Marathon & Garry Bjorklund Half Marathon
     Marathon   Two Harbors, MN   Jun 19, 2021
     7:02:00
24. Morgan Valley Marathon   Marathon   Morgan, UT
     Jun 26, 2021
25. Foot Traffic Flat   Marathon   Portland, OR   Jul 4,
2021
26. Walnut River Gravel Run   Marathon   El Dorado, KS
     Jul 10, 2021
27. Frederick Running Festival   Half Marathon Frederick, MD
     Jul 10, 2021   3:34:00
28. Orange Curtain   Marathon   Cerritos, CA   Jul 17,
2021
29. Bear Brook Trail Marathon & Half Marathon   Marathon
     Allenstown, NH   Jul 24, 2021   5:30:00

30. Riley Trails Marathon & Relay Marathon   Holland, MI
        Aug 7, 2021
31. Tunnel Vision Marathon   Marathon   Snoqualmie
    Pass, WA   Aug 15, 2021
32. Moonlight on the Falls Marathon   Marathon   Davis,
    WV   Aug 28, 2021
33. Mad Marathon Marathon   Waitsfield, VT Sep 12, 2021
34. Bismarck Marathon   Marathon   Bismarck, ND Sep 18,
    2021
35. Akron Marathon & Half Marathon   Marathon   Akron,
    OH   Sep 25, 2021
36. Run Crazy Horse   Marathon   Crazy Horse, SD
        Oct 3, 2021
37. Baltimore Running Festival   Marathon   Baltimore, MD
        Oct 9, 2021
38. Boston Marathon   Marathon   Hopkinton, MA
        Oct 11, 2021
39. Des Moines Marathon Marathon   Des Moines, IA
        Oct 17, 2021
40. New York City Marathon   Marathon   Staten Island,
    NY   Nov 7, 2021
41. Tunnel Hill Marathon Marathon   Vienna, IL   Nov
    14, 2021
42. Little Rock Marathon Marathon   Little Rock, AR
        Nov 21, 2021
43. Little Rock Marathon 10K   Little Rock, AR   Nov
    20, 2021
44. Space Coast Marathon & Half Marathon   Marathon
        Cocoa, FL   Nov 28, 2021
45. St. Jude Memphis Marathon & Half Marathon Marathon
        Memphis, TN Dec 4, 2021
46. St. Jude Memphis Marathon & Half Marathon 10K
        Memphis, TN Dec 4, 2021
47. Dallas Marathon Festival   50K   Dallas, TX   Dec
    12, 2021

Lessons Learned

I have learned many lessons during this quest. If you are seeking to do what I have just attempted, learn these lessons.

Lesson 1. Have a backup plan. I spent a lot more time rescheduling and rebooking and finding another marathon due to covid cancellations. First, have a backup run in mind and explore the logistics for that plan B.

Lesson 2. Don't try to knock out the most popular run first. Do the smaller states like New Mexico and Delaware that only have 2 or 3 good runs. States like Florida or California have a number or races to choose from.

Lesson 3. Don't be afraid to try obscure runs. I didn't know about Daufuskie Island until Chevron, Louisiana Marathon, and Alabama Mercedes canceled. Daufuskie was beautiful as was nearby Skidaway Island. I wouldn't have discovered those if I wasn't forced to look. Take a chance on runs like the picturesque Foottraffic near Portland. I mean, where else could you have a guy on a 20-foot ladder picking cherries off of trees and giving them to runners. Fresh. Juicy. Sweet. You won't get that in Boston, New York, or Chicago.

Lesson 4: Do the big run in every big city. New York is fantastic and has no time limits. If you can't get in through the lottery, raise the funds and run for charity. Boston can be brutal to qualify but it is the pinnacle for most runners. Don't be afraid to try.

Lesson 5: Vary the type of run. Run trails as well as road races. The Bear Creek Marathon in New Hampshire was awesome. Go to

Granite Mountain and see how the steps were hewed out of the granite.

Lesson 6: Don't avoid ultras. Just because a race is advertised as an ultra, doesn't mean they don't have other distances. Aid stations, packed with goodies. 5k out 5k back. Orange Run in CA.

Lesson 7: Do not be afraid to contact the race director if sold out or you have a special request. Do your homework first, then explain it directly to the race director. They want to help. But don't be selfish. They have a job to do and are very busy. Be respectful of their time and resources. Make your request honorable.

Lesson 8: Travel light. Bring only a carry on with what you need to run. Remember, this isn't a vacation. Wear comfortable clothes going and coming. Bring layers. Don't forget something to sleep in.

Lesson 9: Consider low-cost airlines. Every $50 adds up. If you are running 50 states, that extra $50 ends up being $5000.

Lesson 10: Be flexible. This could have been #1. Don't become emotionally attached to a certain race, airline, hotel, or schedule. Be willing to change.

Lesson 11: Don't ignore great opportunities. While a running quest isn't a vacation, don't avoid seeing great sights. When I was running the Crazy Horse Marathon in South Dakota, I knew I wanted to see Mt. Rushmore. It turns out we were going to be driving right by it. I asked my Uber driver, and he pulled off the road so I could take photos.

Lesson 12: Don't assume.

Lesson 13: Ask for donations of miles and points. I've found friends that are working on their 50 states and not in a good financial place. I've used my points to help people. Ask. Points expire so use them.

Lesson 14: Rental Cars, Ubers, and taxis. Plan ahead. Some places don't have any of the above. Others are very expensive. I paid $150 for a cab (each way) to Medina, Wisconsin. That hour and a half ride was still cheaper than the going rate for rental cars of $700 two days. But remember West Virginia and I had to beg for a ride and take turns driving to D.C.? Plan ahead.

Lesson 15: Understand airline hubs. The dominant carrier usually has the lowest cost. United has a hub in Houston, American in Dallas, and Delta in Atlanta, just to name a few. Flying from the hubs to smaller airports will require a connection. You may need to buy segments, switching airlines at the connection. I took United to Denver and then to Billings. But from there I took Cape to Havre Montana.

Lesson 16: People don't share donuts from HURT in Little Rock. Go get your own. I did. They are custom donuts where each one is a masterpiece. It is like having a personalized cake. People spend $40-50 at a time.

Lesson 17: Go to Leonard's in Hawaii. But be prepared for a line. They have custom donuts and cupcakes with unique flavors like avocado and guava cupcakes. You will enjoy them because they are fixed fresh.

Lesson 18: Don't expect great Cajun food at the Louisiana Marathon in Baton Rouge. You've been warned.

Lesson 19: Stay with one airline as much as possible. Because I'm in Houston and that is a United hub, I am now a platinum member. I also fly Spirit as much as I can and have points accumulated with them.

Lesson 20: Book online. Don't deal with people at the counter in the airport. Avoid them at all costs, except New York where they were super professional. Everyone else, they don't care and aren't professional. Besides, if you buy a ticket from Spirit at the airport, it is cheaper than online.

Lesson 21: Sign up for their emails. Look for the occasional discounted links. Even if the link expires, contact them, have a link, or miss a deadline, they will send you another email to book.

Lesson 22: Can only carry a backpack on Spirit. They police it heavily, some don't care. A lot of airlines will not challenge men about backpacks or free carryon sizes. Let husband carry questionable bags. Women get challenged more because they will pay. Men push back. Crew doesn't want to hold up the line. Discriminatory but the way it works.

Lesson 23: Don't even think about cutting the line at TSA. Someone will complain. If you are running late, ask nicely if you can go ahead.

Lesson 24: Checking a bag, be there as the airport suggests. People try to negotiate. Doesn't work. If your bag isn't on the same plane with you, you won't get on.

Lesson 25: Plan to be seated at the gate at least an hour and a half before departure. You are going to wait somewhere, why not wait at the place where you won't miss your flight.

Lesson 26: On long flights, don't sit next to exit doors. Doors on big planes have their own air conditioning and you will freeze in that seat, especially at night.

Lesson 27: Set your clock to your destination's time once you get on the plane.

Lesson 28: Ask for late checkout availability. Call the hotel and let them know you are running a marathon. Since I have chosen Marriott Bonvoy and have accumulated points with them, they often accommodate me. That gives me time to rest, shower, and change before leaving. Be sure to be nice when you ask.

Lesson 29: Tip people that go out of the way for you. Tipping will get what you need. For example, tip $20 to those that grant an early check out. Build rapport with each employee. My rule is to be generous with those you need, and they will be generous with you. I once had a $70 valet removed from my room simply because I was nice.

Lesson 30: Be firm when needed. If you need a certain type of room, ask for it. But if they assign you a different room, state what you need. You have read that I had problems with hotels that messed up my reservation or didn't give me the room upgrade I paid for. Don't give up. Be firm and ask for the manager if needed. Give deserved online reviews. You'll be remembered. A hotel manager comped me one night because I left a well-deserved review.

Lesson 31: Did I mention to write great reviews? When the hotel staff does something amazing, leave a great review on google. Be sure to provide their name (always write it down). When you return the next time, they will remember you and make your stay extra special. Good reviews go toward their employee record. Use your keyboard's microphone to make writing easy and quick.

Lesson 32: Bring the right shoes. This sounds like a no-brainer but imagine showing up for a trail run only to find you packed your road shoes. Beyond trail vs road, you probably have different shoes you wear depending on how your body feels. With my glute, I have several pairs varying in cushion. Depending on how my glute feels, I will need a different shoe. That means you may need to bring a couple pairs and decide on the morning of the run.

Lesson 33: Don't trust the forecast. That's why you bring layers.

Lesson 34: Get good, quality rest. You know I have difficulties sleeping. Remember Montana? I was so tired, I missed the bus, and had to run a 5k to get to the start line and then run the marathon backward. Remember, this isn't a vacation or a party. Get to bed so you can get plenty of rest. You can sleep after the marathon.

Lesson 35: Build your support team. Every week I go to my massage therapist, trainer, and psychologist. Beyond that I have a variety of doctors. Maybe as important are the people who cheer you on. Remember I brought donuts back from Hawaii for my Starbucks team. They are important to me, and I can't neglect them. I must mention writing reviews and calling customer care lines to highlight great customer service. I had the district manager for Starbucks give me a significant amount on an e-e-gift card. Then after learning I was running for Team for Kids, he made a donation.

Lesson 36: Know what you need for a massage therapist. Finding the right one makes a world of difference. But they are not all the same. Some provide relaxation while others focus on deep tissue sports massages. Still others provide mental massages for PTSD. Whoever you choose, they need to read your body in braille, finding the tension points, stressors, and anything else your body is telling them.

Lesson 37: Know your body. You are going to spend money on races and travel. Don't forget to invest in understanding your body. Don't be cheap. Don't ignore pain. Get the help you need. Remember how I found a great massage therapist in Baltimore? When you find a good one, they are a great investment.

Lesson 38: Ask questions of your medical providers. Don't be shy and remember they work for you.

Lesson 39: Focus on recovery. You cannot work on preparation but forget about your body after the race. Drink the cold chocolate milk after the race. That is my go-to for recovery. Take the time to stretch when your muscles are warm. Then, as soon as you can, take an ice bath. Sit in the tub and then fill the tub with cold water. Yes, it's cold, but your body will adjust. Then dump the ice in. It will be cold at first, but your body will quickly adjust. Put a towel over your shoulders if needed. Then once you get used to it, sit as long as you like. That will take the inflammation out of your body, and you will feel better.

Lesson 40: Work on your mental toughness. Remember what I told Pete. Your head is on top of your body because it is mind over matter. You can do far more than you think. Know when you are being a wimp and tell yourself, "Suck it up buttercup. Let's do this. Once you get through this, your recovery will be there."

Lesson 41: Know your why. Many times, I felt like quitting but thought of Gabby and Aiden. I had pushed myself beyond myself, knowing they couldn't quit.

Lesson 42: Only quit when you know you are about to harm your body. Don't cause an injury by pushing too hard.

Lesson 43: Use social media. I've found having a Facebook page helped me to connect with runners and race directors. I've even used it to transfer a bib to another runner when I couldn't make it (with the race's permission.)

Lesson 44: Keep going. Run one more mile and run one more race. Cheer on one more person and offer one more smile. Remember, this is a marathon quest, not a sprint.

Lesson 45: Build relationships. People are what makes the world rich.

For booking Aaron Burros or Loren Murfield to speak at your marathon expos, corporate meetings, or conferences, email Loren@MurfieldCoaching.com

Acknowledgements

First and foremost ,I worship my great God and Savior who delivered me and does deliver from so great perils, the LORD Jesus Christ.

Next, I give honor to Dr. Loren Murfield and his wife Lisa. Many people talk a good game of intentions, but few follow through. Not only did his words match his actions, but his actions matched the character of God in that he did far exceedingly above all I could have thought or even imagined.

Finally, I must thank Lillian Evans, Petra Montgomery, Tonette Mitchell, and Leticia Saddle for their support during the last several years. Mr. and Mrs. William Penrigth.

RACE COMPANIES AND DIRECTORS

Corrigan Sports
The "Crazy" Race Director
John L. Conner, Mississippi River Run
Shawn Cool, Hatfield, and McCoy Marathon
3PR, Pittsburgh Marathon
Jay Wind, Potomac River Run
The Entire Grandma Marathon Staff
St. Jude
Marcus Grunewald, BMW Dallas Marathon
Mrs. Hobbit, Little Rock Marathon
Team 50 New York City Marathon
Akron Marathon
Dori Ingalls, Mad Marathon
Yen Darcy, Orange Marathon
Emily Wheeler, Crazy Horse Marathon
Steve Durbin, Durbin Race Management
Mark Hughes, Two Rivers Marathon

MY TRAINERS AND MASSAGE THERAPIST

Marcus McDade,
MPOWER
Expert Fitness and
Nutrition

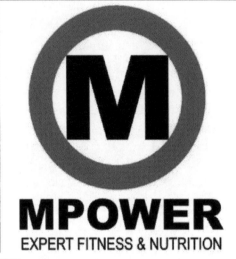

marcusinhouston@yahoo.com

Nwankwo-Ikechi Kanu
Nwankwo
B.S Applied Physics
Personal Trainer

HONORABLE MENTION

Kim Taylor,
S.H.E.E.R. Love

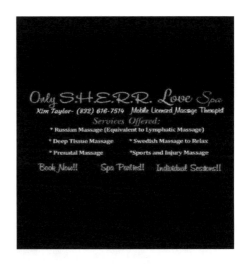

Victor Ly
President , Administration , NuConcept Builders LLC
nuconceptllc@yahoo.com

About the Authors

Aaron Burros is The Running Servant, passionately helping others as God leads. In 2023 he is launching a virtual Birthday Celebration Run as a means of helping individuals celebrate significant milestone birthdays. #RunningServant.

Loren Murfield, PhD is an executive coach, serial entrepreneur, author, speaker, filmmaker, and marathoner. He works with clients to live 100% ALIVE by thinking bigger and reaching higher. He has authored over 30 books, six plays, multiple movie shorts, and several online courses. www.PivotalLiving.org. Loren@MurfieldCoaching.com

Made in the USA
Columbia, SC
17 January 2024

30298811R00215